Two week loan

The Human Factor in Governance

Also by Willy McCourt

GLOBAL RESOURCE MANAGEMENT: Managing People in Developing and Transitional Countries (*with Derek Eldridge*)

THE INTERNATIONALIZATION OF PUBLIC MANAGEMENT: Reinventing the Third World (*edited with Martin Minogue*)

The Human Factor in Governance

Managing Public Employees in Africa and Asia

Willy McCourt
With contributions from Khadija Alarkoubi and Benson Bana

First published 2006 by
PALGRAVE MACMILLAN
Houndmills, Basingstoke, Hampshire RG21 6XS and
175 Fifth Avenue, New York, N.Y. 10010
Companies and representatives throughout the world

PALGRAVE MACMILLAN is the global academic imprint of the Palgrave Macmillan division of St. Martin's Press, LLC and of Palgrave Macmillan Ltd. Macmillan® is a registered trademark in the United States, United Kingdom and other countries. Palgrave is a registered trademark in the European Union and other countries.

ISBN 13: 978–1–4039–4765–9   hardback
ISBN 10: 1–4039–4765–1   hardback

This book is printed on paper suitable for recycling and made from fully managed and sustained forest sources.

A catalogue record for this book is available from the British Library.
A catalogue record for this book is available from the Library of Congress.

10   9   8   7   6   5   4   3   2   1
15   14   13   12   11   10   09   08   07   06

Printed and bound in Great Britain by
Antony Rowe Ltd, Chippenham and Eastbourne

To Glynnis, Róisín and Maya

Contents

List of Tables

List of Figures

Acknowledgements

In research drawing on elite interviews, access is essential. The field studies were only possible because of the colleagues and friends, almost all former students of the Institute for Development Policy and Management in Manchester, who opened doors for us, and it was only their introductions that allowed us to interview the often very senior public officials who are our main data source. Three of those colleagues are or were senior civil servants: Ms Khadija Alarkoubi, formerly of the Ministry of Public Works in Morocco (co-author of Chapter 5); Ms Lee Meng Foon, former Deputy Director of Malaysia's National Institute of Public Administration; and Mr Siripala Wirithamulla, who at the time of writing was Secretary of the Ministry of Trade, Commerce and Consumer Affairs in Sri Lanka. Two more are leading academics in their countries: Dr Benson Bana of the University of Dar es Salaam in Tanzania (co-author of Chapter 4) and Dr Anita Ramgutty-Wong of the University of Mauritius. Finally, Ms Magda Awases, who contributed to the Namibia chapter, is Regional Nursing Adviser (HRD) in the Africa Regional Office of the World Health Organization.

We also benefited from comments and criticisms from many people. The ones we know are Tony Bebbington, Rona Beattie, Derek Eldridge, Brian Goulden, Kit Lawry, Aminu Mamman, Tim Martineau, Martin Minogue, Oliver Morrissey, Colin Murray, Charles Polidano, Tom Redman, Mark Turner and Marinus van Klinken. The ones we don't know are the academic colleagues who provided anonymous reviews of earlier versions of some of the chapters for *Asia Pacific Journal of Human Resources*, *International Journal of Human Resource Management*, *Public Administration and Development*, *Public Management Review* and *World Development*.

Research funding came from the British Council in Malaysia and Morocco, DFID in Ghana, Sri Lanka and Uganda, the European Union in Swaziland, USAID and the World Health Organization in Namibia, and the University of Mauritius. A grant from the British Academy allowed second trips to Malaysia and Sri Lanka. The opening and closing chapters draw on the principal author's contribution to the UN's *World Public Sector Report 2005* (United Nations, 2005b). The annual International Research Symposium on Public Management hosted early versions of the Swaziland and Malaysia chapters in 2001 and 2005. Proto-versions of the Morocco and Sri Lanka chapters were presented, respectively, at the International Human Resource Management conference in Limerick, Ireland in 2003 and the annual conference of the Development Studies Association in 2005.

A year's sabbatical leave from the University of Manchester made room for the later studies and for most of the actual writing.

Last of all, we thank the many public and trade union officials who put up with our obscure interview questions; one of them said we were interrogators, not interviewers. In many places they ventriloquized what we have written: academics are not as different as we would like to think from the legendary consultant who needed to borrow a watch when he was asked to tell the time. The only way we can show our appreciation is to return what they gave us in the form of this book, hoping that it will make their jobs a bit easier, and the service they provide to their citizens a tiny bit more effective.

List of Contributors

Willy McCourt, originally from Belfast in Northern Ireland, started his career as an assistant lecturer in the National University of Nepal. In the UK he worked for a British development NGO, and in adult education and local government, before joining the Institute for Development Policy and Management at the University of Manchester in 1994, where he is a senior lecturer in human resource management.

He has an undergraduate degree from Cambridge, and a PhD from the University of Manchester. He has carried out research and consultancy assignments in Africa and Asia for national governments and for bilateral and multilateral donor agencies such as DFID and the UN. Apart from the interests reflected in this book, he has interests in public management and governance in developing countries. He is married and has two daughters.

Benson Bana (co-author of Chapter 4) holds a PhD from the University of Manchester. He worked in the Tanzanian public service and as a training and development manager in the private sector before becoming a lecturer at the Open University of Tanzania. He is currently a lecturer in human resource management, political science and public service management at the University of Dar es Salaam and consults and researches in the same areas.

Khadija Alarkoubi (co-author of Chapter 5) is a PhD student at New Mexico State University in Las Cruces, New Mexico, USA, and holds an MSc in human resource management from the University of Manchester. A former Moroccan civil servant, she was a lecturer in human resource development at Al Akhawayn University in Morocco from 2002 to 2004.

1
Introduction: The Human Factor in Governance

The human factor

Our book shares its title with one of Graham Greene's latest and most satisfying novels, *The human factor*, whose plot serves as an oblique introduction to our subject. If anyone deserves the title 'novelist of the Third World', it is surely Greene, child of the English upper middle class though he was. His career as a writer was getting into its stride in the mid-1950s when the term began to be widely used, and he and it reached their respective ends almost together, with Greene dying within two years of the fall of the Berlin Wall and the consequent demise of the Communist 'Second World'. His books included all three continents of the South in their settings, with Sierra Leone, Mexico and Vietnam among his locations. Politically he was in sympathy with 'Third Worldism', enjoying friendships with Fidel Castro and with Panama's Omar Torrijos, about whom he wrote a personal memoir (Greene, 1984).

The hero of *The human factor* is an employee of the British Secret Service who betrays his country by passing secrets about his government's activities in South Africa to the Soviet Union. He does so not out of any sympathy with Communism but because of his loathing of apartheid in South Africa as it operated at the time of the novel in the 1970s, and his disgust at what he sees as British and American official collusion with it. His disgust is sharpened by his love for his black South African wife, with whom he has had to flee from a previous Secret Service posting in South Africa. For him the Soviet Union is not party to the collusion, which he hopes that his information will help to frustrate. With his treachery exposed, he ends the novel having fled to an exile in Moscow which, rather endearingly, turns out to be more bathetic than heroic.

1

The 'human factor' phrase appears only in Greene's title and not in the text of the novel. Greene leaves it to the reader to infer that this factor has affected the machinations of Great Powers in a completely unexpected and personal way. At a deep level, the reader senses that the novel champions the individual, not particularly gifted, possibly even deviant human being, overlooked in the calculations of the mighty, whose only claim to greatness is his ability to love. This is a theme that was close to Greene's ambivalent Catholic heart (Greene, 1978).

From cost to resource

We are not privileging 'people management' over the other necessary tasks of government if we point out that it requires a distinctive sensitivity to the complexity of individual human beings; to 'the human factor'. Yet 'sensitivity' is not the word that springs to mind when we look at how public employees have figured in the development discourse over the last quarter-century, during which, as we will see in Chapter 2, they have mostly been represented as drones, often corrupt and a drain on the money that ought to be available for productive private investment rather than a resource that can help to achieve the democratic objectives of the state. With Finance ministries in the lead throughout the 1980s and 90s, egged on by the World Bank and IMF, governments went to great lengths to rein in public expenditure. Policymakers could be forgiven for seeing staff exclusively in money terms, especially as the negative popular image of public employees as corrupt and inefficient gave them no reason to do anything else.

Let us be clear that the governments that devoted so much energy to curtailing spending on staff were partly right: staff *are* a cost: spending on salaries, pensions and allowances consumes the lion's share of public expenditure – around 40 per cent in Benin in the late 1990s, to take just one example (Kiragu and Mukandala, 2004). Many governments *did* need to act to contain spending, and some still do: we explore this case, and the experience of 'downsizing', in Chapter 2. But going through the retrenchment phase has given governments a better understanding of how to keep a grip on their complex spending on staff. There is no longer a need for it to consume as much of policymakers' attention as it did at the start of the structural adjustment era.

Instead, there is the opportunity to recognize that the people who do government's work remain one of the world's great underused resources, unlike the natural resources on which our economies also depend. In the 1980s and 90s economists rediscovered the importance of treating human capital as an economic asset which, uniquely, can increase in value even as it is used, as classical economists like Alfred Marshall had long recognized.[1] This view, which has come to be called 'new (or neo-) endogenous growth theory', is close in spirit to the view that underlies the UN's Human Development Index, which has transformed the discussion of development by showing that that we need to take human capital into account, particularly in the form of health and education, as well as money earnings in order to get a rounded picture of human well-being.

It is ironic that we rediscovered the importance of human capital just as the governments of developing and transitional countries were switching from a post-colonial and socialist phase of developing public services to a phase of retrenchment. There is a gap between the way that many governments still think about their employees and the way we now think about human beings as a whole. More importantly still, there is a gap between the way governments manage their staff and the new development aspirations embodied in the Millennium Development Goals, as we shall see in Chapter 9. This is the gap that our book aspires to bridge.

The argument of the book

How, though, do public employees act as a development resource? In a sense, the answer is obvious: organizations, including governments, employ people to achieve their purposes. But in this and the following sections we set out a more specific argument. In order to develop it, we first locate staff management as an important component of 'governance', a term we use as a convenient shorthand for the overall ordering and management of the public sphere. Despite attempts to distort its meaning, we view achieving good governance as a central task of modern societies (Fukuyama, 2004).

Governance in this sense is a broader concept than the old public administration or civil service reform models whose place it has come to occupy in development thinking and practice. The civil service reform agenda of the 80s and 90s was narrow and negative: with public employees viewed as little more than a financial drain, it boiled down to getting rid of staff that governments didn't need, stopping the ones it couldn't do without from accepting bribes, and so on. The broader governance view leaves room to build a case for staff making a positive contribution.

Governance

Governance and 'governancism'

We begin with the overall governance of the state, and the part that staff management plays in it. 'Governance' is a word that is so ubiquitous and so debased that, like Humpty Dumpty in *Alice in Wonderland*, we can use it to mean almost anything we like. Some radical academics and NGOs have seen it as old wine in new bottles: a new recipe for the old exploitation which has 'served to legitimize and normalize the right of the North to intervene in order to develop the South', and particularly the right of Northern private companies to operate on their own terms; a Foucauldian 'discourse' of power (Abrahamsen, 2000, p.139; see also Bretton Woods Project *et al.*, 2005). Yet it is a sign of the term's vagueness that 'governance' can be stood on its head and used as a euphemism for measures to combat corruption. In the World Bank Institute's work, the two terms go hand-in-hand and are even interchangeable (see World Bank Institute, 2005; and also Rose-Ackerman, 2004).

In this book, by contrast, we view governance as a broader and necessary concept that we may have to rescue from its admirers and its self-serving advocates. Just as there is a distinction between the proper exercise of management and what has been called 'managerialism',[2] we need to distinguish between governance and what we might call, in a suitably ugly neologism, 'governancism'. For, far from an alien imposition, governance is central to the development of the autochthonous New Partnership for African Development (NEPAD), which has developed a voluntary 'peer review mechanism' to allow African countries to 'benchmark' the quality of their governance (NEPAD, 2004). Consequently, it was the African members of the UK government's Commission for Africa (2005) who were most insistent that governance and capacity building should be prominent in the Commission's report, which helped to create the agenda for the G8 summit in Edinburgh in July 2005.

Defining and outlining governance

What, then, does governance consist of? Table 1.1 outlines three current models: NEPAD, developed under African Union auspices; Hyden *et al.*, under United Nations auspices; and Kaufmann *et al.*, under World Bank auspices. They differ principally in their scope. The NEPAD model, for example, includes the private sector, on which it places obligations similar to those imposed on the public sector, thus

Table 1.1 Models of governance

NEPAD (2004)	Hyden *et al.* (2004)	Kaufmann *et al.* (2005)
Definitions		
'creating well-functioning and accountable institutions – political, judicial and administrative – which citizens regard as legitimate, in which they participate in decisions that affect their daily lives and by which they are empowered'	the formation and stewardship 'of the formal and informal rules that regulate the public realm, the arena in which state as well as economic and societal actors interact to make decisions'	'the set traditions and formal and informal institutions that determine how authority is exercised in a particular country for the common good'
Elements		
Democracy and political governance	**'Arenas' of governance**	**Voice and external accountability**
• rule of law	• civil society	• external accountability through national citizen feedback and democratic institutions
• equality and liberty	• government	• competitive press
• freedom, including the right to form and join political parties and trade unions	• government	
• equality of opportunity	• bureaucracy	
• participation in politics	• economic society	
• separation of powers between branches of government	• judicial system	
Economic governance		**Political stability and lack of violence, crime and terrorism**
• promotion of market efficiency		
• control of wasteful spending		
• consolidation of democracy		
• encouragement of private financial flows		

Table 1.1   Models of governance – *continued*

NEPAD (2004)	Hyden *et al.* (2004)	Kaufmann *et al.* (2005)
Corporate governance: disclosure and transparency to enable • compliance with legal obligations • accountability to shareholders • responsibility to stakeholders		**Government effectiveness** • policymaking • bureaucracy • public service delivery
Socio-economic governance • self reliance and capacity for self-sustaining development		**Lack of regulatory burden** (on business)
• sustainable development and poverty eradication		**Rule of law** • protection of property rights • judiciary independence • etc.
• policies and delivery in social development, including education		
• combating HIV/AIDs and other diseases		
• access to water, energy, finance, markets and ICT		
• gender equality, particularly girls' access to education		**Control of corruption**
• broad participation in development		

responding to the criticisms of Abrahamsen and others; the other two models omit it. Most relevant to us is the way they treat staff management. All three share an emphasis on institutions or rules, both formal and informal, and including ones that apply to staff management. Hyden *et al.* and Kaufmann *et al.* both highlight what they call 'the bureaucracy' as an important agency of governance, and it is implicit in the NEPAD emphasis on administrative institutions.

Staff management and governance

How does staff management contribute to governance? Table 1.2 is adapted from Hyden *et al.*

Table 1.2   How governance relates to other concepts and activities

Level	Activity	Concept
Meta	Politics	Governance
Macro	Institutions	Institutional development
Meso	Policy and strategy	Policymaking and strategic management
Micro	Activity	Operational management (including individual staff management)

Source: adapted from Hyden *et al.* (2004, p.17).

We have amended Hyden *et al.*'s table by adding 'institutions' and 'institutional development' at the macro-level, reflecting NEPAD and Kaufmann *et al.*'s emphasis. We have also substituted 'activity' for 'project' at the micro-level, since 'project' conjures up a discrete venture, possibly donor-funded, rather than the network of schools, clinics, district offices and so on which are the basic units of government.

We also qualify the table by pointing out the important interactions among the four levels. The argument that we have already adumbrated, and which this book will develop, is that there may be actions that need to be carried out at the higher levels of politics and policy, including institutional design, in order to improve management at the micro-level. This is a theme of four of the cases we discuss: Mauritius, Morocco, Sri Lanka and Swaziland.

Human resource management, governance and economic growth: the evidence

The bureaucracy model

Our basic argument implies that there are steps we can take to improve staff management which will have a significant impact on governance as a whole. We use two recent bodies of evidence to support it. The first is the group of studies that have converged in the last ten years on the public bureaucracy as an enabler of economic growth. The World Bank commissioned the first of them in the run-up to the 1997 World Development Report. Its authors constructed a 'Weberian' scale of the quality of public bureaucracy (named after the German sociologist, Max Weber, on whose classic model of bureaucracy it was based). Using data from 35 countries, they found a close statistical connection between public bureaucracy and economic growth. Their data suggested that merit-based recruitment was the most important factor, followed by promotion from within and career stability for public servants, with salaries that were competitive with the private sector coming some way behind (Evans and Rauch, 1999; Rauch and Evans, 2000). Henderson *et al.* (2003) have recently extended Evans and Rauch's work by identifying a link between bureaucracy and poverty reduction.

A little later, Daniel Kaufmann, working again under World Bank auspices, constructed a governance index based on the governance model which we outlined in Table 1.1, in which bureaucracy was one of three components of 'government effectiveness', which in turn was one of six components of his overall model. When he tested government effectiveness against data from 175 countries, he found not just the close link with national economic growth that Evans and Rauch had spotted, but evidence that government effectiveness was actually one of the causes of higher national income (Kaufmann, 1999). Moreover, the business people in developing and transitional countries whose opinions Kaufmann and his colleagues drew on ranked government effectiveness ahead of economic factors like high inflation and distortions in the exchange rate regime, and behind only control of corruption in its importance to the success of their businesses.

Finally, a UN study which is the basis of Hyden *et al.*'s (2004) study extended Evans and Rauch's findings into Africa. It found that public agencies do better – they provide better services, and they are less corrupt and more responsive to private sector concerns – if the staff they employ are paid well and have access to internal promotion that

Table 1.3 Staff management in the bureaucracy studies

	Evans and Rauch	Kaufmann	Court	OECD	Manning and Parison
Merit recruitment	✓✓✓				
Internal promotion	✓✓		✓		
Competitive pay	✓		✓		✓
Contracts of employment					✓
'Bureaucracy'		✓			
Agency autonomy			✓		
Pay & employment reform				✓	✓
Anti-corruption and patronage					✓

is not distorted by patronage, and if they have a decent amount of autonomy from the centre of government (Court *et al.*, 1999).

All these studies are only as good as the data they are based on. The World Bank's governance index, for example, leans heavily on surveys produced for overseas investors by agencies like PricewaterhouseCoopers and the Economist Intelligence Unit. They mostly rely on self-report data, where subjects' ratings are based on imperfect knowledge which may be biased by 'halo effect', and also other distortions to which such data are notoriously subject. For example, a perception that corruption is widespread might unduly affect the perception of government effectiveness.

Table 1.3 summarizes those findings and indicates their relative strength, and it also adds the findings of two more studies conducted by Manning and Parison (2003) and the OECD (2004).

The strategic human resource management model[3]

The second body of evidence that we use to support our argument that staff management can have a significant impact on overall governance is human resource management. To someone who comes from a management background, the way the governance literature discusses staff management, which we have summarized in Table 1.3, is bound to seem anachronistic. Evans and Rauch, Hyden *et al.* and Kaufmann all go straight back to Max Weber. They pay only lip-service at most to the criticism of bureaucratic inflexibility and remoteness – that 'Kafkaesque' character which has given 'bureaucrat' its pejorative connotation (see Hyden *et al.*, 2004, p.122), and they entirely overlook all the developments in the way that organizations manage their staff in the little under a century since Weber's death, as if none of them has any value to public agencies.

For, despite the differences between the laws and institutions which govern HRM in the public and private sectors, we too easily forget that both governments and private companies are employers, obliged alike to appoint, pay, train and manage the performance of their employees in order to achieve their objectives. Crucially, where bureaucracy is about compliance, management is about performance (United Nations, 2005b, p.100). There is a body of good practice in areas such as employee selection that has developed over the last 50 years and which is available to both sectors. In particular, there is a body of good practice in *strategic* human resource management which gives an account of how staff management contributes to achieving an organization's purposes. The SHRM model is by now extensively documented on both sides of the Atlantic (seminal texts include Beer *et al.*, 1985; Fombrun *et al.*, 1984; and Guest, 1989). Despite its current competitors, such as the so-called 'resource-based view' (Kamoche, 1996), we judge that it remains the dominant normative model, given the powerful theoretical and empirical support which it has obtained, and which we outline below. We have chosen to analyse selected features of it in detail in this book, rather than to attempt a more comprehensive but inevitably superficial analysis.

While some writers reject the idea of a monolithic SHRM model, distinguishing, for instance, between 'hard' and 'soft' HRM (Storey, 1995) or 'lean' and 'team' production (Appelbaum and Batt, 1994), there are several features on which most writers agree. Probably chief among them is the notion of strategic integration.[4] Strategic integration means aligning staff management systems with organizations' overall strategic objectives and with each other (Anthony *et al.*, 1993; Becker and Gerhart, 1996; Fombrun *et al.*, 1984; Guest, 1989; Purcell, 1995, p.63; Wright and McMahan, 1992). While it has emerged from the normative HR literature, there is some empirical support for the implication that the strategic whole is greater than the sum of the parts (Huselid, 1995; Macduffie, 1995). Indeed Becker and Gerhart (1996) suggest in their authoritative review that it is what they call the 'strategic architecture' rather than individual HR practices that has a universal validity.

It is important to notice that the SHRM model is essentially a sub-set of the larger strategic management model, with which we hope readers are familiar (Johnson *et al.*, 2004). Like that larger model, its essential value lies in giving owners, politicians and senior managers a way of bringing management in line with their political or business objectives. The use of the strategic management model appears to be spreading in the public sector, despite scepticism about its relevance to the political environment of government (McCourt, 2001b). It should be noted that the SHRM model will only be feasible if the paraphernalia of the strategic model – mission statement, strategic objectives etc. – already exist, even if only imperfectly.

Strategic integration implicitly changes the HR specialist's relationship with line managers. The specialist is supposed to design the HR systems that will align with strategic objectives, while the manager is supposed to carry them out. Guest (1989, p.51) observes that almost all writers say that HR must be managed by line managers: 'HRM is too important to be left to the personnel managers.'

Line manager ownership

From this we derive the emphasis we are going to place on the twin issues of 'strategic integration' and 'line manager ownership' of HRM. Readers from a public administration or development background will recognize the latter as corresponding somewhat to 'administrative deconcentration' or 'managerial devolution' (OECD, 1995; Smith, 1985). Studies of the latter usually stop at the level of the administrative unit to which management responsibility is deconcentrated or devolved, and mostly so will we. However, in Chapter 9 we look at the extent to which the Ministry of Health in Namibia has devolved to a lower level, namely its line managers in districts, hospitals and clinics.

It is striking that the HR literature often contrasts this model unfavourably with something very like the bureaucracy model. Tyson and Fell's (1986) seminal characterization of what they called the 'clerk of works' approach to HR, a routine administrative role that consists mainly of ensuring that employees' files are up-to-date, that they were paid on time and so on, was meant to be pejorative. More recently, Ulrich (1998) has argued influentially that there are four roles which HR specialists ought to play: *strategy expert*, in keeping with the SHRM model; *work organization expert* (expert in HR activities like employee selection); *employee champion* (representing employees' concerns: the role which trade unions have traditionally played); and *agent of continuous transformation* (acting as an adviser on change management processes). Significantly, those roles do not include anything that resembles the bureaucracy model.

Employee selection, and performance management[5]

Looking only at the strategic model without considering the HR activities that are its practical expression would be like making bricks without straw. At the expense of other activities which are also important,[6] we have chosen to focus on employee selection and individual performance management and appraisal because:

1 We have good evidence for their effect on organizational performance. The evidence for employee selection is particularly robust (Schmidt and Hunter, 1977). The evidence for performance management is also robust, although oblique: it documents the effect of objective setting and feedback on performance, these being both central features of performance management (Walters, 1995).

2 Both dovetail with the bureaucracy studies that we have already reviewed. Employee selection is one of the two 'Weberian' elements on which they focus, and performance management is implicit in their second element, predictable career progression, since in the public sector promotion is based at least notionally on a satisfactory annual appraisal report. Moreover, we have seen already that *WDR 1997* emphasized merit-based selection, and it also appears in several of the surveys that Kaufmann draws on.

3 We know from previous studies that there are substantial national differences in the practice of performance management. Countries as far apart as Denmark and Japan have resisted the Anglo-Saxon model that focuses exclusively on the individual's performance (Brewster and Hegewisch, 1994; Love *et al.*, 1994; Milliman *et al.*, 1998).

HRM impact on organizational performance

Just as Kaufmann and Evans and Rauch have found evidence of a relationship between public staff management and national economic growth, there is a large and more substantial group of studies of industrialized country private companies which reinforces the message of the bureaucracy studies by showing that the way firms manage their staff is closely related to their overall performance. While the emergence of the SHRM model has attracted much attention among scholars and practitioners in the last 20 years, arguably the emerging view, impelled by the intensification of business competition, that the way staff are managed has a direct impact on organization performance, has an even greater importance. Huselid's groundbreaking study measured firms' staff management in terms of such factors as whether they used occupational tests when they were recruiting new employees. He then measured their performance in terms of turnover, productivity and financial performance. When he put his two measures together, he found that they were intimately connected (Huselid, 1995). A number of follow-up studies have supported Huselid's findings, adding the intriguing suggestion that HRM is an important source of competitive advantage partly because so few firms exploit it properly; unlike new technology, for example, which every self-respecting manufacturing firm knows it needs to spend money on. As with the bureaucratic studies, there is evidence that HRM is not just connected with organizational performance, but is actually causing it (Becker and Gerhart, 1996; Patterson *et al.*, 1997).

Taken together, these studies support our emphasis on the SHRM model. As we have seen, the evidence suggests that it is as much the way an organization aligns the different practices in a *strategic architecture* as the individual practices that matters (Becker and Gerhart, 1996). This is reassuring, as there is a very well established 'contingency' tradition in management thinking which insists that the practices may differ – and should differ – from place to place (Pugh and Hickson, 1976). For example, pay contingent on performance, an aspect of performance management, is notoriously subject to national and sectoral differences, as we will see in our chapters on Mauritius and Malaysia.

HRM a 'magic bullet'?

Our discussion has reviewed the evidence from a number of quarters that governments should take staff management more seriously because it is an important factor in their effectiveness and contributes to overall economic growth. It is probably still too early to claim that HR is a 'magic bullet' that will reliably improve governments' performance if only they take the trouble to invest in it. The bureaucracy and firm performance studies discussed earlier are not wholly consistent, although that is mainly because they have chosen to emphasize different aspects of HR. Use of self-managed teams, for example, which Huselid omitted from his research, is associated with firm performance in four other HR studies. Moreover, we have suggested that we may have to adapt particular practices if we want to transfer them successfully from one country to another, or from one sector of the economy to another. 'Vice may be virtue uprooted', is how the great Anglo-Welsh poet David Jones put much the same point (Jones, 1974, p.56).

So we are not yet in a position to read off prescriptions from the studies that we have reviewed. But we believe that we would be missing an opportunity if we ignored what staff management may be able to offer and dismissed it as nothing more than 'managerialism'. Instead, we think it is justified to test the value of the staff management hypothesis in the real world conditions of developing country governments. In the next section we explain how we went about that in the studies on which this book is based.

Methodology

The case study method

Many, perhaps most, studies of HR and staffing, whether at organization level in industrialized countries or at national level in developing countries, are quantitative and cross-sectional, typically based on a questionnaire sent through the post (examples appear in Brewster and Hegewisch, 1994; Evans and Rauch, 1999; and Huselid, 1995). Such studies allow comparisons across organizations and countries, uncovering patterns and allowing generalizations whose strength can be calibrated using standard statistical techniques. As we have seen, the Huselid paper inaugurated a whole body of research into the relationship between HRM and organizational performance. Brewster and Hegewisch's survey uncovered national differences that we will draw on below.

But that is not our approach. We have used a case study methodology, for four reasons. The first is that it is especially appropriate to research on government, since in the nature of things each country has only one government to study, precluding a quantitative, multi-firm study, at least at country level (Yin, 1994). The second is that it complements the quantitative methodology used in both the private and public sector studies. Quantitative researchers themselves have seen the value of doing this. Becker and Gerhart's review of the HRM and performance literature calls for 'deeper, qualitative research to complement the large-scale, multiple firm studies that are available' (1996, p.796; see also Guest, 1997). Third, the single-case study approach is appropriate when a single case represents a critical example for testing a theory or model (Eisenhardt, 1989).

The fourth reason is that having a reasonable number of cases does allow us to generalize, albeit with more than the usual limitations. Although there are themes that were constant across all the studies, as we will see, each study had its own flavour. That was first of all because our interests evolved. The studies were conducted sequentially by the main author, not in parallel. Later studies were 'in the light of' earlier ones.

Our 'sequential' research in fact spread out over six years, from 1999 to 2004, with the downsizing research taking place in 1997 and 1998. While it was not possible to update the interview data gathered in the earlier studies, published and Internet sources were used to bring the picture up to date: the Mauritius chapter (Chapter 3) is an example of how we did that.

It would be strange if a study of HRM, of all things, did not have learning built into its design. It would be equally strange if we failed to apply to this research project what we have learnt elsewhere about 'process project' methodologies. We have realized that 'logical framework' development project designs need to be flexible enough to adapt to the developing interests of their stakeholders. It was academics like Mintzberg (1989) and Korten (1980) who discovered this, and the lesson has been digested in most corporate boardrooms and development projects on the ground. Yet we academics have been reluctant to practise what we preach: academic research, ironically, is the last bastion of the blueprint project.

The literature review and the scope of our analysis

Researchers comparing staff management in two hospitals or two firms in the same country will concentrate on what distinguishes them; on organization-level factors like the different cultures of the two organizations. What they can afford to ignore, however – the national social, economic and political factors that they have in common – becomes crucial as soon as one makes qualitative comparisons across countries. Moreover, it is a feature of the public sector to be more deeply dyed with a national hue than, to take an extreme example, the local subsidiary of a multinational firm like IBM, with its employees who may have been hand-picked for their affinity with the parent company and country's ways. Public staff management, we hope to show, is intimately affected by national factors. In our literature reviews we have therefore drawn widely on the social, economic and political literature of the study countries.

Taking a broad view of influences on staff management allows us to hope that some of the conclusions about staff management that we will present in our final chapter will have implications for other areas of governance, so that readers whose interest in governance is broader than the one that this book mostly takes will find something to repay their study.

The data

Secondary data consisted mostly of government and donor agency reports and other documents. As the research progressed, the development of the Internet and the partly related climate of transparency meant that secondary data was easier to access, even from abroad. Knocking on a ministry or donor agency's door was no longer the only way of getting it.

Our main primary data-gathering method was interviews with key stakeholders (Burgoyne, 1994). A semi-structured format (Lee, 1999) was used, based on the themes outlined in the previous section (strategic integration, line manager ownership, employee selection and performance management). Interviews were conducted face-to-face and lasted from 60 to 90 minutes. In Malaysia, Mauritius and Morocco, the author and a researcher from the country in question conducted the interviews, with a couple of exceptions. In Tanzania, the interviews were conducted by Benson Bana, the co-author of the corresponding Chapter 4. All other interviews were conducted by the main author alone.

A non-probability judgement sampling approach was used, targeting government officials up to the most senior levels. Officials were identified by a national or (with the downsizing interviews) by a donor official familiar with the structure of the public service as having a key responsibility for the design and operation of HRM systems. To get at the strategic level, we interviewed the Head of the civil service or equivalent, which we managed to do in four of the countries, and Heads of line ministries, which we managed in every case. We also interviewed top officials in central agencies responsible for HR matters: the Ministry of Finance, which controls the payroll; the national civil service training academy (such as Sri Lanka's Institute of Development Administration); and the central staffing agency (such as Morocco's Ministry of Public Service, but also Sri Lanka's Public Service Commission). We also talked to the officials who were responsible for HRM in selected line ministries and agencies; the line ministry level (Health and Social Services) was the focus of the Namibia chapter (Chapter 9). In the later studies we made a point of interviewing retired officials, hoping, correctly as it turned out, that their views would be less inhibited.

Our success in getting interviews with very senior officials created the danger of hearing exclusively the 'view from above'. We skirted that danger by conducting 'focus group' interviews (Morgan, 1997) of relatively junior civil servants from different Ministries to give the point of view of a lower level in the hierarchy. We did this in Malaysia, Mauritius, Namibia and Tanzania. We also avoided it by interviewing trade unions representing civil servants in all but one of the countries. In a few cases we interviewed donor representatives and academic experts from the countries in question as well. The semi-structured format based on identified themes was again used.

Our judgement sample had limitations. First, only in Mauritius and Namibia did we manage to speak to a minister. This was unfortunate, given how much we will have to say about the political dimension, but the 'glass ceiling above' the official level proved hard to pierce (on this point see especially Chapter 6 on Swaziland). We tried to use the political literature as a proxy, and our two minister interviews tended to confirm rather than contradict our analysis.

The second limitation is to do with the frankness of our interviewees. We should not expect complete candour from senior officials, properly conditioned to do the bidding of the government of the day.

The author of a recent oral history of France under German occupation in World War Two, whose principal source was interviews with French people who sometimes had an interest in disguising the extent of their collaboration with the Germans or their approval of the transportation of French Jews to the Nazi death camps, talks about a 'rupture in the narrative', when the 'hidden transcript' beneath the rehearsed narrative begins to play (Gildea, 2002). Our less dramatic procedure was the uneventful, judicial one of letting interviewees have their say, and then sifting the different accounts in order to reach our own view, with the added dimension of the literature review to flesh out the picture.

Interviews and focus group meetings were conducted in English (or French in Morocco), and contemporaneous notes were taken. In most cases interviews were also taped and subsequently transcribed. A content analysis was carried out in which interview transcripts, interview notes and government reports and other documents were coded using the themes previously identified. We follow the convention of using italic type to indicate direct quotations from our interviews.

Choice of countries

Our main sample comprises Malaysia, Mauritius, Morocco, Namibia, Sri Lanka, Swaziland and Tanzania. For the downsizing chapter (Chapter 2), we also drew on interviews in Ghana and Uganda. Listing the countries makes plain the limitation of our sample: Latin America, for instance, is wholly excluded. But we did manage to go to lower and middle-income countries, both English- and French-speaking (Mauritius is both), in different regions of Africa and Asia, with Morocco additionally on the edge of the Arab world. As with much recent development research, there is a bias towards sub-Saharan Africa, an area facing dramatic development challenges, as Chapter 9 (on Namibia) makes particularly clear.

Country data

The information in Table 1.4, where countries are listed in chapter order, is mostly taken from the current UN *Human Development Report* and the World Bank's *World Development Indictors*, and data is for 2003 unless shown. Arrows in the first column indicate the direction of change in recent years. Namibia and Swaziland's absolute ratings have deteriorated and Tanzania's relative rating has stood still, the result of the HIV/AIDS pandemic in sub-Saharan Africa, especially southern Africa (see Chapter 9).

The following ratings in Table 1.5 are taken from the World Bank governance index.

Bearing in mind the data limitations we have already noted, and despite the strong tendency for governance ratings to be correlated with wealth – bluntly, rich countries are better governed than poor ones – there are interesting anomalies which we will examine in individual country chapters and in our concluding chapter. For example, Kaufmann's survey respondents rated government effectiveness in Malaysia even more highly than its wealth would lead us to expect. At

Table 1.4   Basic indicators for study countries

Country	Human development	GNI per capita (US dollars)	GDP growth (%age)	Aid as %age of GDP	Debt service as %age of exports
Mauritius	64th (out of 177) ↑	4100	3.2	0.5	8.2
Tanzania	162nd →	300	3.5	13.1	8.9
Morocco	125th ↑	1310	5.5	1.8	23.9
Swaziland	137th ↓	1350	3.5	2.1	1.7
Sri Lanka	96th ↑	930	4.3	2.1	9.8
Malaysia	57th ↑	3880	3.2	0.1	7.3
Namibia	126th ↓	1930	3.7	3.4	9.1

Sources: IMF (2004a); UNDP (2004); World Bank (2003). The figure for debt service in Mauritius is for 2000 (Earthtrends, 2005).

Table 1.5 Governance indicators for study countries (percentile rankings)

Country	Government effectiveness	Voice and accountability	Political stability	Control of corruption
Mauritius	70.7	74.8	78.2	67.0 (54th)[1]
Morocco	56.3	32.5	39.8	56.7 (77th)
Tanzania	40.4	38.3	35.0	36.0 (90th)
Swaziland	31.3	10.2	53.9	13.8 (–)
Sri Lanka	45.7	41.3	14.1	52.2 (67th)
Malaysia	81.3	37.4	58.7	64.5 (39th)
Namibia	63.5	61.2	60.2	62.6 (54th)

Source: Kaufmann *et al.* (2005).
[1] Ratings in brackets from the 2004 Transparency International Corruption Perceptions Index.

the other end, they rated Tanzania more highly on this dimension than Swaziland, despite Swaziland's relative wealth.

Summary of chapters

Chapter 2 HRM as Downsizing: From Cost to Strategy

Our second chapter deals with the HR initiative that dominated public staff management in developing countries throughout the 1980s and 90s: what was variously called 'civil service reform' or (more narrowly and accurately) 'employment reform' or (more brutally but still euphemistically) 'downsizing'.

Efforts to curtail the size of the public workforce were the staffing expression of the 'small state' ideology on which the World Bank and IMF's structural adjustment lending programmes in the 1980s and 90s were based: we therefore refer to them as the 'Washington model' of staffing reform. These efforts, as the Bank and IMF came to admit, rarely succeeded even in their own terms. The Bank/IMF's predominant explanation is that there was a failure of 'political commitment'; in other words, developing country governments had failed to follow through on the commitments they had made to donors. We compare this view with explanations for the similarly poor outcomes of downsizing in (mostly private) organizations in industrialized countries, explanations that emphasize weaknesses in strategy, diagnosis, incrementalism and provision for retrenchees. We then present the results of field research in Ghana, Malaysia, Sri Lanka and Uganda, and – providing an industrialized country comparison – the UK.

The various findings converge on the need to move from a cost-driven approach, with Finance ministries in the lead, to a strategic approach, one based on diagnosis and drawing on HRM expertise. Such an approach should take account of process factors in reform, make provision for the 'victims' of reform, loosen the link between down-sizing and pay reform, and refine the role of donors in supporting reform. We suggest also that HRM practitioners and scholars have an important contribution to make in developing a new approach.

Chapter 3   Mauritius: Economic Growth and Strategic Human Resource Management

The chapter on Mauritius, the first of the single country studies that constitute the remainder of our empirical data, takes up where the previous chapter left off by exploring the value of a strategic approach to staffing in the form of the SHRM model that we have outlined already in this chapter. We also explore the putative relationship between public staff management and economic growth identified by Evans and Rauch, and others.

SHRM was not practised in Mauritius at the time of our interviews, nor was it feasible in the near future. It was not widely known, there was no strategic management framework, staff management was highly centralized, and, lastly (here we echo the World Bank/IMF explanation of the failure of employment reform) 'political will' to make radical changes in staff management was lacking. Mauritius' undoubted economic success could not be attributed to the quality of the civil service.

However, a change of government in 2000 created political will where none had previously existed. Influenced rather more by Malaysia than by Western countries, government was becoming more strategic, with evidence of piecemeal improvements, although there were still gaps in the strategy, and the fear of nepotism and favouritism was still evident in the government's reluctance to implement performance management.

The case study does not support either the claim that SHRM and its associated practices have a universal validity, or that public staff management is a 'magic bullet' that reliably delivers economic growth. We conclude that rather than applying a template from abroad, improvements to staff management in Mauritius, and arguably other developing countries, will require a creative and piecemeal adaptation of Anglophone 'good practice' that respects political, economic and social realities.

Chapter 4   Tanzania: Laws and Institutions

We saw earlier that our current thinking about governance has learnt from the New Institutional Economics the importance of political and other institutions. How those institutions affect the way public servants are managed is the main concern of our study of Tanzania. Tanzania is one of two countries discussed in this book where staffing institutions have been subjected to upheaval in the post-independence period (the other is Sri Lanka). Tanzania rejected the Westminster model of separation between politics and administration, deliberately placing institutions like the Civil Service Commission under the control of the ruling party in the period of *Ujamaa* socialism so that they would serve national development objectives. Although the government subsequently moved back towards the Westminster model, features of the single-party period remain, contaminating the efficiency and integrity of government.

Even the framework of laws in place at the time of our study conferred excessive powers on the President, and there were few procedural checks on how he exercised them. The centralization of power in the President's office was replicated one level down in the centralization of power in the Civil Service Commission and Civil Service Department, which meant that line ministries had little discretion to make staffing decisions, despite the fact that in most cases the central agencies' decisions represented the rubber-stamping of a decision that a line ministry had already made. There was also considerable duplication of functions between central and line agencies, and even between the central agencies themselves.

In a climate of corruption and favouritism that was admitted on all sides, it was clear that civil servants and the public at large had lost confidence in the integrity of civil service staffing. There was therefore a need to strengthen the independence of staffing decisions from political control, and to delegate to lower levels. However, this would need to be done sensitively in order to ensure that the civil service was properly responsive to political objectives, and to prevent corruption and favouritism from creeping in at the lower levels to which decisions might be delegated.

Chapter 5   Morocco: The Politics of HRM

Once again our next chapter takes up where the previous one left off, presenting an analysis of the political context of staffing reform. We find several reasons why HRM in the Moroccan civil service has stagnated, notably unfamiliarity with HRM models, and the French administrative heritage. But the fundamental reason is Morocco's political system, where power resides in the Palace despite the apparatus of democratic government, and where political actors are reluctant to take bold initiatives. Thus a focus on the management level is currently misplaced, and fundamental political action harnessing the authority of the Palace without disempowering other political actors is needed. It follows that in Morocco – and once more we argue that the finding can be applied to other countries – a political analysis is sometimes a prerequisite for improving HRM in both public and private organizations.

Chapter 6   Swaziland: Political Commitment

Attributing both the stagnation of HRM and then its revival following the 2000 election in Mauritius to 'political will' begged the question of what that cloudy concept might consist of. This is the focus of our study of Swaziland, a country with a history of unsuccessful attempts at reform which stretch back almost to its independence in 1968.

Political commitment has figured as a principal reason for the failure not only of staff management reforms, but also of development programmes in general. We propose a new model of commitment, and we apply it to Swaziland's experience. The failure of repeated reform attempts there up to the time of writing is indeed due to a lack of commitment that has its roots in Swaziland's unusual political system, in which 'traditional' rulers have effective power: like Morocco, the Palace is where the real power lies. Prospects for reform therefore depend either on fundamental political change, or on engaging with rulers' fear that reform represents a threat to their interests. Applying the model of commitment to the case study allows us to suggest ways of overcoming the current deadlock in Swaziland. Analysing commitment, which entails a broader political analysis, also allows us to predict whether a government's ostensible commitment to reform will translate into action.

Chapter 7   Sri Lanka: Political Patronage

Our next chapter enlarges on the problem of patronage, an aspect of the political system which previous chapters have touched on. It builds on an earlier study to present a review of the progress of HR reforms in Sri Lanka up to the time of writing. As in some previous chapters, HR is found to be unstrategic, highly centralized and lacking sophistication in the practice of key HR activities. However, it is suggested that the failure of previous reform efforts is rooted in the patronage system that has been a major political driving force for almost 50 years. The latest reform, which concentrated on institutional design *via* a constitutional amendment at the expense of putting professional HR considerations on one side, made sense as an attempt to tackle patronage head-on. However, it had the side effect of increasing familiar bureaucratic pathologies. While the reform was worthwhile in itself and deserved to be continued, there was a need to address the perceived remoteness of government that had caused patronage to arise in the first place, and also to strengthen the reform's political support base, recognizing politicians' expectation that the bureaucracy should be able to respond to their constituents' needs.

Patronage, in other words, is found to be a political problem that requires a political solution, although institutional reform is still one of its elements, just as in Tanzania. Once that solution has been found and the integrity of government is established – but not before – attention can return to more recognizable HR concerns that will improve efficiency and responsiveness to citizens' needs. As in Morocco, HR and managerial improvements must wait on a solution of the political dilemma.

Chapter 8   Malaysia: History and Path Dependence

In this study we descend to the historical level of analysis *via* a critique of the currently influential notion of 'path dependence', and we also recapitulate themes explored in earlier chapters. Path dependence refers to the way in which an industry's or a country's choice of a particular technology or mode of governance is a 'critical juncture' which 'locks in' the choice and closes off alternative paths of development. It implicitly denies that governments can do much to influence long-term direction; donors still less. The article explores similarities and contrasts with the treatment of these questions in mainstream historiography, particularly the work of Braudel.

Relative to the other countries discussed in this book, HRM in the Malaysian civil service is found to be performance-orientated, though also emphasizing affirmative action; strategic; centralized; and displaying evidence of use of normative approaches in activities like personnel selection. We suggest ways in which the government might further improve on a performance that is already relatively strong.

In terms of the 'path dependence' theory, we find that the consolidation of the civil service around 1954 was indeed a 'critical juncture', but that its subsequent evolution, in which individual 'agency' was important, has been equally significant in giving it its overall shape.

The abiding value of the path dependence view lies in its insight that history shapes and constrains policymaking. It is an insight that both academics and policymakers, drawing on historiography, would do well to develop.

Chapter 9   Namibia: The Human Resource Crisis in Health in Africa

In the last of our country studies we address an important practical challenge to staff management. In 2000 the United Nations committed themselves to the ambitious targets embodied in the Millennium Development Goals (MDGs). Only five years later, it was clear that poor countries were not on track to achieve them. It was also clear that achieving the three out of the eight MDGs that concern health would only be possible if the appropriate human resource was in place.

Chapter 9 explores the steps that Namibia, a country facing severe health problems that include an alarmingly high AIDS infection rate, has taken to manage its health workers. In the 15 years since independence, Namibia has patiently built up a relatively good strategic framework for health policy in the context of government policy as a whole, including strong training arrangements at every level of health staffing, and it has brought HIV/AIDS under the strategic umbrella through its National Strategic Plan for HIV/AIDS. Its major weakness is that the strategic framework has not kept pace with the rise in HIV/AIDS and TB infection: the community counselling service, still at the pilot stage when we did our study, was the only specific response. That has created a tension between building long-term capacity in a strategic context and responding to the short-term demands of the AIDS and TB crisis.

We suggest that countries like Namibia need a new paradigm for staffing their health services. Building on the existing strategic framework, it should target the training of 'mid-level cadres'. Higher-level cadres should take on the role of supporting and monitoring the mid-level cadres. To do that, they will need management training and a performance management framework for staff support and monitoring.

Chapter 10   Conclusion: Improving HRM in Developing Country Governance

In our final chapter we synthesize our findings in two models. The first is a two-stage normative model of HRM in which countries whose political dispensation and institutional structure as they affect staff management are flawed concentrate initially on correcting those flaws, emphasizing compliance with organizational norms. Countries whose political dispensation and institutional structure are sound are able to move to Stage Two, concentrating on refining their strategic frameworks and improving the professional conduct of HR, with a view to improving staff performance, and with that the performance of public services.

However, the model does not give us a formula for generating plans of action. Instead, actions must be informed by a 'thick description' of the political, economic, social and historical influences on staff management. Actions to improve staff management require a 'total explanation' of those influences, and of the interactions between the four levels of our governance model. This will be demanding to conduct, but it gives us our best chance of taking actions that will stick and will make a difference.

2
HRM as Downsizing: From Cost to Strategy

Introduction: the significance of downsizing

This chapter raises the curtain on the empirical studies which are the core of the book by examining a little-studied Human Resource initiative taken by developing country governments especially in the 1980s and 90s, one entirely unrelieved by the application of HRM specialist knowledge. This is the phenomenon of what has usually been called 'civil service reform' or, more narrowly, 'employment reform' in developing countries. Reform in this context refers to those deliberate measures that developing country governments have taken to alter the employment and payment of their staff, typically within some larger programme of macroeconomic reform. 'Reform' is often a euphemism, since in practice the most prominent measure has been job reduction, with which civil service reform has frequently been synonymous (Pronk, 1996). That is why our chapter has the title it does: 'downsizing' is a suitably ugly label for an ugly phenomenon.

It is appropriate to discuss it early in this book, as it is the HR measure that ushered in the age of reform in the early 1980s. For despite the bullish claims made for the emerging strategic HRM model which we reported in Chapter 1, it is downsizing that has towered over the HRM landscape in developing country governments. Between 1987 and 1996 the World Bank assisted no fewer than 68 developing and transitional countries with reform programmes (Nunberg, 1997). China, the world's most populous nation, embarked in 1998 on a reform programme designed to cut the number of its civil servants by half – in other words, by a projected four million people (Economist, 1998), and studies reported below demonstrate that it has made good on its intention. Similarly dramatic reports from individual countries are also available, such as Ghana and Uganda (McCourt, 1998a). Even in industrialized countries the scale has been dramatic: staff retrenchment programmes were carried out between 1987 and 1992 in the public sectors of 22 of the 27 member countries of the OECD, making it by some distance their most widespread Human Resource initiative (OECD, 1994). The number of public employees in Germany went down from 381,000 in 1992 to 315,000 in 1998; the US reduced by 17 per cent over roughly the same period (Manning and Parison, 2004).

This chapter presents an integration of the rather disparate literature that bears on employment reform in developing country governments and in industrialized country (mainly North American) private companies. It also incorporates material from field interviews in six countries, including Malaysia and Sri Lanka, two countries whose HR experience we look at more broadly in later chapters.

The experience of reform

With the important exception of China, which we discuss below, a review of the literature on downsizing in developing countries is largely a review of what World Bank and IMF staff have had to say on the subject.[1] It is impossible to exaggerate the dominance of the twin Bretton Woods institutions over the reform debate. Their Washington headquarters are veritable research factories, and the leverage which their lending powers give them in the field (both institutions are lending institutions first and foremost) means that when they evaluate the success of reform, it is largely the success of their own prescriptions that is being evaluated, and that their perspective influences what they study (Mallaby, 2005); hence the Bank President's characterization of its role in the 1990s as having been that of a 'professorial policeman' (Mathiason, 2005, p.11). By contrast, the capacity of developing countries to undertake their own research is weak. A HRM specialist wishing to understand, let alone influence, the conduct of reform must therefore engage with the Washington literature.

In studying the downsizing experience, we can regard 1982, when Ghana's bellwether programme began, as a *terminus ab quo*. As country after country followed in Ghana's footsteps, a blueprint emerged in which a reduction in the size of the civil service, typically expressed as a conditionality or 'structural benchmark' in a World Bank or IMF loan, was specified in the context of a reduction in overall government expenditure whose aim was to restore macroeconomic stability and facilitate growth (Lindauer and Nunberg, 1994). Crucially, in other words, this was a cost-driven model of reform. Recognizing that the alleged overstaffing had often been at the expense of lower wages, the blueprint included provision for the savings from retrenchment to be used to raise wages for the survivors, especially the higher-paid for whom *salary decompression* was indicated, since their salaries were said to have fallen relative both to their juniors and their private sector counterparts. Stevens (1994b) provides a textbook example of how all this was to be done in practice.

Clearly other analyses were possible. At the macroeconomic level, for instance, development activists have pointed to the effect of foreign debt on government finances or the decline in development assistance from rich countries (Commission for Africa, 2005). Others have priori-tized improved revenue collection rather than cutting government expenditure as a way of balancing government income and expendi-ture (Dia, 1996). Nonetheless there was a presumption that govern-ment was overstaffed in any case (Nunberg, 1997), and, as one of the Bank's staff put it, 'That no government or little government was better than big government' (Chaudhry, 1994, p.199).

From a HR point of view, the favoured reform instruments were a mixture of familiar and unfamiliar. Certainly the familiar tools of voluntary and compulsory redundancies figured among them. But other options have included the elimination of 'ghost workers', a colourful phrase which refers to the practice, widespread in sub-Saharan Africa in the early 1990s (Nunberg, 1994), of interpolating fictitious names into a payroll so that wages can be diverted fraudu-lently. Since such practices can only occur when a payroll is in disar-ray, reform was predicated on first carrying out a payroll census (Stevens, 1994a).[2]

Dealing with the impact of reform on its victims was not an integral part of the blueprint, although the Bank has become more sensitive recently, particularly in relation to women retrenchees (Rama, 2002; World Bank, 2004b). Severance packages could be seen as too generous (Abed *et al.*, 1998), possibly at the expense of needier groups in society (Graham, 1994); the informal and agricultural sectors might have a robust capacity to absorb retrenchees, even in the absence of any sever-ance packages (Nunberg, 1997; Wescott, 1999), despite evidence that the jobs in those sectors were not often the ones that ex-public employees were best equipped to do (Alderman *et al.*, 1994; Solinger, 2002). Attempts to supplement compensation packages with retrain-ing, counselling or other measures were seen as ineffectual (Alderman *et al.*, 1994). The effect of reform on civil service performance was also outside the blueprint, and was rarely mentioned.

As mentioned above, China is exceptional in being the subject of several independent studies (Brødsgaard, 2002; Burns, 2003; Cai, 2002; Cooke, 2000; Li *et al.*, 2004; Solinger, 2002; Straussman and Zhang, 2001). Its approach displays distinctive 'Chinese characteristics' (Warner, 1993), notably in the leading role that the Communist Party continues to play, but it also echoes experience elsewhere, such as the difficulty of achieving cost saving targets, the book transfer of staff from one agency to another which gives the appearance but not the reality of job reduction, and the ineffectual nature of re-employment schemes for displaced workers.

The outcomes of reform

How have the World Bank and the IMF evaluated the performance of downsizing reforms, even in their own terms? It has been disappointing. Abed *et al.* report an annual 0.5 per cent drop in numbers in 22 countries assisted by the IMF, but also an annual 1 per cent decrease in real wages, suggesting that wage cuts played a critical role in reducing the wage bill – the exact opposite of what the blueprint envisaged. By 1995 the World Bank had rated 40 per cent of its own civil service reform projects as unsatisfactory at completion (Nunberg, 1997). Lienert and Modi (1997, p.32) concluded that 'most sub-Saharan African low-income countries have made only limited progress towards achieving the objectives of civil service reform', and Schiavo-Campo (1996) contended that elsewhere there was even more to be done.

Why the failure? Nunberg (1997) baldly lists factors identified in World Bank project evaluation reports. Pride of place goes to lack of political commitment and ownership by reforming governments – a factor that we will dwell on in this book, particularly when we look at Mauritius and Sri Lanka (Chapters 3 and 7 respectively). Other factors listed are political and economic crisis, lack of administrative and financial capacity and flawed project design and project staffing, along with two factors which relate purely to the role of donor agencies: poor donor co-ordination and Bank-country dialogue.

The Bank/IMF explanation of failure might be a little sketchy, but the remedial proposals were assured. Countries should consolidate and extend the existing reform programme but should also supplement it with a 'second generation' of reform measures (Abed *et al.*, 1998; Lienert and Modi, 1997; Nunberg, 1997; Schiavo-Campo, 1996). These would include wider staffing issues such as pay and appraisal, but also systemic factors such as the link between the personnel and finance functions in government, the introduction of a strategic approach, modulated to take account of differences between countries, and an emphasis on increasing government ownership of reform. Only Nunberg addressed the part that donors had played in the failure of reform.

In short, the Washington reaction to the failure of their own reform prescriptions was ambivalent. The earlier approach was not repudiated: for example, reform as cost reduction still has pride of place in a recent Bank publication (Manning and Parison, 2004: see especially p.26). But it now coexisted uneasily with the sense that something was needed to supplement it, possibly work on systems, institutions and strategies. The Bank's recent emphasis on the role of government as a vehicle for pro-poor service delivery has further complicated the picture (World Bank, 2003).

The industrialized country experience

Points of corroboration

While industrialized country studies of downsizing do not address some of the specific problems of reform, such as the role of donors, they are relevant to us because of the scale of downsizing – IBM's reduction from 406,000 to 202,000 jobs between 1986 and 1995 (Economist, 1996b) is hefty, even if not quite on the Chinese scale – and because they disclose some surprising similarities.

There are four ways in which the industrialized country experience echoes the Washington analysis. The first, and perhaps the most striking, is that downsizing has frequently flopped here as well. It was established quite early on, counter-intuitively, that firm performance tended to worsen rather than improve following downsizing (De Meuse *et al.*, 1994). The reasons are interesting. Profits might go up, as wage costs, including pay levels, went down, if only because downsizing represented a simple transfer of wealth from labour to capital. But productivity targets, and even simple cost-cutting targets, were often not met, and workers' morale and trust often suffered (Baumol *et al.*, 2003; Bennett, 1991; Henkoff, 1990; Peak, 1996). Companies' share prices tended to deteriorate as well: again contrary to some popular belief, investors largely disapprove of cost-cutting for its own sake, believing it shows that a company has lost its way (Cascio *et al.*, 1997; Rigby, 2002).

The second and third echoes are the stress on the importance of ownership (Cameron, 1994), and on the cost dimension. On the latter, Greenhalgh and McKersie (1980) point out that downsizing could paradoxically increase costs, at least in the short term, because of severance and other expenditure.

Finally, and notably, the American studies strongly emphasize the importance of a strategic approach, explicitly contrasted with the cost-driven approach. Again and again, writers point to the failure of organizations to downsize in the context of a strategy for improving organizational performance, one whose elements include restructuring, performance appraisal and articulating a vision of where the organization wants to go. Stock market reaction to downsizing is only favourable where it is geared to refocusing the business (Chalos and Chen, 2002; Rigby, 2002), and where it is simply one component in an integrated package of measures which will enable the organization to realize its new vision (Cameron, 1994 and Roach, 1996 are representative). Henkoff (1990, p.34) sums up the view of many:

> Downsize if you must. But don't expect a pay-off unless you do so with a well-thought-out strategy.

Qualifications

However, the industrialized country studies also qualify the Washington analysis in two ways. First, they place the strategic and the cost-driven approaches in opposition: the cost-driven approach, it seems, is unlikely to succeed even in reducing costs, let alone improving performance. Second, the striking similarity between the failure of downsizing in the two domains paradoxically calls into question the major element in the Washington explanation of reform failure, political commitment and government ownership. When downsizing fails, it has as much to do with the process followed as with the commitment of the downsizers.

Distinctive factors

Cameron's study: success factors in downsizing

In other respects, the American studies take the explanation into new territory. In a perceptive study, Cameron (1994) found that increased participation by the workforce, systematic prior analysis of tasks and personnel and, to a lesser extent, use of a gradual, incremental approach were statistically associated with downsizing success. (More detail on prior analysis and incrementalism is given below.) He also identifies HRM expertise as a bridge between organization-level staffing decisions and their operational implementation (see also Kozlowski *et al.*, 1993; and Sahdev *et al.*, 1999).

Diagnosis

Prior analysis of tasks and personnel – diagnosis, in other words – appears crucial. Whetten and Cameron (1994, p.272) found that failure to diagnose led to 'a protracted implementation process often marred by multiple false starts'. Identifying the causes of overstaffing is an important element. As a US general manager said, 'Costs exist for a reason. If you don't take the reasons away, the costs will return' (quoted in Henkoff, 1990, p.27). Moving to the public sector, Rose (1985, p.xiii) argues similarly that the size of the public workforce is the result of past programme commitments perpetuated in the present. The inference is that in order to control staffing numbers it is necessary to understand the policymaking process, since that is the root of staffing size.

Incrementalism

The importance of a phased approach is highlighted in the separate but related literature dealing with the phenomenon of 'turnaround', i.e. programmes for the recovery of sickly firms (e.g. Slatter, 1984). Arogyaswamy *et al.* (1995) have presented a two-stage model of corporate recovery, where emergency actions to cut costs lead on to strategic planning for the future, generating stakeholder support and strategic development of the organization's staff (see also Pandit, 1996).

Victims of downsizing

As we saw, the Washington analysis has mostly been sanguine about the fate of retrenchees. The fate of their American private sector counterparts is the subject of many articles in the downsizing literature. In contrast to the reform studies, American retrenchees, despite operating in a robust economy, are seen to have suffered financially, with severely reduced earnings that persist for as much as six years after retrenchment (Stevens, 1997). Retrenchees suffer in other ways too: the negative impact of unemployment on health and well-being is firmly established (Argyle, 1989).

Employers have concerned themselves with their employees' fate for a mixture of expedient, legal, and ethical reasons. First, it is expedient for employers to treat victims decently, if only because survivors whose retrenched colleagues have been badly treated are likely to react by working less hard (Brockner *et al.*, 1987; Ting, 1996). Second, employers are of course obliged to obey the law and to honour employment contracts which have the force of law. Third, many employers go further than the law requires for ethical reasons (Brytting, 1994), doing their best to avoid redundancies altogether, or to mitigate hardship when redundancies are inevitable. Methods used have included giving adequate notice; providing outplacement and job search advice, and staff counselling; and involving trade unions (Perkins, 1987; Sutton, 1987).

Inappropriate reasons for downsizing

If the gains from downsizing are so uncertain, why do organizations keep doing it? An innocent explanation is that they are playing follow-the-leader: downsizing companies have tended to imitate fashionable models (McKinley *et al.*, 1995). Sometimes the model is their own previous practice: Henkoff (1990) found that one of the best predictors of downsizing is whether a firm has downsized before. Echoing the preference for smaller government in the Washington analysis, there is also a preference for 'lean' staffing structures as good things in themselves (Peters and Waterman, 1982). More darkly, we have seen already that owners or managers have benefited financially from downsizing, and they may also have benefited by seeing their power increase at workers' expense (Baumol *et al.*, 2003; Downs, 1995; Tomaney, 1990). Klein (1997) and Ruggles and O'Higgins (1987) have argued that in the public sector downsizing has advanced a right-wing ideological agenda.

Downsizing and pay

Finally, it is worth mentioning that pay, an integral part of the reform package, is barely mentioned in the downsizing literature. The Western equivalent of salary decompression, where some egregious CEOs have received generous pay increases at the same time that their staff were being sacked, has not impressed Western public opinion, becoming an issue in elections in both the USA and the UK in the 1990s (Economist, 1996b).

Lessons of the reform and downsizing studies

Recognizing the limitations in the data, we can draw some tentative conclusions. Both the reform and the downsizing studies agree that programmes that emphasize cost reduction in isolation have frequently failed even to reduce costs, let alone improve performance. They also agree on the importance of a strategic approach, and of the commitment of the reformers. The developing country studies empha-size the role of donors. The downsizing studies emphasize the impor-tance of diagnosis, and of the process factors of incrementalism, communication and participation. They also emphasize the role of the HRM function in brokering the reform process, and they point to the distortion caused by doing reform for inappropriate reasons. On the other hand, the sources are contradictory on the relationship between cost reduction and strategic approaches, on the care of the victims of reform, and on the importance of pay as a reform element.

Interview findings

Countries studied

Semi-structured interviews were held in 1997/98 with government, trade union and donor officials in Ghana, Malaysia, South Africa, Sri Lanka, Uganda and – in order to provide an industrialized country comparison – the UK. Countries were chosen to give a geographical spread of low, middle and high-income countries which have sign-ificant downsizing experience. Government officials comprised Heads of the Civil Service or their nearest equivalent in four of the five deve-loping countries, and relevant senior officials in the Ministries of Finance and Public Service, or their equivalent, and in local or provin-cial authorities. In the UK, where published documentation is more extensive, interviews were confined to staff of the Cabinet Office, one executive agency, one Health Trust and one local authority. The coun-tries studied were also chosen to include examples of both success and failure as defined in the reform studies which we have reviewed. Ghana, Malaysia, Uganda and the UK had carried out substantial staffing reforms; South Africa and Sri Lanka had not. Given that the original data was collected some years ago, more recent secondary sources have been used where possible to bring the picture up to date, and fresh field research was carried out in Malaysia and Sri Lanka in 2004. However, readers should be aware that the picture is more reli-able as an account of general trends and patterns than of any particular country. Our data is therefore grouped by theme rather than country.

The costs of reform

Our interviews suggest that the failure of reform may be more serious than the reform studies report. Even Ghana, Uganda and the UK, which have been represented as success stories, had serious problems in containing staffing costs. While Ghana's civil service numbers fell by 26,766 between 1987 and 1992 (albeit against a target of 45,000), payroll expenditure at the beginning and the end of the reform period were almost the same (Burton *et al.*, 1993), and in 2004 an overrun in the civil service wage bill was obliging the government to increase borrowing (World Bank, 2004a). Unlike Ghana, the UK did meet – indeed exceed – its early job reduction targets: by 1985 total numbers had already dipped below 600,000, a target they were expected to reach only three years later. But there too, payroll spending did not decline commensurately, instead rising somewhat through the early 1980s (Dunsire and Hood, 1989). Numbers employed in Uganda fell sharply, but have risen slightly again; and the overall pay bill actually rose from 2 per cent to 3.6 per cent of GDP between 1989 and 1996.

Explaining reform outcomes: factors already identified

Clearly some of the elements of an explanation of reform outcomes are purely local. Sri Lanka threw a spanner in its reform machinery when it mistakenly extended the enhanced voluntary redundancy package to its regular retirees. South Africa did likewise, yoking a retrenchment target that was in any case unrealistic to a three-year pay agreement with trade unions. But we wish to concentrate on factors that are generalizable. We begin with factors that we have already identified in the reform and downsizing literatures.

Strategy

The early stages of reform in Ghana, Uganda and the UK were not strategic at all. Number- and cost-reduction were geared to reducing overall government expenditure. Ironically, it was the two countries which have not succeeded in reducing numbers or costs which were most strategic. South Africa's Department of Public Service and Administration had an elaborate HRM strategy, where a 'transformed' public service was harnessed to providing services to the previously disadvantaged majority population (Government of South Africa, 1995, 1997). Its approach to downsizing, which began as a classic cost reduction exercise, had now been aligned with the overall strategy through the adoption of a review methodology. Sri Lanka was implementing a package of measures which included a rolling programme of management reviews of all its major departments, and the formulation of mission statements for each department to clarify its purpose (Government of Sri Lanka, 1998).[3]

In general, political reluctance and official incapacity to think strategically acted as brakes on the development of a strategic view.

Review methodologies had their own problems. Addressing whether a particular function was carried out efficiently was useful, but still begged questions about whether the function was needed, whether it was duplicated by another agency, and its priority relative to other functions. This required action at the level of the civil service as a whole. Reports of the ubiquitous administrative reform commissions (Government of Sri Lanka, 1987; Government of Uganda, 1990; see also Polidano, 1995), provided a strategic basis, but were sometimes confined to efficiency issues. Moreover, governments often overlooked fundamental issues of strategy, as in Sri Lanka (McCourt, 2001a). Malaysia went furthest in this respect, eliminating duplication between agencies, as with the amalgamation of the Rubber Licensing and Rubber Research Boards.

Political commitment and ownership

The importance of commitment and ownership was not in doubt, being argued forcefully by Sri Lanka's Cabinet Secretary among others (Wijesinghe, 1997). In Uganda, President Museveni's personal commitment to reform was clear (Museveni, 1997). Prime Minister Mahathir showed his commitment by himself chairing all ten meetings of the committee which reformed Malaysia's civil service pay (Government of Malaysia, 1991). In pluralist systems, however, commitment was necessarily the outcome of an agreement among multiple stakeholders which had to be painstakingly constructed. *'There was a hell of a consultation with the stakeholders,'* as one South African official put it. His government, and that of Sri Lanka, were coalitions which included trade unions, and their views mattered (World Bank, 1996b; see also Kiragu and Mukandala, 2004).

Stakeholder support was affected by the nature of the various programmes. The South African government hesitated to embark on a radical programme which would have thrown many employees out of work in former homelands such as the Transkei region, causing hardship and possibly damaging the government's electoral support; but they implemented a modified but still substantial proposal to eradicate ghost workers in the same areas – ghosts do not suffer hardship or, as a rule, vote in elections.

Donor behaviour also affected commitment. Where political commitment was already strong, as in Ghana and Uganda, donor involvement contributed to more sharply focused programmes. But in a more complex stakeholder environment, donors were apt to be heavy-footed, and even to create a focus for opposition to reform. South

Africa politely rejected the *'expert but inflexible'* advice proffered by British civil servants. The perception in Sri Lanka that donors, particularly the World Bank, were pressing for a harsh package of reform measures created a focus for opposition to reform, so that even an innocuous measure like performance appraisal could be portrayed as a World Bank imposition.

Donors were sometimes insensitive to governments' actual reform priorities, as opposed to the ones that donors wanted them to have. One major donor saw a major restructuring of central-local relations in Sri Lanka as an expensive irrelevance. In the context of downsizing that was certainly true. But the plan was motivated mainly by a desire to confront the problem of Tamil insurrection by conceding greater autonomy to regions, and to Tamil areas in particular (although we will see in Chapter 7 that the donors weren't so far wrong). Governments did not always agree with the Washington analysis of the importance of pay decompression. Even in Ghana, where the ratio changed from 2.2:1 in 1984 to 10:1 in 1991, decompression was moderated by across-the-board pay increases (Burton *et al.*, 1993). Uganda was at least as concerned to improve the pay of its primary teachers, an aspect of its Universal Primary Education policy, and to return overall civil service pay its 1960s level, as it was to decompress the pay of senior civil servants.[4] These corroborate previous findings of support among civil servants and the public for greater pay equality (Fosh, 1978; Robinson, 1990).

Diagnosis

'The first redundancy exercise was a disaster,' said one Ugandan official, while a Sri Lankan union official believed that *'1990* (the date of the first redundancy exercise) *failed because it was too hasty.'* Like American companies, governments tended to reform publicly in haste, only to repent discreetly at leisure. Rising costs alongside falling staff numbers is one example, but there were others: expensive and ill-targeted voluntary retirement packages in Sri Lanka (World Bank, 1996b) and South Africa; the first batch of retrenchees in Ghana believing that they would be rehired when the economy recovered; and their counterparts in Uganda dismissed on the basis of grotesquely unreliable appraisal reports.

Governments and donors alike appeared unwilling to admit that they did not fully understand public staffing, though its complexity and the customary absence of reliable data at the beginning of reform made misunderstanding almost inevitable. Targets for staffing cuts were usually arbitrary, to be over- or undershot to equal amazement. Uganda's initial target for staff reduction of 34,000 jobs looked tough until it discovered no fewer than 42,000 ghosts (Government of Uganda, 1994). Numbers were to decrease eventually by about 150,000, or almost 50 per cent. Ghana's initial annual job reduction target of 15,000 jobs was beefed up after 11,000 ghosts came to light (Burton *et al.*, 1993).

Process factors: participation, HRM expertise and incrementalism

The Ugandan official who commented that *'The whole reform process was welcomed, but the way it was handled is now detested'* highlighted a pervasive failure. Thus, for instance, the participation of employees and their trade union representatives was occasional at best, even though it appeared to have positive effects where it did take place.[5] The Civil Servants' Association in Ghana *'gave its blessing'* to reform; a UK official went so far as to say that the unions were his key change agents, and that pushing through job reductions would have been 'one hundred times' more difficult without them. In other cases there was no participation. The civil servants' union was not recognized in Uganda at the start of reform. In Sri Lanka the management side did not consult unions: *'Government believes we are hostile to reform,'* said one union official, *'But we support reform. If reform is constructive and in the interests of the country, we support it.'*

Downsizing is a staff management issue. HRM expertise is relevant, but is generally thin on the ground in developing countries (Taylor, 1992). Only in South Africa was there evidence of an ability to take a strategic HRM view of overall staffing issues (Ncholo, 1997). It is arguable that HRM expertise might have helped avoid the fiasco in Uganda where appraisal reports were the basis for redundancy decisions, with the result, in the words of one official, that *'50% (of retrenchees) were victimized, through tribalism or because they were supporters of Obote or Amin.'*

The complexity of reform meant that taking an incremental approach which built on developing experience would be important, and all the countries duly did so, even if it was more by accident than by design. The most impressive example was South Africa, which progressed even during the period of our research from a crude number-cutting approach to a sophisticated review methodology. In an already strong strategic context, they telescoped 18 years of UK experience (on which they drew heavily) into 18 months of learning and policy redesign. Generally however there was little evidence of a deliberately incremental, process approach based on an appropriate admission of ignorance.

Victims of reform

Despite the sanguine view of the reform studies, governments worried a great deal about the hardship that their reforms might create. There was genuine remorse among Ugandan officials over the harsh terms on which their first retrenchees had been dismissed. At the time of our interviews South Africa had not embarked fully on reform, partly because of fears about its potential impact on poor regions like the Eastern Cape. Roughly half of those who had left were White or Coloured; the number of Black and Indian employees increased slightly (Fourie, 1998). Trade union representatives in Malaysia and Uganda echoed officials' concerns. Their accounts of loss of status in villages, marriage break-ups and the like are anecdotal, but echo Western accounts such as Argyle's.

While the value of financial help to victims was taken as read, our interviews corroborated the finding that resettlement plans such as Ghana's were often ineffectual – but for specific reasons. Ghana's provision of retraining and business start-up help (Government of Ghana, 1987) started a year late, at a point where sensible retrenchees would already have made their own arrangements. Uganda's never started at all, foundering on the mistaken assumption that banks and the Ministry of Labour would be willing to participate. One British government agency, embroiled in union negotiations, woke up to the importance of making arrangements only when its retrenchees were about to leave.

Thus a generally poor record of implementation leaves room to argue that more skilful measures could still have helped. To take one example, communication with employees was clearly necessary to alleviate employee anxiety about the threat of retrenchment. Uganda's first retrenchment exercise, said one official, was *'shrouded in secrecy, and the news that they were to be retrenched came as a shock to most retrenchees.'*

Inappropriate reasons for reform

Ostensible job reductions were sometimes the result of transferring staff from one part of the public payroll to another, making life difficult for anyone wanting to produce a reliable estimate of numbers: one government adviser (actually a donor-financed expatriate) commented on the publicity value of such ostensible but insubstantial 'reductions' when dealing with donors. Government officials in the UK were instructed by ministers during the 1980s to present the transfer of staff responsible for housing benefits payments from central to local government as a reduction in the central government workforce. It was contracting out of public services in the UK that had the largest impact on numbers in the mid-1990s (Cabinet Office, 1996). It seemed reasonable to infer the influence of the 'small government' ideology in such measures, especially where they did little to reduce the cost of government.

Explaining reform outcomes: additional factors

Unsurprisingly, some generalizable factors emerged from our interviews which do not appear in studies we reviewed, and we now deal briefly with them, in a rough order of priority in terms of their effect on numbers and costs.

The insignificance and expense of redundancy

Contrary to the popular image, and to the reality of downsizing in Western private sector firms, compulsory redundancy was a small, sometimes even trivial component of overall job reduction. In Uganda, only 15,000 of the 160,000 job reductions came through compulsory redundancy (Government of Uganda, 1996). In the UK, a senior official estimated that not more than 1000 annually of the 250,000 job reductions between 1976 and 1996 came in that way. Elsewhere proportions are unclear, but redundancy was at most only one of a range of measures (Nunberg, 1994).

Despite this, reform was expensive, with the lion's share of costs going on severance payments. While the UK makes an impressive bid for the record with the eight billion pounds spent on making coalminers redundant between 1979 and 1992 (Wass, 1996), elsewhere too the cost was sizeable. Ghana's severance programme cost an average of 2 per cent of government expenditure in its first five years (Younger, 1996); Uganda's had cost US$18.6 million by 1995 (Government of Uganda, 1996).

Recruitment control. Public recruitment is a complex area in itself, with tight control by a central employee selection agency co-existing with discretion for local managers to make lower grade and temporary appointments. Failure to control ongoing recruitment was a major reason why numbers did not drop by as much as expected in Ghana (Burton *et al.*, 1993).

Controlling staff numbers and controlling costs

There was a frequent insensitivity to costs, with the pervasive assumption that if numbers fell, costs would follow suit. Waters already muddied by movement of staff from the core civil service to agencies and the like were further muddied by increased expenditure on other budget heads, notably on consultants. Many of them were recycled civil servants who had 'taken the package': *'Last week the government disposed of the Transport Board. The people may get golden handshakes and then come back in again! I wouldn't be surprised,'* said a senior Sri Lankan official. The UK solved the problem by moving to a simplified budget structure, removing the incentive for 'manpower substitution'. But experience in South Africa and the UK showed that this required basic budget reform for which detailed preparation would be needed.

Controlling numbers was sometimes socially regressive. The temptation was to reach a numerical target by focusing on lower echelon staff, of whom there are many, even though the cash saving may not be greater than focusing on a much smaller number of higher echelon staff. *'Getting rid of a support person ... is worth as much as getting rid of a Permanent Secretary!'*, as one official in Uganda exclaimed. It is striking that, for this very reason, the Uganda Civil Servants' Union had a preference for a cost-based approach.

Co-ordination

Co-ordination was crucial, but difficult. At the same time that the retrenchment team in the Ministry of Public Service in Uganda was working towards job reductions, colleagues on the other side of the building were carrying out a rolling programme of reviews whose net result was to recommend a staff increase! Rightsizing mechanisms were important. The key steering committee in Ghana, the Redeployment Management Committee, had cross-departmental membership with Finance closely involved (Government of Ghana, 1992). In Uganda there were three levels of committees: the Public Service Review and Reorganisation Commission, the Civil Service Reform Co-ordination Committee, which was a committee of directors-general of departments, and the Implementation and Monitoring Board, which took operational decisions about rightsizing.

The problem of co-ordination was compounded by frequent mistrust between Finance and Public Service ministries. Despite the stress in the Washington analysis on the link between them, Public Service have often been seen by Finance as a 'trojan horse' inside government, acting as an informal trade union, especially on behalf of senior civil servants (Corkery and Land, 1996). Staff in the Ministry of Finance in Ghana openly declared that their Public Service colleagues were the biggest single threat to the success of reform.

The political process and fresh commitments

We pointed earlier to the importance of understanding why staffing costs arise, in terms of programme commitments. Embarking on reform does not mean suspending the normal political process, through which fresh commitments constantly arise. The number of prison officers in the UK (Cabinet Office, 1996), and of police officers in Uganda, rose even while both countries were bearing down hard on staffing, reflecting law and order commitments. Government commitments often come with a staffing cost attached, which may (as in Uganda) be presented to the staffing ministry as a *fait accompli*.

Equally, governments generally tried to protect services which had a political priority, especially education and health (Burton *et al.*, 1993; Government of Uganda, 1994). But there was no *prima facie* reason why abuses such as ghosts would respect those areas. There was also a tendency for numbers to rise again like a seat cushion, once pressure to reduce was relaxed; one reason being that managers sought to restore a *status quo ante* which they still saw as normal.

Summary of interview findings

There was a general, though fitful movement towards a strategic approach. Commitment was clearly important, but derived from an interaction between stakeholders and the nature of the reform programme. The latter reflected governments' own reform priorities, as they developed through normal politics. In terms of process, employee participation was helpful where it occurred, and countries did take an incremental approach; this, however, would have been more coherent if it had been based on thorough diagnosis. Savings and overall impact were both lower than expected. This was because of an exclusive focus on the number of civil servants, exacerbated by poor co-ordination between the finance and staffing functions and the ideological preference for small government, together with weak recruitment control and disproportionate spending on the retrenchment of relatively few staff. Although the number of retrenchees was small, governments did make provision for the 'victims', though delays in implementation made it hard to judge its value.

Discussion: lessons from the downsizing experience

As with all aspects of HR in developing country governments, there are many gaps in our knowledge of downsizing. Data are often unreliable, and analysis has been scanty relative to the size of the phenomenon. Further research is desirable in a number of areas, including the relationship between downsizing and the macroeconomic reform programmes to which it has been so closely linked in the past; and the development of appropriate human resource management models (see also Nunberg, 1997). However, it is important to outline possible lessons for the design of reform.

Strategic reform

Reflecting on what other countries might learn from his country's experience, one official in Uganda commented:

> *Think carefully about where you want to make reductions, and why. Think about the shape of the service – where do we want to go – and have reductions follow from that.*

There is general agreement that reform should be more 'strategic', and that cost cutting is not a strategy in itself. Strategy cannot ignore costs, but affordability, taking account of performance in revenue collection and other factors, is merely one among other strategic elements. What then would a strategic approach look like? It is possible to point to some relevant experience. Malaysia's administrative reforms, which included some 'rightsizing' of the civil service, have been based on a conscious reform philosophy in the context of the overall government objective of attaining developed country status by the year 2020 (Sarji, 1995). There is also the example of New Zealand's well-known reforms, carried out in the context of a vision of a public service harnessed to achieving specified goals such as higher quality of life and higher employment (Boston *et al.*, 1996: see especially Appendix 2). Among the countries studied in our research, South Africa and Sri Lanka showed evidence of a movement towards strategy, as we discussed earlier. The UK used 'prior options' reviews as a vehicle for introducing strategic management into its executive agencies (Office of Public Service, 1995). It is true that 'strategic' actions have sometimes been partial and reactive in reality, as in New Zealand (Boston *et al.*, 1996). However, it is still possible to extract from experience such as the above a strategic model of employment reform.

Strategy in this context means starting from first principles with a view about the fundamental tasks of the public service which covers the role of the state in economic activities and delivery of services. In the light of that view a review is carried out of the alignment of the existing structure of government with strategic priorities. Review at the level of an individual department or service is a further stage, and the final stage is review at the level of the individual job or family of jobs. Thus job reduction 'falls out' of the strategic process – or job increase: strategy is neutral on this score. It follows from the experience reported in this chapter that all of this should be done incrementally. This is in keeping with the strategic tradition that derives from Lindblom (1959) and Mintzberg (1989), which emphasizes the importance of just such an incremental, 'emergent' approach.

Such an approach may still appear unrealistic. But an emergent model of strategy, as opposed to classical 'top-down' blueprint models, may be attainable. Thinking strategically is at least as important as producing detailed, possibly unrealistic blueprints (Johnson *et al.*, 2004). Some governments do have the capacity to operate in that way: national movements such as Namibia's and South Africa's have come to power with a clear vision, and downsizing was actually part of the 'Ten Point Plan' with which Uganda's National Resistance Movement came to power. Other governments probably do not have that capacity at present, though even in such governments a strategic approach could still be piloted in an individual department or agency.

Strategy, by definition, is stable and addresses long-term issues (Johnson *et al.*, 2004). But what about urgent problems? Applying the turnaround concept of a two-stage recovery, there may still be a need for a first stage where glaring blemishes which do not have systemic implications, such as the elimination of ghosts and the enforcement of retirement ages, are removed. Such steps give government a tangible early success (Cameron, 1994) which public opinion is likely to support, as South Africa found with its 'ghostbusters' initiative in 1997. They also bought time to carry out diagnosis and to plan strategy. But drastic measures to retrench serving employees, which in principle can still arise, should follow rather than precede strategic planning. Identifying poor performers is not straightforward, as Uganda found, and identifying redundant jobs requires some process of job inspection or review. Moreover, the downsizing literature shows that hasty retrenchment without a strong justification has a catastrophic effect on the morale and the performance of survivors.

Political commitment

Commitment is crucial, but is best understood as the outcome of the interaction between reform stakeholders on the one hand and the nature of the reform programme to which commitment is sought on the other. This echoes the view of the World Bank's *Public Expenditure Management Handbook* that 'In many respects, political will is a function of the quality of advice provided to politicians' (World Bank, 1998b, p.iii).

Diagnosis

Governments need to conduct a thorough diagnosis of political, economic, social and institutional factors (McCourt, 1998b). Such diagnosis will take time, and may seem a luxury that governments cannot afford. But without it, reform is likely to be misconceived, and governments will end up starting again, with their stocks of political and financial capital heavily depleted. Specifically, diagnosis should allow for the adaptation of generic reform models to the circumstances of particular countries.

Process factors

Both downsizing studies and our own interviews point to the importance of an incremental, process approach, if only because hasty interventions in a complex and only partially understood system have so often been botched in the past. Institutional reforms need not be rushed (Klitgaard, 1997). The participation of employees and their representatives in the design and execution of reform is desirable and possible, assuming reasonable good will – '*Involve worker representatives from beginning to end*' was how one official put it.

Human resource management: developing new models of practice

Downsizing, which by its nature should be exceptional and temporary, during the 1980s and 90s became the regular condition of public staff management (Polidano and Hulme, 1999). But Maoist permanent revolution is destabilizing and distracting. Reform should eventually give way to normal human resource management, combining financial control of staffing (led by Finance) with procedures for managing performance (led by Public Service or its equivalent), even though the point at which that will happen is some way off in many countries. There is an urgent need for the development of HRM models appropriate to developing country governments.

However, our analysis suggests that governments will only be free to concentrate on HR, which is a 'Stage 2' activity in terms of Arogyaswamy *et al.*'s turnaround model, when they have got a grip on their staff spending in Stage 1.

Victims of reform

Compulsory redundancy was a minor component in all the countries which we studied, so it is not surprising that resettlement schemes were insignificant. But where redundancy is important, there are legal, expedient and ethical reasons why resettlement provision should be taken seriously. Financial compensation will remain the biggest element, but the failure of resettlement schemes in Ghana and Uganda shows that there is room to design schemes for communicating with retrenchees. As one Ugandan official put it in very personal terms, *'Handle people with extreme care and love.'*

Loosening the link between downsizing and pay reform

Employment and pay reform are two sides of the same coin in the Washington analysis. Certainly measures to increase the transparency of remuneration, notably through monetizing benefits, are desirable, and the pay of employees in priority services ought to rise (Chew, 1990). But privileging senior civil servants in the teeth of public opinion over other priority groups such as primary teachers is questionable, especially when including allowances qualifies the overall picture. Moreover, the linking of employment and pay reform implies that savings from the former will pay for the latter. But we have seen that savings have often not been substantial, and in any case other government functions such as primary education – or even foreign debt repayment – will make their own bids for what savings there are. Pay rises in Malaysia and Uganda were financed by economic growth, not by reform. The desirability of pay increases in the light of catastrophic pay decreases is clear, but unmet pay expectations may contaminate other aspects of reform if pay and downsizing issues are linked too closely.

The role of donors

The downsizing literature identified pressure from outside as a negative factor in building ownership. Donors should take care to ensure that their efforts increase rather than undermine government ownership. They should also have the courage of their growing convictions, and move to support governments' efforts to reform strategically. Admittedly the difference between careful strategic planning and outright procrastination can be hard to detect on the ground. But donors should be readier to trust governments that choose the gradualist strategic route. Resources should be brought into alignment: it may be more productive to use aid to give governments the breathing space they need to carry out strategic reform than to fund the heavy costs of severance packages. The move in recent years away from project aid towards sector-wide approaches and general budget support are in line with this.

Conclusion: towards a strategic model of employment reform

In this chapter we have reviewed the experience of downsizing in developing country governments. We have summarized the Washington analysis of the progress of reform, and compared it with the (mainly) North American analysis of downsizing. In the light of those analyses we have presented the findings of field interviews, and we have presented tentative implications for the conduct of reform.

Looking back at the time of writing over the experience of a quarter century of efforts, it is clear that reform cannot be a single finite event. Even the African countries that went furthest in the 1980s and 90s were still facing problems at the start of the new century (World Bank, 2000a, 2004a), and one of the countries that we focus on later in this book, Morocco (see Chapter 5), was only embarking on downsizing for the first time in 2005. Most of the sources point to the necessity of a strategy- rather than cost-driven model of reform, one which proceeds incrementally from a diagnosis that takes account of local factors. This has the advantage of encompassing other HR reforms which we discuss elsewhere in this book. The broadening of the debate to take in such reforms, recapitulating to an extent the concern of the immediate post-colonial period with capacity building, is a wholly positive development: there was definitely a need to supersede the reductive and exclusive emphasis on downsizing. Yet such a model makes heavy demands on the capacity of developing country administrations, demands which many cannot currently meet. But the experience of countries which are some way down the reform road shows that capacity can develop through learning from experience. South Africa is a good example.

At any rate the failure of reform remains the context for our discussion. Moreover, if Baumol *et al.* are right, and downsizing is an inevitable aspect of the 'creative destruction' which Schumpeter famously saw as inherent in capitalism, we will always need ways of carrying it out. But it seems reasonable to suggest that the approach should be different from the one practised in the 1980s and 90s, whose success was partial at best. It also seems reasonable to suggest that HRM practitioners and scholars, whose stock-in-trade is the development of strategic approaches to the management of staff in organizations, are in a strong position to work together with the economists who have dominated the discussion up to now.

3
Mauritius: Economic Growth and Strategic Human Resource Management

Social, political and economic influences on the civil service

Our next study focuses on Mauritius, an island in the Indian Ocean conventionally grouped with the developing countries of sub-Saharan Africa, but whose status as a middle-income, recently industrialized economy also links it with the emerging economies of Asia, where members of its Chinese and Indian communities have astutely exploited ancestral ties to promote trading relationships (Economist, 1995). While the official language is English, French is more widely spoken. African and Asian, Anglophone and Francophone, developing but with a growing export-orientated industrial sector, Mauritius is highly exposed to global influences.

Given the strength of the Mauritian economy and, as we shall see, the explicit recognition by the government of the importance of the civil service's role, this chapter will focus on the relationship between economic growth and civil service performance, and on the extent to which staff management was strategic: exposure to international influences should make Mauritius a fertile environment for the SHRM model to take root.

Society: the salience of ethnic identity

The key feature of Mauritian society is ethnicity. 'The inhabitants of Mauritius have made a success of multiculturalism,' says one sanguine account (The Courier, 1998, p.14). But with highly differentiated and mostly endogamous population groups (Hindu, Muslim, Sino-Mauritian, White and the 'general population', or Creoles) speaking 15 languages between them, 'the very construction of the social person is

49

based on ethnicity' (Eriksen, 1998, p.15). Minogue has asserted that 'Mauritian politics (is) ... overwhelmingly the politics of ethnic competition' (1992, p.646). As recently as 1999, some parts of the island were convulsed by riots that had a strong ethnic dimension (Economist, 1999). It is not surprising that nepotism is assumed to be widespread in the labour market, including in the civil service. A former minister insisted in one of our interviews that

> *Opportunities in the private sector ... are not within the reach of certain segments of Mauritian society. Therefore the government had ... to provide employment opportunities, otherwise there would have been social chaos.*

Those opportunities have not been evenly spread: Creoles have been apt to remark bitterly, 'Tu pu malbar' ('everything is kept for the Indians') (Eriksen, 1998, p.177).

But nepotism doesn't have it all its own way, so to speak. 'Principles for recruitment to the labour market are no longer unambiguously ethnic' (Eriksen, 1998, p.177), and there is a national ideology in which 'communalism' is a cardinal sin. This is in keeping with the gradual shift from what anthropologists call an ascriptive to an achievement orientation that tends to accompany the growth of an industrial economy such as that of Mauritius (Linton, 1936).

Economy: 'managing success'

Mauritius is classified by the World Bank as an upper-middle-income country, with a per capita GNI of $4090 and GDP growth of 3.2 per cent in 2003, somewhat lower than in the 1990s: between 1994 and 1998 growth was 5.3 per cent. Overall unemployment was estimated at 9.8 per cent for 2003, up from 6.0 per cent in 1996, when employers were importing workers from China and elsewhere to work in textiles and construction (Economist Intelligence Unit, 1999). Like many African countries, Mauritius plunged into severe balance of payments trouble in the late 1970s, with a catastrophic drop in the sugar price, on which the island's plantation economy then depended, coming hard on the heels of global oil price increases. Unlike many of those countries, however, Mauritius made a success of its IMF-assisted structural adjustment policies in the 1980s (World Bank, 1989). Economic progress has been facilitated by a series of reforms, notably the pioneering island-wide Export Processing Zone, established in 1971 to exempt investors from government taxes and labour legislation. The reforms led to the growth of a substantial clothing and textiles export industry, with more than 200 foreign manufacturers present by 1994 (Heenan, 1994) and exports worth $1.2 billion in 1999, up 11 per cent on 1998 figures (De Giorgio, 2000). With tourism well established and an incipient financial services sector (Ashurst, 1998), the days of the plantation economy are over.

Despite continuing problems, such as increasing competition in textiles from other developing countries whose production costs are even lower than those of Mauritius, a major reason for the slackening of economic growth at the start of the new century, the claim that Mauritius has Africa's most successful economy was a good one (Economist, 1996a, 2003).

Politics: coalition, not revolution

Politics in Mauritius is characterized by a commitment to parliamentary democracy and a tendency to coalition government. Like many former British colonies, Mauritius has an independence constitution which established Westminster-style multi-party democracy. The ethnic groups that are the fundamental feature of Mauritian society have ultimately identified their interests with the continuation of multi-party, parliamentary government: 'the interplay of communalism and class in politics led to coalition and cohabitation rather than coup or revolution' (Dubey, 1997, p.219). The National Assembly comprises 62 elected representatives and up to eight 'best losers', appointed to ensure adequate representation for all ethnic groups. The coalition government in power at the time of writing[1] won all but six of the contested seats in the 2000 general election. Its main members were the Mouvement Militant Mauricien (MMM), a radical party founded in 1969 in the afterglow of the 'Paris spring' of 1968 by an alliance of intellectuals and trade unionists, and the smaller Mouvement Socialiste Mauricien (MSM), which broke away from the MMM in 1983. The MMM leader, Paul Bérenger, was prime minister at the time of writing, his predecessor Sir Anerood Jugnauth having handed over, and then acceded to the Presidency, under the terms of a pre-election pact for the second half of the five year mandate obtained in October 2000. This was the first time that a non-Hindu had become prime minister. The government defeated in the 2000 election had been another coalition, headed by the Mauritius Labour Party (MLP), a moderate socialist party founded in 1936 which led the campaign for independence during the 1960s.

The civil service itself

In this section we set out the contradictory picture we gain of HRM in the Mauritian civil service from published sources. Certainly the civil service is an important actor in the formal economy: in 1997, the public sector employed just under 12 per cent of the active labour force (Economist Intelligence Unit, 1999). Government recognizes that the civil service has an important role to play in building the economy. Addressing the senior civil service in 1996, the then prime minister said that

> If we are to attract and keep foreign investment, the lifeblood of the economy, we must have an efficient bureaucracy, which is not there to resist and hinder – but to assist and facilitate (quoted in PRB, 1998, p.20).

The prime minister would have been preaching to the converted, according to a number of writers who give the civil service much of the credit for the island's economic success. 'Widespread political agreement created a stable atmosphere for the growth and functioning of a capable public service ... the state was only able to implement export-linked industrialisation because it had some significant degree of autonomy and bureaucratic capability,' says Meisenhelder (1997, p.283 and p.296; see also Subramaniam, 2001). Dilating on Meisenhelder's theme, Carroll and Carroll (1997) find a dynamic and innovative bureaucracy that has avoided the classic bureaucratic dysfunctions. Echoing Evans and Rauch, they point to an emphasis on merit in employee selection, something they attribute to the constitutional entrenchment of the PSC. 'Promotion and recruitment at the most senior level are based on merit, not seniority as in West Germany nor cronyism as in Italy', making the civil service, according to Carroll and Joypaul, a model for other countries, developing and developed alike (1993, p.432).

But not everyone sees it that way. An early analysis quoted with approval a report from the colonial period that had described the civil service as 'lagging behind the stages reached in constitutional, economic and cultural development', and found that 'Mauritius exemplified the classic faults of bureaucracy, and nowhere more so than in the tendency to avoid the difficult business of administrative reform ... (which) is vital and urgent' (Minogue, 1976, pp.162, 164, 166). In the key economic area, Gulhati and Nallari (1990, p.36) noted 'many weak areas' in core economic ministries, and were uncertain what role the bureaucracy had actually played in the recovery of the 1980s.

Interview findings

Interview details

Our field research attempted to resolve the contradictions in the published sources. Eleven officials were interviewed, identified as having a key responsibility for the design and operation of HRM systems. They were:

- a former cabinet minister who had a role in setting HR policy
- the heads of statutory agencies responsible respectively for employee selection (the Public Service Commission, or PSC), pay determination (the Pay Research Bureau, PRB) and training (the Mauritius Institute for Public Administration and Management, MIPAM)
- permanent secretaries heading three of the line departments where most civil servants work: Health, Economic Development, and Civil Service Affairs
- senior officials in the central departments responsible for civil service staffing and the payroll
- senior officials in the Management Audit Bureau within the Finance ministry

We also interviewed a senior official whose responsibility cuts across departments. In addition, in order to give the point of view of important stakeholders outside government, we held interviews with an official of the Federation of Civil Service Unions and an official of an international development agency active in Mauritius.

Finally, we conducted a focus group which brought together a mixed race and gender group of junior civil servants attending courses at the University of Mauritius.

Developments following the 2000 election

It is important to note that our interview data was gathered in the final days of the MSM-led coalition ejected in 2000. The turn of the century was a turning point of another kind. Once the new Minister for Civil Service Affairs got his feet under the table, the Ministry launched its first ever Action Plan (Ministry of Civil Service Affairs and Administrative

Reforms, 2001), a comprehensive framework document. By 2004, 12 agencies had obtained ISO certification, and Client's Charters were being introduced: the influence of Malaysia, which had furnished an expert under Commonwealth Secretariat auspices, will be clear to readers who go on to read our chapter on Malaysia (Chapter 8). The government had proceeded to draw up a second Action Plan, for 2004–05 (Ministry of Civil Service Affairs and Administrative Reforms, 2004). Significantly, it talked about moving from a personnel administration to a HRM role, and of the need to develop the Ministry's 'strategist' function, and about picking up the performance management gauntlet which had been lying at its feet since 1987. While actual implementation was unclear, at least the intention to reform had appeared, with some tangible evidence of progress. All of this will require us to qualify the rather negative picture that we report below based on our 1999 interviews.

The SHRM model: strategic integration and line manager ownership

In this section we deal in turn with the three elements of the SHRM model on which we focused: strategic integration, in both its vertical and horizontal aspects, and line manager ownership.

Strategic (or vertical) integration (the integration of staff management with overall organizational strategy: see Chapter 1). Integration was, very simply, not practised. Minogue's analysis held true, a quarter of a century after it was written: despite government's strategic intentions (Ministry of Economic Development and Regional Co-operation, 1997) the civil service, in the unanimous opinion of our informants, remained essentially unstrategic and unreformed. Here are two representative comments:

> *The reform unit is there. But the question is: What is it doing?*

> *They don't have any action plan.*

The setting up of the Burrenchobhay committee, the first comprehensive attempt at reform, came only after 28 years of independence in 1996. It reported two years later, although it was to be another two years before its report was published. As in Aesop's fable, the mountain laboured and brought forth a mouse, a nugatory addition to the island's 'history of forgotten reports' (Titmuss and Abel-Smith, 1968). Its advocacy of such measures as mission statements, TQM and citizens' charters was in line with reform elsewhere, but lacked operational detail. One senior official called it *'superficial – and worth throwing in the dustbin.'* Even one of the committee's own members told us that *'The report considers mainly the immediate problems. It does not really try to bring radical changes'.* The approach to reform had been *'piecemeal rather than strategic'*, and another official report admitted that 'There is need for a more integrated and holistic approach towards reforms' (PRB, 1998, p.25). In this strategic vacuum, inevitably *'personnel managers in the service are more involved in applying the rules'* than in taking a strategic view, according to a very senior official.

In the absence of comprehensive reform, central government seemed to be hoping that individual ministries would fill up the strategic vacuum:

> *In every ministry you always have a few good civil servants ... (who) bring about changes in their area of responsibility, which is called 'pocket development' ... Our hope is that we will be able to multiply these pockets.*

Certainly the global language of strategy had reached a few of the ministries, if not the centre of government: one of them had adopted the slogan 'Initiate, innovate, interact' as its mission statement. But such statements were little more than pious declarations. They were not fleshed out into strategic objectives, and strategic thrust was dissipated in a host of worthwhile but piecemeal initiatives. One of the more dynamic permanent secretaries listed his ministry's initiatives: quality circles, names on all the doors, weekly meetings of Heads of Section and potted plants.

What was true of strategy in general was equally true of HR strategy. Asked what had been the main HR initiatives of the last ten years, a central official with a major HR responsibility asked rhetorically, *'Well, have there been any?'* After some prodding he listed three decidedly unstrategic items: the rationalization of 'schemes of service' (essentially job descriptions), the recognition that senior managers should have managerial capacity, and the provision that posts left vacant for two years could be abolished. From the point of view of the junior staff who attended our focus group meeting, there was simply *'no policy of HRM in the civil service'*, an opinion echoed by another senior respondent, who saw the civil service as being

> *addicted to rules and regulations, (having) no sense of direction (and) not fully aware of the vision for the country.*

Line manager ownership

In this section we review the degree of 'horizontal integration' in the civil service, defined in Chapter 1 as the integration of staff management activities with each other. It was no more practised than the vertical variety. A permanent secretary lamented:

> *This is how our hands are tied as regards the management of people. We have no say in the determination of salaries. It's determined by somebody else, the PRB. Recruitment, promotion and discipline are done by the PSC. For training, we have to go to MIPAM. So human resource management is frag-men-ted* (his emphasis).

An example came when the PRB carried out the worthwhile exercise of asking jobholders to rewrite their own job descriptions as the basis for grading decisions. There was no hint that this might carry over to training for the jobholders or later on to the recruitment of their replacements.

It follows that line ministries, let alone line managers, had little role to play in staff management, even in the minutest particulars ('walking allowance' paid to forest guards, set centrally at Rs75 per month in 2000). Several officials listed the predictable effects: *'The actual centralized system favours "passing the buck"'*, said a central official on whose desk certain bucks were liable to fetch up. From a permanent secretary's point of view,

> *You want people to behave as managers, but you're not giving them the opportunity ... I have to bear with people like (x), (y), (z) and others. They are chosen elsewhere ... People are even removed from my organization without my knowledge!*

Another permanent secretary echoed this:

> *You are at the mercy of the Minister of Civil Service Affairs. We should be able to hire ourselves, not take from other ministries.*

Moreover, officials were alive to the advantages of line manager ownership: as one permanent secretary pointed out,

> *Once you determine pay levels, it should be left to the ministry to recruit. If I do the selection decision myself, I know that I will be stuck with a bad decision for life.*

HR activities: employee selection and performance management

Employee selection. Where employee selection is concerned, it is true that the remit of the responsible agency, the PSC, is specified in the national constitution (Articles 88 and 89), just as Carroll and Carroll point out. But this in itself is merely the norm in British-influenced administrations as far apart as Nepal and Swaziland (McCourt, 2001c, 2003). What was more significant was the way the PSC was going about its business, for which it was roundly criticized even in the mostly anodyne Burrenchobhay report. Noting that it had been the subject of much internal and external criticism, the report found a lack of transparency in the recruitment and training of officers, an over-centralization of power, decisions not subject to scrutiny except by the Supreme Court, no clear criteria for decision-making or proper communication channels with ministries, delays in recruitment and in disciplinary cases, and a wide belief that undeserved favours had been granted to some public officers. It was easy to understand why a union official told us that

> *After each exercise of the PSC, the curve of confidence slopes downwards.*

Nor did the PSC's constitutional status ensure its independence. As a commissioner pointed out,

> *The cycle of appointments (of commissioners) is fundamental. There is no continuity across changes of governments.*

Appointment of commissioners invariably followed general elections and as a trade union official put it,

> *You must dance to the music of the one who appoints you.*

Complaints of abuses abounded: police officers drawn disproportionately from the new prime minister's constituency; candidates suddenly appointed after the formal appointment procedure had ended; ministers engineering the appointment of permanent secretaries from their own ethnic communities. All this, said one informant, *'breeds a culture of suspicion'*, one where staff relations were characterized by 'méfiance' (distrust) rather than 'confiance' (trust). In the absence of transparency (even a PSC official was prepared to admit that there was *'no transparency in selection or recruitment'*), it was impossible to verify the numerous complaints against the agency, but they were taken seriously in the

Burrenchobhay report. No one could be found to defend Carroll and Joypaul's view that merit was sacrosanct.

For initial employee selection, suitably qualified candidates sat for a test of general knowledge, so there was an 'examination' in Evans and Rauch's sense. Shortlisted candidates attended an interview conducted by two commissioners and an adviser, issuing in a consensus decision based on personality, fluency in English, experience relevant to the job and additional qualifications. Again all this was very similar to the practice of the PSC's counterparts in other former British colonies, both rich and poor, and largely continues pre-independence practice. There was no professional selection expertise in the PSC, and no evidence about whether this selection approach actually managed to identify able staff, and there appeared to have been no innovations in employee selection in recent years.

Performance management. The picture was the same when we turned to performance management. Like many former British colonies, Mauritius continued to use the old British system of annual 'confidential reports', written by 'supervising officers' and not shown to or discussed with the supervisees. No one defended them: 'In the final analysis (they) boil down to an annual ritual of stocktaking' (PRB, 1998, p.37). As long ago as 1987 a new performance appraisal system, including a procedure for linking pay to performance, was piloted but not implemented:

> In 1987 ... I started performance appraisal. In 1997 it still hadn't been accepted.

This was despite the fact that a modified system was actually piloted in 1994. The Burrenchobhay report recommended yet another system, characteristically omitting any operational detail. A central official who had had a leading role in introducing appraisal attributed its failure to the fact that *'Different communities are sensitive – "Mauritian specificity".'*

Promotion from grade to grade remained effectively automatic, based on seniority rather than merit (Government of Mauritius, 2000, p.141), a practice that one senior official described as *'the scourge of the Mauritius civil service'* (again, the contrast with Carroll and Joypaul's view is stark). It was so firmly entrenched that the PSC actually required a written explanation if a ministry recommended the promotion of an officer over the head of a more senior colleague. As so often, the question of nepotism was relevant: according to one informant, the requirement was intended to discourage ethnic discrimination.

It follows that pay was not linked to performance. Indeed, the attempt to make the link is one reason why earlier attempts to introduce performance appraisal had failed. A union official commented on performance-related pay (PRP):

> *Mauritius isn't ready. Now we are coming to election time. Politicians will interfere.*

The same official we interviewed viewed the existing system as a *'mal nécessaire'*, given the prevailing 'culture of suspicion'. Pay awards emerged from tripartite negotiations based on the recommendations of the PRB. The system was *'inherently inflationary'* as a Ministry of Finance official put it: significantly, one of the new government's first actions in 2000 was to refuse to implement the outgoing administration's pay award.

We should note that some 'pocket development' had taken place, with at least two ministries experimenting with appraisal, and with some success:

> *In our department it has really worked. We used it to improve work performance. We designed our own form.*

But in the absence of central direction they were swimming against the tide: staff in two ministries complained that lack of commitment from senior management had prevented appraisal from getting past the pilot stage.

Discussion: strategic HRM and economic growth

The civil service and economic growth: 'a heavy-handed bureaucracy'

To what extent had staff management in Mauritius had the dramatic effect on economic growth that Evans and Rauch have claimed for it elsewhere? The answer is clear. At both the strategic level and the level of HR activities there was evidence of stagnation rather than strategic reform. Despite some worthwhile departmental initiatives, Mauritius was far from being a meritocracy in Evans and Rauch's sense. Overall, in fact, it was difficult not to agree with the government's own summing up: 'A pervasive and heavy-handed bureaucracy still rules and it is a miracle, no less, that in these circumstances, industrial development did take place at all' (Ministry of Economic Development and Regional Co-operation, 1997: 1.11; see also Government of

Mauritius, 2000, p.132). This corroborates Minogue's (1976) early analysis, although it contradicts the more adulatory accounts. In short, economic growth in Mauritius up to the end of the twentieth century occurred in the teeth of the public bureaucracy, not because of it. Very ironically, the Action Plans from 2001 onwards were a sign that the government had woken up to the importance of staff management just as economic growth was faltering. But the slackening of growth, affected by the ending of preferential trading arrangements and competition from low-cost textile producers in Asia, had very little to do with the civil service, just as the appearance of what looked like a real commitment to civil service reform had more to do with a change of political leadership than with economic factors.

The SHRM model: 'frag-men-tation'

We also wanted to see whether the SHRM model had had – or could have – the same dramatic effect on organizational performance in a developing country that it seems to have had in the Anglophone world. Our answer is somewhat involved. Let us recall what we found. At the strategic or meso-level, there was little overall strategy with which HR could be integrated, precluding vertical integration; and the heads of ministries who were the senior line managers had virtually no control over their staff, precluding horizontal integration. At the activity or micro-level, we found that the agency responsible for employee selection, the PSC, had lost the confidence of both senior officials and staff representatives, while the professional conduct of selection itself merely continued pre-independence practice. Pre-independence practice also subsisted in performance management, where attempts at reform going as far back as 1987 had failed to get off the ground. We conclude that neither SHRM nor good practice in key HR activities was being practised at the time of our interviews.

The applicability of strategic HRM in Mauritius

In the earlier article based on our interview data, in trying to understand why the SHRM model had not had the dramatic effect in Mauritius that has been claimed for it in the Anglophone world, we suggested four conditions which would need to be met in order for SHRM to be applicable. We list them together with our assessment of the position in 2000.

Familiarity with HR models. SHRM and HR 'good practice' have to be known before they can be adopted; and they were not widely known in Mauritius, especially not in the government. Only one out of all our informants had any familiarity with the SHRM model. Being yoked to the single, inflexible model of staff management with which it was familiar reduced government's room to manoeuvre. For example, the model of performance management that was unsuccessfully attempted in 1987 included a PRP element which, for reasons we shall discuss, was never likely to be accepted, whereas an alternative model that did not include PRP might have taken root (Cleveland *et al.*, 1989; Long, 1986).

A strategic framework. The problem of familiarity with SHRM applied equally to the larger strategic management model of which SHRM is a sub-set. As we saw, the government was paying only lip service to the need for a strategic framework.

Devolution of staff management. HR was *'frag-men-ted'*, as one of our informants forcefully put it, being shared among several different agencies: the PSC for employee selection, MIPAM for training and development and so on. This responsibility would need to be devolved to line ministries to make horizontal integration feasible. We found the arguments for and against devolution to be finely balanced. We noted Eriksen's (1998) analysis that the ethnicity factor, while certainly ubiquitous, is in decline. By the time of writing, both the Prime Minister and the Head of the Civil Service were non-Hindus for the first time (a former minister said that such an appointment would have been *'inconceivable in the past'*); and, as we have seen, a non-Hindu is scheduled to become prime minister. Thus we heard arguments both for and against devolution. Most tellingly, of the two most senior commissioners of the PSC in Mauritius, one was for and the other against.

Yet we also suggested three reasons why devolution might not occur:

1 It would require fundamental structural reform and a constitutional amendment in the case of the PSC; and therefore a substantial investment of political resources.

2 Clientelism and nepotism may be in decline, but having been fundamental to politics in Mauritius, they are not going to disappear overnight. One informant said that

   It is not in the interests of politicians to change, even though they criticize while in opposition.

The same informants who criticized the PSC's propensity to patronage defended its existence as a bulwark against clientelism. They believed that as the single point for making many staffing decisions it would contain clientelism better than devolved decision-making in a large number of ministries. It was, as a trade union official put it, *'the lesser of two evils'*.

3 The third factor was the capacity of lower levels to operate delegated functions.

> *Delegation rebounds on us. We delegated appointment of nursing officers. They (i.e. the Ministry of Health) were submerged with thousands of applications. At ministry level people are not properly trained. They don't have the knowledge. We see hundreds of mistakes.*

Line ministries in a small island are also small, and their capacity base is slender. Management from the centre is possible and justifiable in a way that it would not be in a larger country.

Political will. Finally, 'political will' was absent, every bit as much as it was in the many countries where downsizing programmes failed, as we saw in Chapter 2 (we will explore the concept of political will or commitment in Chapter 6). A former minister, nursing burnt fingers, reached this gloomy conclusion:

> *I would say, without any hesitation whatever, that there is no political will, really, to change the civil service.*

In addition to the factors we have already listed, and very ironically in the light of Evans and Rauch, economic prosperity militated against political will. Writing in 1991, and noting that a coalition government headed by Sir Anerood Jugnauth had managed to stay in power for most of the 1980s, Bowman (1991, p.88) observed that 'It is the economic miracle of the 1980s that has enabled the Alliance to weather an endless succession of intra- and inter-party feuds and remain comfortably in control of the government.' Prosperity had allowed government to stave off the need to reform the civil service along with political challenges to its rule. As one tactful official put it:

> *The PM (prime minister) has not realized the necessity to get the issue to be discussed at cabinet level.*

The feasibility of SHRM in the Mauritian civil service

In the light of the analysis above, the conclusion of our earlier study (McCourt and Ramgutty-Wong, 2003) was that SHRM was not feasible. We were also unsure whether it was even desirable, at least if implementing it meant devolving staff management to agencies with the danger that nepotism would increase. Noting that knowledge of SHRM was increasing, with a Masters degree in HRM being offered by the University of Mauritius with an intake that included serving public officers, we suggested that

> the appropriate strategy for the government to pursue (is) a modulated one: creating the conditions for SHRM by training civil servants and experimenting with devolution, and making piecemeal improvements by selecting from a wider range of approaches to individual HR activities such as employee selection and performance management (McCourt and Ramgutty-Wong, 2003, p.613).

Six years on from the date of our original research, how would we revise our conclusion? It is a pleasure to confess that we erred on the side of pessimism. Despite recognizing the importance of the political dimension and of political will, we had failed to anticipate what a difference a change of government might make. It was clear that the MMM/MSM government had sustained a commitment to reform through the implementation of two Action Plans over its five-year period in office. To some extent, moreover, political will was dragging familiarity with strategic and professional models in its wake, with the reorientation of the central ministry from what we called a 'clerk of works' role in Chapter 1 to a 'strategist' role. This was abetted by the increasing use of the strategic management model by governments in other countries such as New Zealand (Irwin, 1996), a trend that our earlier study overlooked. There were also signs that the government would improve the conduct of employee selection, and would move towards introducing performance management.

The direction of reform also took us by surprise. We betrayed our Western orientation by assuming that if reform did happen, it would follow an industrialized country model such as SHRM. Instead, however, Mauritius chose to look east and model itself on Malaysia, under the influence of Malaysia's success and, in particular, of the Malaysian expert appointed through the Commonwealth Secretariat (though it is fair to note that Malaysia's reforms, in which ISO 9000 and Client's Charters had pride of place, largely originated in the United Kingdom).

In other respects we were perhaps not mistaken. There was no sign in either of the Action Plans that the government was even considering delegating powers to departments, despite some evidence that the gradual decline of communalism was continuing (Mauritius News, 2005). It was unclear whether this was because of a reasonable fear of nepotism increasing, or politicians' simple reluctance to lose control of the patronage machine, or some mixture of the two. Similarly, strategic integration remained weak, with issues like performance management and HRD being handled separately just as before, even though the basic strategic framework was being strengthened through the refining of mission statements and, indeed, of the Action Plans themselves. One reason was that familiarity in government with professional HR approaches was still limited.

Moreover, the notorious 'Mauritian specificities' were still acting as a constraint. The PRB's 2003 Report reported strong support among staff for a performance management scheme linked to pay, but it also noted that

> Though staff associations are not against the notion of (PRP), they are sceptical as to the manner in which such schemes would be introduced. To them, there is a strong fear that the scheme may be used as a tool opening the door to favouritism and abuse, and believe that the time for its implementation is not appropriate.

By this point in the chapter, readers will not be surprised that it was the unions' scepticism which won the day, so that the performance management scheme being piloted at the time of writing did not include a link to pay. The PRB report tersely justified this by invoking 'the specificity of the Mauritian fabric': there is no need to spell out what that means to a Mauritian audience (PRB, 2003, p.57). Nor was there any sign of merit triumphing over nepotism. Significantly, the last recommendation – indeed the very last sentence – of the *second* Action Plan was '*Introduce* the merit principle' (Ministry of Civil Service Affairs and Administrative Reforms, 2004, p.33; our italics).

With the necessary strategic framework only partially in place, no evidence that the government was committed to the profound devolution of managerial authority that full-blown SHRM would require and a general election that had just occurred at the time of writing, there were clearly still limits to the application of SHRM, though less severe than they had been in 2000. Moreover, just as in 2000 there was a danger of the reform thrust being dissipated in a large number of worthwhile but piecemeal initiatives: the Action Plan 2004–05 contained almost 100 separate actions, ranging from development of Action Plans by ministries to sports and keep fit activities. On the other hand, a modified form of SHRM was becoming feasible. Knowledge of SHRM was beginning to spread out, and the political will which was weak at the time of our interviews had strengthened following the 2000 election and the implementation of two Action Plans, though it was unclear what difference the election of the Social Alliance in 2005 would make, under a prime minister who had personally assumed the civil service and administrative reform portfolio, but whose party had historically not been very reform-minded.

Prospects for HR in the Mauritian civil service

Looking ahead from the time of writing, overall the signs were more positive than negative. In the short term, Mauritius was likely to practise a mixed model of HRM, with strategic elements jostling uneasily alongside central control of key HR decisions, notably employee selection and pay determination. Having set its own reform agenda, however imperfect, it was important for the government to consolidate it. But our analysis suggests that the time had come to profit from declining particularistic pressures in the wider society and experiment with staffing devolution. After all, even the union official who, like his counterparts elsewhere, had a preference for central bargaining could see the case for some devolution:

> *Certain powers should be delegated to (ministries) to do away with redtapeism.*

Devolution should probably be incremental, taking note of the caution expressed by one of our informants, who was alluding to the wider political context when he said that the government should

> *Be cautious about reforms. If you want to perform in a democratic way ... we have to be cautious and we can't go at the speed of the private sector. Others (i.e. other countries) are willing to have a military regime, but ... here there is hope for the civil service.*

The government could also move faster to improve the conduct of HR activities such as employee selection and performance management, even within the existing structure of government, as becoming familiar with a range of professional models was within government's reach in a country so highly exposed to global influences. We saw, however, that it would be important to choose an appropriate approach. Performance management had failed to get off the ground largely because it had come to be associated with performance-related pay, with all the risks of nepotism that PRP entails. Models of performance management that stress assessment or development rather than pay (Randell, 1994) were more appropriate.

To sum up, at the time of writing the appropriate strategy for the government to pursue seemed to be a modulated one: consolidating its existing agenda, continuing to invest in disseminating knowledge about SHRM and recent management developments by training civil servants, devolving in incremental stages, and making piecemeal improvements by selecting from a wider range of approaches to individual HR activities such as employee selection and performance management. Clearly some experimentation would be needed to determine the most suitable composition of such a strategy.

Conclusion: lessons from the case

The case study methodology that we have used limits obliges us to be cautious about reading too much into a single study, but a single case study can qualify the findings of even robust correlational studies like those of Huselid (1995; see also Chapter 1) and Evans and Rauch. What appears promising in a cross-sectional study is apt to break down when we address particular cases.

The first specific question that this chapter has explored is the relationship between staff management and economic growth. We have found that despite the views of authors like Meisenhelder and Carroll, economic growth, in the eyes of observers like Minogue but also of most bureaucratic insiders, has occurred in the teeth of the bureaucracy rather than because of it. If there is a causal relationship between growth and staff management, the direction of causation is from growth to staff management, for the simple reason that in Mauritius, Evans and Rauch's suggested effect (economic growth) has come before its suggested cause (good staff management). But it is politics rather than economics that has been crucial: after years of post-independence stagnation, it was the election of the MMM/MSM coalition in 2000 and the appointment of a minister for the civil service committed to reform which were decisive.

Our second specific question concerned the applicability of SHRM. Our earlier study was pessimistic about it in the short term, but we failed to anticipate the difference that an election might make. However, the sudden strengthening of political will had not led to full-blown HRM, but instead to a modulated approach, with strategic elements emerging in a structure that remained centralized, partly owing to the 'Mauritian specificities' – that fear of nepotism which militates against the line manager ownership dimension of SHRM. Those elements jostled alongside piecemeal improvements to HR practice which threatened to dissipate the strategic thrust, and which were themselves constrained by the same social pressures that affected the applicability of SHRM: the debate about the viability of a pay element in performance management is an example of this.

No single factor explains the development of staff management in the Mauritian civil service. Social influences, economics and politics and, at the level of staff management itself, the existing structure of government, familiarity with models like HRM and the capacity of lower levels to exercise delegated functions all play their part. Macro-, meso- and micro-levels in our model of governance (see Chapter 1) are all involved, and they interact. But what we are trying to explain is still in an important sense a single phenomenon: the interaction between professional models on one hand and local conditions on the other to produce a hybrid practical model which to an outside observer has recognizable features, but which is unique to the situation that has elicited it. It is an interaction that we will continue to explore in the later chapters of this book.

4

Tanzania: Laws and Institutions

Benson Bana and Willy McCourt

As we saw in Chapter 1, institutions are an important component of the new model of governance. They are a meso-level phenomenon which arises out of politics, even though once established, they take on a life of their own and proceed to shape the conduct of politics (we discuss the reciprocal relationship between politics and institutions – the meta- and macro-levels in our governance model (Table 1.2) – in Chapter 10 in this book). Moreover, they are lifeless until imbued by a particular style of operation at the micro- or management level, as with the SHRM model in the case of HRM. In this chapter we focus on the institutional framework of HRM in the public sector *via* a study of the Tanzanian civil service.

Highlighting one issue, even a central one, obscures others that are also significant. We hope that reading this chapter in the context of the other studies that we report in this book will allow readers to correct our tactical overemphasis. Our choice of Tanzania to do this is not arbitrary: we will suggest that Tanzania's institutional framework lends itself to studying the impact that institutions can have on the way HRM is conducted in Tanzania and elsewhere.

Social, political and economic influences on the civil service

A poor society

Downplaying other factors does not mean neglecting them entirely. We start with a review of the social, political and economic factors that affect HRM in the Tanzanian public sector. Tanzania has a special place as the only low-income country among the countries whose experience we report in this book: poverty is the dominant social factor. As we saw in Chapter 1, Tanzania is near the bottom of the UN Human

Development Index, ranked 162nd out of 177 countries in 2002, and it was poor enough to be eligible for the UN's Highly Indebted Poor Countries initiative.

Poverty is both widespread and deep. Estimates for 2000 suggested that well over 50 per cent of the population was living in poverty, with approximately one-third of them in extreme poverty (United Republic of Tanzania, 2000). Income poverty is compounded by low levels of other social indicators. Despite some recovery in the last few years, social development has gone backwards over the last quarter century: the impressive expansion of social services in the 20 years following independence has not been sustained. In 1982 life expectancy was 51 years; in 1999, it was 45. The crude death rate rose from 14.2 per cent in 1982 to 16.7 per cent in 1999 (World Bank, 2002), which in turn was partly a reflection of deteriorating infant and under five mortality (UNICEF, 2002; United Republic of Tanzania, 2001; World Bank, 2002).

The outbreak of AIDS has made a lethal contribution. With an estimated 1.5 million people HIV positive, including 520,000 of them with full-blown AIDS, representing over 10 per cent of the active labour force (Stepforward, 2003), there were profound implications for HRM in organizations, including in the civil service, the country's biggest employer. Employers' need to replace employees who passed away or simply retired or left was complicated by the increase in the adult illiteracy rate, which in 1999 was estimated at 25 per cent. Alarmingly, primary school enrolment, 93 per cent in 1980, had dropped to 78 per cent in 2000, though it was at least showing signs of recovery at the time of our study.

Luckily, not all the achievements of the post-independence period had been lost. Tanzania, as Jeffrey Sachs (2005) has recognized in his recent book, is a harmonious country despite its ethnic diversity, relative to its similarly endowed neighbour Kenya, and also to the richer countries of Malaysia, Mauritius and Sri Lanka discussed in this book. We do not need to dwell on ethnicity when we discuss Tanzania in the way that we have to do with those countries.

Politics

Political stability is another enduring achievement. The United Republic of Tanzania was born on April 26 1964 out of the union of two sovereign states, Tanganyika and Zanzibar, which had become independent from British rule in 1961 and 1963 respectively, making Tanzania the biggest sovereign state in Eastern Africa, sharing borders with eight countries.

Following independence the country moved away from the 'Westminster' model of governance, with its elements of parliamentary supremacy, multi-party democracy and separation of power between the legislature, the executive and the judiciary. Julius Nyerere as first president became head of state, executive head of government and commander-in-chief of the armed forces, with the power to dissolve parliament (Republic Constitution, Article 44[2]). The interim constitution of 1965 (superseded in 1977 by a permanent constitution) turned Tanzania into a *de jure* single party state dominated by the ruling party of the time, the Tanganyika African National Union (TANU). All political activities were carried out under party auspices, and civic organizations and governance institutions, including the civil service, were deliberately politicized. In 1967, the country moved further still from the Westminster model, adopting the populist socialist ideology of *'ujamaa'*, enshrined in the Arusha Declaration.

In a tacit admission that single-party rule had failed, the government reverted to a multi-party system in 1992, and 13 parties duly participated in the 1995 general elections. Yet multi-partism is still more apparent than real. Opposition parties are weak, lacking a firm political base and adequate finance, and their representation in both central and local government is insignificant. At the time of writing, for example, the ruling party, *Chama Cha Mapinduzi* (CCM), formed from the merger of TANU and the Afro-Shiraz Party of Zanzibar in 1977, had 258 seats while the opposition had only 34. Tanzania remains what Hague and Harrop (2001) describe as a 'dominant party system'.

Tanzania's stability has allowed both Nyerere and his presidential successor Benjamin Mkapa to resign voluntarily when they reached the end of their period in office. CCM's dominance means that their successors have emerged from within the ruling party, but still have a broad popular acceptance. At the time of writing, CCM had just chosen the former Foreign Minister Jakaya Mrisho Kikwete as successor to Mkapa, who left office in October 2005. The intra-party nomination process appeared to be accepted both by the public and external observers, including donors.

Economy

Tanzania's enviable stability has not been enough to generate economic growth and relieve its chronic poverty. Repeated attempts to invigorate the economy through the 1980s and most of the 1990s did not succeed.

They included the National Economic Survival Programme (NESP) of 1980–82; the Structural Adjustment Programmes (SAP) from 1982 onwards; the Economic Recovery Programme (ERP) in 1986 under the auspices of the World Bank and IMF; and the Social Action Programme in 1989. Reform programmes in progress at the time of writing included the Public Service Reform Programme, Public Financial Management Reform Programme, Local Government Reform Programme, and Legal Sector Reform Programme. There were some indications of economic growth and public service delivery improvement.

Agriculture, the mainstay of the economy, contributed only 48.2 per cent to GDP in 2000 (United Republic of Tanzania, 2001), despite the involvement of 82 per cent of the employed working age population. Much farming is still carried out for subsistence. Farmers depend on rainfall, and tend to use unsophisticated and unmechanized methods. Industry, meanwhile, remains undeveloped. The import substitution strategy from the 1970s onwards failed, with the import dependent industries that it created increasing structural dependence on imports.

The civil service post-independence: building services and political control

Institutional continuity and change

The countries in this book fall into two groups. The first group comprises those where the basic civil service structure bequeathed by the departing colonial power has endured: Malaysia, Morocco and Swaziland. (In Malaysia's case, the essential continuity of the structure of civil service management from the pre-independence period despite considerable innovation in its content is a paradox which Chapter 8 will try to resolve.) The second group consists of two countries, Sri Lanka and also Tanzania, where the basic institutions have been redesigned. Moreover, having rejected Westminster-style administration in favour of a politicized system meant to be more responsive to national development needs, both countries later reverted to something resembling the *status quo ante*, as elements of the Westminster model rather unexpectedly re-emerged.

Africanization and service building

Independence produced tangible achievements. Tanzania, like other former colonies, pursued 'Africanization', the deliberate removal of expatriate predominance in senior positions. At independence there had been only 12 qualified local doctors; by 1985 there were 782. There had been only 98 hospitals, 22 rural health centres and 975 dispensaries; by the mid-1980s there were, respectively, 149,239 and 2644 (Legum, 1988, p.4). Where only 486,000 children in Tanzania had access to a primary education that for most lasted only four years, over two million children were working their way through a seven-year primary education in 1984.

Africanization was initially a success. Other post-colonial African countries such as Swaziland may have seen an immediate drop in quality and standards (Dlamini, 1992), but Tordof found that 'In the decade following independence ... there was less corruption among public servants in Tanzania than in Ghana and efficiency was better in poor Tanzania' (1967, p.150). Looking back, the former Chief Secretary and Head of the Civil Service remarked that

> At that time, we had a civil service, which was visibly vibrant, motivated, and disciplined. In many, if not most, ways the civil service then epitomized the rising glory of our nation. Thus, those civil servants who were inducted into public service in those years still harbour nostalgia for what today may be regarded as the golden era of our civil service. (Lumbanga, 1995, p.20; see also Bryceson, 1988; Mukandala, 1992; Nyerere, 1977; and Pratt, 1976, pp.224–5)

His elegiac tone is explained by what came next.

Politicization and egalitarianism in the *Ujamaa* era and after[1]

The independence constitution had assumed an apolitical civil service that would be loyal to the government of the day, operating within a multi-party political system where power would change hands periodically. Employee selection was to be based on merit, seniority and performance. However, political leaders, and especially Nyerere, came to believe that this approach was designed for 'the administration of a nation, not for its development' (Nyerere, 1975). The famous Arusha Declaration of 1967 had set out Tanzania's commitment to a socialist path of development, influenced as so many newly independent governments were by the achievements of the socialist states, and especially China. Those states had deliberately fused politics and administration to prevent the civil service from remaining the mandarin class serving elite interests that it had been under colonial or imperial rule. The belief was that the civil service would thwart the government's socialist aspirations unless it was brought under strict political control.

Thus the Tanzanian civil service, along with all the organs of the state, was placed under the control of the ruling party (Constitution, Article 3 [3]). What this meant in practice was that every civil service office now had a party branch with leaders who were mostly employees in junior grades. The party policy document known as '*Mwongozo*' (Party Guidelines) of 1971 stated that

> There must be a deliberate effort to build equality between leaders and those they lead. For a Tanzanian leader it must be forbidden to be arrogant, extravagant, contemptuous and oppressive. The Tanzanian leader has to be a person who respects people, scorns ostentation and who is not a tyrant. He should epitomise heroism, bravery and be a champion of justice and equality. (Clause 15)

The party branch leadership had the authority to summon any civil servant right up to the permanent secretary of a ministry, whom the law recognized as the employer, and therefore the disciplinary authority. While the guidelines spelt out managers' responsibility to workers, they said nothing about workers' responsibility to management, or indeed their obligations as public servants. The effect on discipline was predictable. Managers had no wish to exercise their authority if it meant being branded as 'colonialists' by their politically liberated workers. Ironically, *Mwongozo* and the climate of liberation that it embodied contributed to the indiscipline and corruption that crept into the civil service from the 1970s onwards.

Emasculation of trade unions

Yet through four pieces of legislation[2] shortly after independence, the government took away with one hand the power it had given workers with the other, virtually outlawing strikes, and collapsing all the existing unions into a single national union, NUTA, affiliated (one need hardly add) to the ruling political party. The President had the power to close even this puppet union if it displeased him.[3]

Consolidation of party power

These measures that appeared to increase and decrease workers' power at the same time were not really contradictory. The consistent thread running through them was to increase the power of the ruling party, which now permeated every area of government and, indeed, national life. At the highest level of the administration, the President led the army, acted as chairman of the ruling party, and personally made appointments to senior official positions. Loyalty to the party became an essential requirement.

Similarly, the colonial regulations which forbade civil servants to belong to a political party were now rescinded, allowing civil servants to join TANU *en masse*, and with impunity: Nyerere was convinced that in a one-party state it would be absurd to exclude 'a whole group of most intelligent and able members of the community from participating in the discussion of policy simply because they happen to be civil servants', and his conviction was duly echoed almost to the letter by the subsequent Presidential Commission that led to the establishment of the one-party state (Government of Tanzania, 1965, p.24; Nyerere, 1962, p.26). Once the logical conclusion was reached of civil servants being able to stand in elections, many civil servants skipped over the by now rather low fence that separated politics from administration, taking what was left of the doctrine of separation of powers with them.

Decentralization, economic crisis, overstaffing and underpayment

Having consolidated its control over central government, CCM moved to absorb local government, ostensibly to encourage popular participation in decision-making. Local authorities were to be reinstated in 1984 in a tacit recognition that decentralization had failed, but by then the damage was done. The number of civil servants had increased by about 88 per cent in the decentralization period (and the number of ministries increased from ten to 22 in the 17 years up to 1978). However, the government chose the worst possible moment for its decentralization experiment, with the economy reeling from a severe drought in 1974, the effects of the overthrow of Idi Amin in Uganda in 1979 and the steep oil price rises of the early 1970s and early 1980s. In a stagnant economy, the increase in overall civil service size was inevitably at the expense of individual civil servants' pay, with senior civil servants disproportionately affected (Kiragu, 1998), as Figure 4.1 shows.

Civil service reform

With an undisputed acceleration in the corruption and absenteeism which had already crept in, at some point the need for reform would

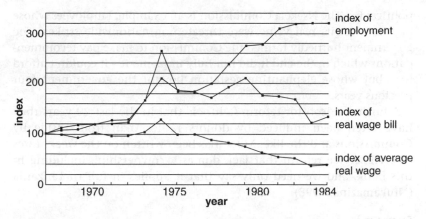

Figure 4.1 Overstaffing and underpayment
Source: Doriye 1992, p.107.

have to be addressed. Of course every generation of administrators finds immemorial stagnation which it alone has been vouchsafed the task of reforming. But since the creation of the civil service in Tanzania in 1927 there have in fact been repeated reform initiatives, albeit limited ones that have mostly concentrated on salaries and structures in isolation from other HRM practices, and even then on adjusting pay levels in isolation from the commitment and performance for which pay is meant to be a reward. For instance, while skills deficiency is sometimes identified as an impediment to performance, little attention has been given to training and development.

These limited reforms did not lead to lasting changes. The corruption that began in the 1970s has persisted. It is identified in both the World Bank's Governance Index and the Transparency International Index (see Chapter 1), and is freely admitted by the Tanzanian government. Consequently, each reform served mainly to breed another. For example, the recommendations of the Nsekela Commission of 1985–87, which themselves built on the recommendations of preceding commissions, were largely repeated by the Civil Service Reform Programme of 1991–98.[4]

The reasons why reforms so often fail is one of the central themes of this book. Reform commissions as a vehicle for reform have inherent limitations (Polidano, 1995). Their Terms of Reference are always restricted, and their investigations tend to be narrow and to address symptoms rather than causes. Sometimes they are set up as a short-term political fix. The Nsekela Commission is an example. Employees whose pay had lost its real value were threatening nationwide strikes. The government hurriedly formed the Commission to make pay recommendations which in the end it did not fully implement – it couldn't afford to – but whose elephantine gestation bought the government four precious years.

A further reason for reform failure is that in the last 20 years they have often been induced by donors rather than from inside by Commissions and the like. Much has been written on the weaknesses of civil service reform that lack domestic 'ownership', including in this book, and we need only say that it applies in full to Tanzania (Ntukamazina, 1998).

Summary

The early promise of the independence period was gainsaid by the mistakes of the *Ujamaa* episode, although there were signs of recovery at the turn of the century. The British, confining themselves mostly to law and order and revenue collection, had not invested in developing an indigenous administrative class, and at independence there was much for the new government to do. The 15 years that followed saw real achievements: health and education services built up almost from scratch, and impressive improvements in adult literacy and other social indicators. But in the mid-sixties things started to go wrong through a combination of internal factors, notably the well-intentioned but misguided *ujamaa* experiment, of which the politicization of the civil service and the failed attempt at decentralization were the elements relevant to us, and external factors which included high oil prices and a heavy debt service burden. The government put off corrective action for too long and when it finally acted, it confined itself to the subsystems of salaries and structures rather than taking the broad view of strategy and HRM that the scale of its problems required.

Interview findings

Forty-eight officials, identified as having a significant responsibility for the design and operation of HRM systems, were interviewed by the first-named author in 2002. They were government officials in senior positions, including HR practitioners in the Civil Service Commission, the Civil Service Department and line ministries.[5] Two technical advisers for the World Bank-funded Public Sector Reform Programme were also interviewed.

We also interviewed leaders of government of the United Republic of Tanzania and Tanzania Union of Government and Health Employees (TUGHE) to get the point of view of important stakeholders outside government. Finally, two focus group sessions were conducted, bringing together 33 staff with experience of HRM practices.

In an addition to the procedure of the other studies in this book, we administered a questionnaire to junior civil servants to get the perspective of recipients of the government's HRM practices. 207 questionnaires were returned (a return rate of about 8 per cent), and they were coded and analysed using SPSS. We draw on both interview and questionnaire data below, and also on secondary data gathered during the field research.

The laws and policies

Bana (2004) gives a comprehensive account of HRM in the Tanzanian government. Many of its features are not unique to Tanzania, and we explore them in other chapters. This chapter focuses on the legal and organizational framework on which HRM is based.

A legal and organizational framework which is more elaborate and binding than in the private or NGO sectors is one of the things that make HRM in the public sector distinctive. The legal framework, which we discuss in this section, consists of Acts of Parliament, principal and subsidiary legislation as well as administrative standing orders. The organizational framework, which we discuss in the next section, consists of statutory administrative organs that are meant to facilitate staff management.

The Tanzanian legal framework's principal element was the Public Sector Act No. 8 of 2002. It came into operation without corresponding subsidiary legislation in the form of regulations and Standing Orders. Consequently our discussion will be based on a combination of the Act and the regulations and standing orders made under the repealed Civil Service Act of 1989, which remained in force as stipulated in section 36 (1) of the new Act, pending their replacement.

The powers of the President
The civil service in Tanzania was based on the British system, but founded on statute rather than common law. We have seen already the enormous power which the President accumulated after independence, and his office duly remained the fulcrum of the institutional arrangements that govern the employment relationship (Mwaikusa, 1998):

The authority of the government of the United Republic shall be exercised by either the president himself or by delegation of such authority to other persons holding office in the service of the United Republic ... All executive functions of the government of the United Republic shall be discharged by officers of the government on behalf of the President (Constitution, Articles 34, 4 and 35, 1; see also Article 36, 1).

The Public Service Act stated explicitly that:

A delegation or authorization made under this section shall not preclude the President from himself exercising any function which is the subject of any delegation or authorization. (United Republic of Tanzania, 2002, p.283).

Except for high court judges and the Controller and Auditor General, the President was able to hire and fire at will. There was no institution which could properly question his staffing decisions. The high court could only examine his actions through cumbersome procedures which aggrieved civil servants seldom exercised. From time to time the President flexed his legal muscles in an almost casual way. For example, he personally appointed two permanent secretaries to the Ministry of Finance in 2003 (Guardian, 2003). Table 4.1 lists the powers which the Public Service Act has conferred on the President.

The 'public interest'

We draw readers' attention to the 'public interest' power set out in Section 24, 1. We were told of several instances in which civil servants

Table 4.1   Powers of the President over the Civil Service

Section number	Presidential powers
4, 1	Appoints Chief Secretary who is also head of civil service and Secretary to cabinet.
5, 1 (a–c)	Appoints, promotes, terminates, revokes appointments, transfers and dismisses: • Head of the civil service who is also Chief Secretary, and Secretary to the cabinet • Permanent Secretaries and their deputies • Heads of heads of independent departments

Table 4.1   Powers of the President over the Civil Service – *continued*

Section number	Presidential powers
	• Regional Administrative Secretaries • Regional and District Commissioners • Clerk to the National assembly • High Commissioners and Ambassadors • Directors of city councils/commissions
5, 3	May appoint such a number of other public servants known by titles, as may from time to time be provided for by any other written law.
9, 1	Appoints members of the Public Service Commission. Appoints the chairperson of the Commission.
9, 7 (b) & 9, 10	Removes Public Service Commissioners from office.
14, 1	Appoints the Secretary to the Public Service Commission.
15, 2	Approves establishment of departments, divisions and sub-divisions, and committees of the Public Service Commission.
17	Approves or consents for the production or disclosure of the Public Service Commission's annual report in any legal proceedings.
21, 1 (a)	May, by regulations, delegate the exercise of any of the functions conferred upon the president by Article 36 of the constitution other than the power of removal.
21 (b)	May delegate to a public servant the exercise of any such functions in relation to a public servant or a public service office.
21, 2	May, by regulations, authorize the Commission or any public servant to whom he/she has delegated functions to depute to the public servants to whom the president is authorized to delegate the exercise of such functions.
24, 1	May remove any public servant from the service of Republic if the President considers it in the public interest to do so.
25, 2 (a) & (b)	May order the compulsory retirement, dismissal of any officer in the public service.
25, 1 (a) & (d)	Has appellate jurisdiction for all civil servants. May confirm, vary, or rescind any decision of the civil service employees' disciplinary authority. Has a final decision on all appeals of public servants.
25 (e)	May, in regulations made under section 20, provide for appeals for other cases other than those provided for in section 23.

had been dismissed by the President without right of appeal. For example, some employees accused of corruption but cleared by the courts were still dismissed from the service, making a mockery of the independence of the judiciary. Others had been retired on the same ground of 'public interest'. Barry has argued that public interest 'is used emotively to add honorific overtones to policies which are in reality merely to the advantage of individual or private group interests' (2000, p.269). Certainly it is amenable to abuse in a country like Tanzania where there is no authoritative interpretation deriving from case law to which courts might refer or which aggrieved individuals might invoke. Moreover, those civil servants had no right of appeal once dismissed, because

> The question whether the President validly performed any function conferred on him by Article 36 of the constitution or by this Act ... shall not be inquired into by or in any court. (Public Service Act, Section 32, 2 [a–b])

Adequacy of civil service primary legislation

Apart from the excessive power which it vests in the President, how adequate was civil service law in other ways? The Organization for Economic Co-operation and Development (OECD) has developed a checklist in its work in central and Eastern Europe (OECD, 1996). We use it as a benchmark in Table 4.2 on next page.

Secondary legislation and line manager ownership

Secondary legislation operationalizes primary legislation. In Tanzania the subsidiary employment legislation consisted of the Civil Service Regulations and Government Standing Orders. It is notable that government agencies had no discretion to make regulations to suit their own needs. In this respect Tanzania was following the standard practice of the Commonwealth countries represented in this book, though it differed from Morocco, which follows the French pattern, and also industrialized countries like New Zealand and the UK, where line agencies have gained considerable autonomy. Although we did not specifically examine the viability of line manager ownership in this study, an earlier study conducted by one of us showed that favouritism was at least as widespread as it is in countries like Mauritius, and even line agency staff often preferred not to have discretion to make decisions because they believed their politicized agencies were not capable of using it fairly (McCourt and Sola, 1999).

Table 4.2 Adequacy of primary legislation

Provisions in the OECD checklist	Explicit	Implicit	Absent
A statement of objectives the Act is designed to achieve		✓	
Establishing a professional and an apolitical service			✓
Definition of institutions empowered to manage staff	✓		
Selection of staff on merit after fair and open competition		✓	
Specification of qualifications for entry in the civil service		✓	
Equality for entry, promotion and career advancement		✓	
A regime of duties for civil servants directed to quality, continuity, impartiality and accountability in performance			✓
Requirement for neutrality, probity, loyalty to government, efficiency and accountability		✓	
Conditions of employment, rights and benefits	✓		
Protection of job security or tenure of office		✓	
Categories of public employees to be subject to the legislation		✓	
Other laws that other public employees are subjected to			✓
Employees in the service on contract terms or precise purpose	✓		
Conditions that permit mobility within the service	✓		
Central management authority with policymaking and secondary legislation powers for the whole civil service		✓	
Independent monitoring of the civil service legislation			✓

Table 4.3   Adequacy of secondary legislation

Provisions in the OECD checklist	Explicit	Implicit	Absent
Legally enforceable rights and privileges	✓		
Legally enforceable duties and statutory restrictions		✓	
Structure of service; designation, categories and number of posts		✓	
Ways in which disciplinary proceedings are to be conducted	✓		
General procedure for recruitment, promotion and mobility		✓	
Penalties and remedies on non-compliance with the Act		✓	
Prescription of circumstances excluding or exempting civil servants from a right or a duty created by the primary Act			✓
Provisions having implications for the central budget			✓
Conduct and discipline: General principles and rules	✓		
Disciplinary authorities	✓		
Civil service code of conduct			✓
Procedures regulating appeals and legal representation	✓		
Grievance handling procedures			✓
Terms and conditions of service		✓	
Discretion to ministries and agencies to develop terms and conditions of service for their staff			✓
Individual staff handbooks			✓
Guidance on conducting performance appraisal	✓		
Health and safety at work	✓		
Procedural rules and steps to particular administrative process			✓
Interpretative guidance and use of discretionary powers		✓	
Procedures to be followed in making statutory rules			✓

Table 4.3   Adequacy of secondary legislation – *continued*

Provisions in the OECD checklist	Explicit	Implicit	Absent
Recruitment code and selection procedures	✓		
Grading and classification of staff	✓		
Hours of work holidays and attendance	✓		
Staff movement and redeployment	✓		
Leaving the civil service	✓		
Pay and allowances	✓		
Staff training and development	✓		

Once again we use the relevant OECD checklist to assess the adequacy of the secondary legislation, see Table 4.3.

Assessing the legislation

In assessing the legislation, we must begin with the caveat that the fact that the law provides for something does not necessarily mean that it actually happens. There was a procedure for performance appraisal, but it was a dead letter in most Tanzanian public agencies. That said, in many ways the primary and secondary legislation conformed to the OECD's guidelines, but with important omissions. First, there was no requirement for the Regulations to be approved by any statutory organization, and there was no obligation to consult anyone about them, not even trade unions or the Joint Staff Council. There was no civil service code of ethics or staff handbook, and staff responsible for HRM told us in interviews that little effort was made to ensure that employees understood the regulations.

The most striking area of weakness was in relation to discipline. There was no grievance procedure, and an accused civil servant facing a disciplinary hearing might be denied the right to be represented by a lawyer or anyone else. This was especially onerous since the disciplinary authority was also the employees' superior. As he or she might previously have conducted the initial inquiry, that made her policeman, prosecutor, jury and judge all rolled into one (Regulation 40, 7). This was of a piece with the President's freedom to make his own arbitrary staffing decisions.

The policies and strategic integration

Government policy on employment was embodied in a policy manual entitled 'Public Service Management and Employment Policy' (United Republic of Tanzania, 1999). This was one of the products of the Civil Service Reform Programme (CSRP), which was implemented from 1991 to 1999, and prior to which there was no policy. The manual spells out the Vision, Mission and Values (VMV) for the public service. They were aligned with the 'Tanzania Development Vision 2025' (United Republic of Tanzania, 2003), Tanzania's blueprint for macroeconomic stability and poverty eradication. Individual ministries, though not government as a whole, had formulated their own visions and missions. However, between the high-level national vision or ministry missions on one hand and the highly operational employment policy framework which the Policy sets out on the other, there was a huge strategic hiatus. Neither the civil service as a whole nor the individual ministries had a specific HRM policy or strategy, even some years after the production of the Employment Policy; nor could we find evidence, in the absence of such a strategy, of a link between individual HRM practices such as employee selection and the various visions and missions. Vertical integration, in other words, was wholly absent, and likewise horizontal integration in the form of links between the individual HRM practice areas such as between employee selection, again, and performance management. In short, despite the development of an overall strategic architecture, nothing resembling strategic HRM was practised in the civil service.

Perhaps in the last sentence we should have used the word 'rhetoric' rather than 'architecture', because despite the prominence of Vision 2025 in government documents, it was not widely known at the time of our field research. Only 18 per cent of our questionnaire respondents said they were familiar with it. One of our focus group participants was speaking for many when she said:

> Some of us in the public service read the government Vision 2025 ... in the press. Others have never seen the blueprints. We never had thorough discussions on the contents, let alone the implementation strategies. Perhaps our bosses know the rationale and necessity of the so-called vision and mission ... There are many sceptics ... Some employees in middle and lower civil service positions tend to equate the VMV to initiatives for further retrenchment.

The institutions

The division of responsibility

Such staffing authority as the President chose to delegate was shared between several authorities: the Civil Service Commission (CSC), the Chief Secretary and the Civil Service Department (CSD) in the centre; and the Chief Executive Officers (CEOs) and 'Special Committees on Employment' in line Ministries.[6] Their respective responsibilities are shown in Table 4.4.

Given our emphasis on institutions, we confine ourselves in this chapter to the agencies which have a statutory role in civil service staffing. Readers should be aware that there are other 'stakeholders' which we do not discuss: they include the Ministry of Finance, responsible for the payroll, and the trade unions which represent public servants. We give them due weight in other chapters in this book.

Table 4.4 Distribution of staffing responsibility

Locus of power	Appointing authority	Staff category	Disciplinary authority	Staff category
President	Yes	TGS M–TGS Q	Yes	TGS M–Q
			Appellate	All civil
			Jurisdiction	servants
Civil Service Commission	Yes	TGS C–TGS J	Yes	TGS 3–9
			Appellate	TGS 9–17
			Jurisdiction	
Chief Secretary and Head of the Civil Service	No	TGS J1–TGS O	Yes	TGS M–P
			Appellate	TGS A1–B10
			Jurisdiction	TGOS A1–C12
CEOs of Ministries	No	–	Yes	TGS F–TGS I
Special Committees for Employment (KAMUS) in Ministries	Yes	TGS A1–B10* TGOS A1–C12*	No	–
Heads of Divisions/ Departments in Ministries	No	–	Yes	TGS A1–B10 TGOS A1–C12

* = TGOS A1–C12 and TGS A1–B10 are operational service grades in the civil service.

The Civil Service Commission

The Commission is probably the most important of all the staff management organizations. In a country where the civil service, despite its vicissitudes, retains considerable prestige, if only because the private sector is relatively undeveloped, the public and particularly the civil servants need to have confidence in it. Its commissioners should be seen to be impartial, upright and (an attribute highly prized in Tanzania) well educated; and the process by which commissioners are appointed must itself be impartial. Fundamentally, the Commission needs to be independent from the Executive.

The crucial fact about the CSC, founded in 1955, is that despite periodic reforms (in 1962, 1989 and, most recently, 2000), it does not have a constitutional status but rather owes its existence to primary legislation, and statute law is insufficient to stop legislators from tinkering with its role through simple changes to regulations and standing orders. Constitutional bodies like the CSC's counterpart in Malaysia do not have to put up with this.

Moreover, the CSC's particular statutory basis gives the Executive controls which are specified in the Public Service Act No. 8 of 2000. Among them is the power of appointment and removal that is particularly significant since, as a trade union official commented in relation to the CSC's counterpart body in Mauritius: *'You must dance to the music of the one who appoints you'* (see Chapter 3).

When we did our study, the CSC had five part-time commissioners (three male, two female) including its chairman, all appointed by the President. Two of them were former employees of the Ministry of Foreign Affairs, where by coincidence the President had spent most of his career, including as ambassador and Foreign Minister. Conversely, expertise in staff management did not appear to be an appointment criterion.

One of the Commission's functions was 'to advise and assist the President on matters relating to appointments as he may require,' yet the President was not obliged to accept its advice. The Public Service Act (Section 22) goes out of its way to emphasize this:

> For the avoidance of doubt it is hereby declared that the conferment on the Commission of the duty of giving advice to the President in respect of the exercise of any of the functions vested in the President, shall not preclude the President from seeking advice in respect of the exercise of any functions from any other person.

In consequence, the perception among civil servants was that CSC was not independent. This was reflected in the pattern of disciplinary appeals. The Commission fielded only an average of 11 appeals in the three years prior to our field research, despite being the designated appeals body. The Permanent Commission of Enquiry, Tanzania's ombudsman, however, was fielding around 50 complaints annually on this score, for which it had no specific remit. Civil servants had greater confidence in the ombudsman than they did in their own Civil Service Commission.

In any case, as Table 4.4 shows, the Commission's authority went no higher than middle-level grades. Above that level the executive had total discretion.

Rubber stamping and financial constraints

Our interviews with CSC staff as well as our review of CSC's procedures showed that the Commission was largely a 'rubber stamping' body:

> *I know of no case where the Commission overturned a decision of a ministry, independent departments or regional administration. The commissioners in all occasions approve all documents the secretariat submits, which are of course, compiled from the information obtained from Ministries and Regions. The Commission intervenes only when there are contentious issues like a denial of promotion for a civil servant by designated authorities.*

When a ministry recommendation was rejected – this occurred in only 10.9 per cent and 2.6 per cent respectively of promotions and confirmations between 1992 and 2001 (Civil Service Commission data) – it was almost always on procedural grounds.

Even after several rounds of downsizing, the Commission remained overstaffed. Handling the very small number of disciplinary appeals was the sole task of a Discipline Section which had four staff. But if the Commission had too many staff, it also had too little money. It ran an average deficit of 18.6 per cent in the ten years up to 2003. Consequently, meetings of commissioners were curtailed, contributing to the delays that resulted from the rubber stamp not being applied in a timely fashion, so that staff often had to wait an inordinately long time for their appointments or promotions to be confirmed. Computers and other work tools were also inadequate.

> *Even the little that parliament allocates to us may not be made available to the Commission. Sometimes we do not get the money when we require it to implement our action plans. The Chairman and the Executive Secretary quite often march to the Treasury to ask for disbursement as if they are beggars. The Ministry of Finance has almost an absolute power in allocation of funds.*

The obvious solution was to cut staff costs in order to increase resources, and the scope for savings would have been even greater if its rubber stamp functions had been devolved to Ministries and Regions.

In addition, the Commission submitted its annual reports to the President and not to Parliament. Parliament had no legal oversight of the Commission despite allocating its funding. The public had no way of holding the Commission to account through its representatives.

The Civil Service Department

The Department was the central government's HRM unit, headed by a minister of state in the President's office, with a Permanent Secretary as CEO who, as usual, was a presidential appointee. In a highly centralized system, CSD was responsible for formulation, implementation, review and evaluation of HRM policies and practices in the civil service.

CSD was supposed to perform 107 separate functions at the time of our study. Among them were several areas of intra-departmental and inter-departmental overlap. Within CSD itself, training policy was a responsibility of both the policy development and HR development divisions, and remuneration of both the policy development and establishment divisions. Similarly, both the establishment and management service divisions monitored staffing levels, while the ostensibly separate roles of policy formulation and policy monitoring within the policy development division were indistinguishable in practice.

In terms of inter-departmental overlaps, CSD's HRD division was nominally responsible for evaluation of management training and co-ordination of management training programmes in the ministries. This was a function for which line ministries were also responsible, which CSD had no practical way of performing, and which we could find no evidence of CSD actually doing. 'Scrutinizing staff grade appointments' was the victim of a three-way overlap. CSD, line ministries and also CSC all had a remit.

A review of the government Staff Orders showed how little freedom line ministries had in this centralized system. They had to seek permission from CSD before filling a vacancy; making an appointment in an 'acting' capacity; granting, withholding or deferring a salary increment; changing office hours; granting leave without pay; or paying a responsibility allowance. Developing country governments, as we show elsewhere in this book, often justify central controls as a bulwark against nepotism, but it is hard to see why even the design of official forms for every ministry had to be done by CSD and no one else.

The cadre system

A quirk of civil service management which Tanzania shares with other New Commonwealth countries, including those represented in this book, is the *cadre system*. This is not to be confused with the political cadre system of socialist countries like Vietnam, but refers to an arrangement where professional civil servants have 'parent ministries', as shown in Table 4.5 below:

Table 4.5   Parent ministries and civil service cadres

Parent ministry	Civil service cadre
Finance	Accountants, Auditors
Agriculture and Food Security	Soil scientists, Crop scientists, Agronomists, food scientists
Civil Service Department	Administrative officers, Human Resource Officers, Management Analysts, Office Management Secretaries, Receptionists, Executive Assistants, Security Guards, Office Assistants, Records Officers
Works	Civil, mechanical and electrical engineers, Materials management officers, Supplies officers, Procurement officers, Stores officers
Industries and Trade	Trade officers
Community Development, Women's Affairs and Children	Community development officers
Lands and Human Settlements Development	Surveyors, Land Valuers, Evaluators, Land Officers, Land Surveyors, Town planners, Housing officers, Rent Inspectors
Planning and Privatization	Economists, Planning officers, Demographers, Statisticians
Water and Livestock Development	Sanitary and environmental engineers, Water engineers, Veterinary tutors, Veterinary officers, Livestock field officers, Livestock research officers, Hydrologists
Justice and Constitutional Affairs	Lawyers, State attorneys, Law reformers

Thus, to take the extreme case, an administrative officer who may be posted to a number of different ministries during her career will always remain an employee of CSD. The adverse management implication is obvious. Employees of a parent ministry employed in a different ministry have a dual allegiance. Their parent ministry can transfer them at will, and retains the final say on their promotions, because the parent ministry owns the all-important scheme of service for its cadre. Likewise on discipline: as one interviewee quaintly declared, *'It is phenomenal in the civil service that an employee who is under-performing in one ministry or region can be returned to his/her parent ministry for relocation.'* This is what Mawhood (1983) had in mind when he observed that 'an employee's loyalty should be single – to the authority which employs him'.

The line ministries

The Chief Executive Officers. The CEOs are recognized as the employer in their ministries, but their power is constrained, in the ways we have already seen and in other ways too. They are not appointing authorities even for the appointments delegated to ministries. They can fire but not hire: hiring is conducted by a committee in each ministry, as we shall see. Staff management in the Tanzanian civil service was, if anything, even more fragmented than we found it to be in Mauritius.

The nature of the CEO's own appointment is odd. The President's personal power, never delegated, to appoint and dismiss Permanent Secretaries means that their title was a misnomer as their tenure was impermanent, verging on precarious:

> *Very few permanent secretaries can claim permanency in the job in some ministries. Within five years, for instance, the ministries of Education and Culture, Community Development and Women Affairs, Planning and Privatization, Trade and Industries, Agriculture and Food Security, only to mention a few, have been under the executive leadership of either two or three different permanent secretaries. The President changes these top officers in the service in a similar way as he changes attire.*

A presidential appointee told us that

> *In my position anything can happen at any time. The security of my tenure in this ministry is not at all guaranteed. I may be transferred at any time or given a different appointment against my interest or profession. This prompts one to take precautionary measures all the time. Some individuals do it even crudely.*

The KAMUS system. Each ministry had a committee known as the 'Special Committee for Employment' (KAMUS is the Swahili acronym), which was responsible for employee selection for the relatively junior officers who were not managed centrally. It was chaired by the CEO, and the Director of Administration and Personnel acted as secretary. But it also had three members appointed by the minister or Regional Commissioner as the case may be, plus a trade union representative.

By this point in the chapter, readers should be able to recognize the influence of the party supremacy model: sure enough, the KAMUS system was a vestige of the single party era. The political element created the opportunity for decisions based on favouritism, as a focus group participant told us:

> *KAMUS was, in principle, established to combat patronage and favouritism ... However, it has not deterred those in power positions to get employment opportunities for their relatives and friends ... I was a KAMUS member for eight years. I know several occasions in which decisions were directly or indirectly made to accommodate the wishes of power holders.*

Law, organizations and fairness in appointments

How did the framework of laws and organizations translate into HRM practice in the key area of appointments, including employee selection? Here we confine ourselves to their effect on the perceptions of employees about the way in which appointments were made (more detail is given in Bana, 2004). Table 4.6 shows employees' perceptions about different kinds of appointments.

For all three kinds of appointments, more civil servants in our survey were dissatisfied than satisfied. Given the pervasive nature of corruption in Tanzania, including in the civil service, we went on to ask our

Table 4.6   Employees' views of appointment decisions (rounded %ages, N = 207)

Kind of appointment	Very satisfied	Fairly satisfied	Fairly dissatisfied	Very dissatisfied	No response
New appointments	9	33	30	23	4
Promotions	8	24	44	18	6
Transfers	7	30	51	9	3

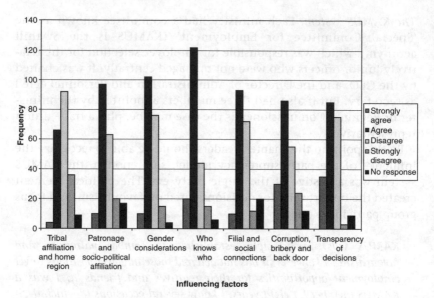

Figure 4.2   Perceptions of fairness in appointments (N = 207)

questionnaire respondents for their views on the fairness of appointment decisions, and they are set out in Figure 4.2 above.

The perception of unfairness was clearly widespread. From our point of view, the results for the last item ('transparency of decisions') are particularly interesting. For in a situation where senior appointments were not made on the basis of open competition, where internal and external checks on appointments did not exist, where many vacancies were not advertised, where criteria for appointments were unknown, and in a broader context in which corruption and unfairness were pervasive, the suspicion that many decisions were made unfairly or even corruptly was almost inevitable.

Discussion: strengthening laws and institutions in Tanzania

Once again we emphasize that this chapter has not given a comprehensive view of public staff management in Tanzania, but has concentrated, in the context of the other studies in this book, on the institutional framework of laws and organizations for HRM in government. We have seen that HRM in the civil service was carried out within a constitution and primary and secondary legislation that satisfied most of the requirements for such legislation set out in the

OECD checklist that we used as a benchmark. However, there were unsatisfactory aspects. Tanzania may have become a formal multi-party democracy but the President retained most of the single-party era formal powers over the civil service: control over creating and abolishing functions, authority over all senior appointments and promotions, and the power to dismiss civil servants in the 'public interest'; and there were few procedural checks on the way he exercised them. He also indirectly controlled the CSC, notably through his power to appoint and remove Commissioners. From all of this flowed civil servants' (and the public's) distrust of the impartiality of staffing decisions, a distrust that we saw reflected in the pattern of disciplinary appeals. Even the most senior officials lived in constant fear of arbitrary executive decisions.

Dropping down a level, power was also highly centralized in the organizations that the laws had created, particularly the CSC and the CSD. Among other things, it meant that there was duplication of functions and role confusion between these central agencies and line ministries, so that the central agency role was far too often confined to rubber-stamping decisions that in reality had been made lower down. Yet the line ministries and Regions were obliged to wait for the stamp to be applied, resulting in delays that reduced efficiency and demoralized civil servants.

In a stable and notionally multi-party democracy, there seemed every reason for the President to devolve his powers to the staffing organizations beneath him, and in so doing to strengthen the organizations' independence by specifying procedures on which the law was silent at the time of writing. For example, the CSC could be transformed into a freestanding constitutional body *via* an amendment to the Constitution, which could require the President to be advised by a committee whose members might include the Head of the Civil Service and the Chief Justice, as is the case in countries like Nepal and Sri Lanka (McCourt, 2001c; and Chapter 7 in this book). A CSC with a constitutional status would be the appropriate body to devise the staffing procedures to guide the President that we have argued were deficient in the prevailing arrangements.

Other things being equal, there was also scope to devolve functions from the Centre – from CSC and CSD alike – to line ministries and Regions, to increase efficiency by eliminating duplication and delays. However, that would require a judgement about the ability of the lower levels to carry out their functions fairly which it is outside the scope of this chapter to make. We should recall that even in a relatively prosperous country like Mauritius, the subject of Chapter 3 in this book, there was a well-grounded fear that devolution would increase favouritism.

Conclusion: aligning institutions with new objectives

While Tanzania shares features of its institutional framework with other developing countries, especially those in the Commonwealth, it has a unique post-independence political history which has conferred enormous power on the Head of State, greater in the case of the civil service than even the two semi-absolute monarchies discussed in this book, Morocco and Swaziland. This is a specific reason for the general methodological rule which we take the opportunity to rehearse, not for the first or last time in this book, that we should not read too much into a single case.

However, we suggest that Tanzania's experience illustrates the way in which institutions convey powerful messages about the integrity of government to the people they affect: civil servants but also the public at large, given the prominence of public sector employment in a country like Tanzania. Equally importantly, the extent to which they are adequate affects the work of government. In this respect they correspond to the structure of private companies, differing only in their scale of operation and their derivation from laws rather than the discretionary decisions of senior managers (Mintzberg, 1983). Like company structure, they are an unobtrusive and unglamorous, but powerful influence on public management. In developing country governments, institutions are sometimes no more than a façade, but buildings still need façades. Patronage and inefficiency can subsist in the interstices of even a solid institutional framework, but fairness and efficiency will be impossible in public agencies without such a framework.

Tanzania's institutional history also suggests a more specific lesson. Having moved decisively away from the Westminster model by fusing politics and administration under the leadership of the dominant party, Tanzania has moved back towards it, and, based on our analysis, our view is that it ought to move closer still. Tanzania's experience shows that the civil service is, ironically, better equipped to serve political and development objectives when it has some degree of autonomy from politicians, because autonomy fosters civil service capacity and confidence. Yet the single-party era has left much of the single-party institutional architecture behind, persisting as what

Mahoney and Snyder have called a 'frozen constraint' (1999, p.18) on the government's current objectives, as opposed to those it once had, and restricting the autonomy of line ministries and agencies.

The Tanzanian government has tacitly admitted that single-party rule was a failure. But it was still the attempted solution to a real problem, that of reorientating the ship of state from the objectives of colonial administration to the objectives of development. Moreover, we will see when we discuss Sri Lanka in Chapter 7 that the problem has not wholly disappeared, even at the start of the twenty-first century. How developing country governments can achieve the contradictory goals of strengthening the autonomy of the civil service while making it more responsive to political objectives at the same time is a dilemma that we will try to resolve in our concluding chapter.

5
Morocco: The Politics of HRM

Willy McCourt and Khadija Alarkoubi

The political context of reform

Two things make Morocco an interesting case. First, Morocco, like Mauritius, has made an explicit link between the efficiency of its civil service and the health of its economy: 'Morocco has undertaken reforms to ensure sustained economic growth, macro-economic stability, opening up to the global economy ... Their success ... is intimately linked to the quality of the civil servants involved' (Ministère de la Fonction Publique, 1998; see also Proulx, 1999). Second, Morocco is a North African middle-income country whose public administration is coloured by the French colonial legacy, distinguishing it from the Anglophone countries in sub-Saharan Africa and Asia that make up the remainder of the cases in this book; the Francophone/Anglophone divide is a major fissure in the post-colonial developing world.

This is the first of three chapters which explore the politics that underlies public staff management. It aims to establish the intimate way in which Moroccan politics affects staff management, a function which readers from a management background might expect to be the domain of pure 'good practice'. The chapters that follow, on Swaziland and Sri Lanka, will develop that insight by exploring particular aspects of politics: patronage and political commitment respectively.

The Moroccan political system: 'disparate centralism'
Politics in Morocco is becalmed by two settled features of Morocco's governance. The first is the centralized yet disparate nature of government. Power centres on the palace. In formal terms, the 1996 constitution envisages a multi-party system of democracy, but also

allows the king a lot of executive leeway (Economist, 2004). He personally appoints the Prime Minister, key central ministers and regional governors. While he often delegates his authority over more junior appointments (including officials), the practical contrast with, say, the British monarch, who also enjoys the theoretical right to select the Prime Minister, is stark. Moreover, the late King Hassan did pass a strong legacy of skilful government in its own terms to his son at his accession in 1999, whatever one's misgivings about certain aspects of it. Finally, even at the start of the twenty-first century one should not underestimate the king's *baraka* (roughly charisma), a quasi-religious quality which derives from the monarch's important religious role,[1] and which he shares with Muslim saints (Munson, 1993): the popular grief at the death of King Hassan II in 1999 attested to it.

But it is a surprising fact that some have argued that the monarchy's power essentially consists of holding the ring between strong autonomous élites: the urban bourgeoisie, including senior government officials; professors and intellectuals; the army; and the rural notables (Clement, 1990). The model statement of this view is still Waterbury's (1970). For him, the king was like a Nuer chief who, in Evans-Pritchard's classic analysis (1940: see especially pp.172–6) had little formal authority, and merely mediated between tribes in the event of disputes, in a society where rebellion had been endemic for much of its history,[2] and which was held together, paradoxically enough, by opposition between its 'segments'. In this analysis, the king finds himself having to placate and trim between powerful rival groups. Some have found Waterbury's analysis over-ingenious (Eickelman, 1998; Gellner, 1981), but there is agreement that whether from a position of strength or of weakness, the palace has played élite groups off against each other by the well-judged use of patronage, albeit the modernizing bent of both the present king and his father means that its recent beneficiaries have often been highly qualified technocrats[3] (Joffe, 1988; Pennell, 2000; Tessler, 1987; Zartman, 1987).

The Palace's resort to patronage is an expression of Morocco's deep-rooted clientelism (Willis, 2002). While in other countries favouritism relates to a single feature of identity, such as ethnicity in Rwanda or religion in Northern Ireland, in Morocco it is 'fluid', to use Gellner's word (1981, p.72): 'Any individual ... will seek a person who can help him from any place in the country, any position in the official hierarchy and on the basis of any personal connection that best serves his particular purpose at that moment' (Rosen, 1979, p.53). Individuals are thus reluctant to commit themselves irrevocably to any single aspect of their identity if that precludes emphasizing another aspect that might be to their advantage later on; and by extension, to nail their colours to the mast of a single policy, as they might need to espouse a different one in due course.

Both 'strong' and 'weak' king views agree on some features of Morocco's politics. A positive feature is that, within a stable system, political actors have developed the instinct to consult and seek consensus: Morocco was a practitioner *avant la lettre* of what we have come to call 'stakeholder politics' (Hutton, 1995). The IMF stabilization programme of 1983 illustrates this. In the face of IMF pressure to adopt a rapid, if not brutal approach to reform, the Moroccan side entertained a wide range of opinions across government, and even the IMF came to admit that the gradual pace of the reform programme that emerged and the care taken to address the public's anxieties contributed to its success (Azam and Morrisson, 1994; Nsouli *et al.*, 1995). Involving reform stakeholders has also been central to the government's administrative reform strategy, as we shall see.

However, a negative feature, to which the particular character of Morocco's clientelism also contributes, is a tendency to passivity or *attentisme* in political actors, leading to an 'abhorrence of bold initiatives, and the overall stalemate that characterizes Moroccan politics' (Waterbury, 1970, p.8). Government is fundamentally quietist, and does not so much take initiatives as arbitrate between opposing interests when action is unavoidable, as in the stabilization crisis of the early 1980s. Even the dramatic 'Green March' which culminated in the 'liberation' of the Spanish Sahara was arguably precipitated by the impending collapse of Fascism in Spain (Pennell, 2000). This tendency, which has deep roots in Morocco's royal history, is compounded by the hostility to innovation of the mainly conservative rural notables who are an important part of the monarchy's power base (Hammoudi, 1997; Leveau, 1985).

In this analysis, royal intervention becomes the only way of overcoming political stalemate; and, partly for this reason, other political actors have tended to accept it: 'Everyone wants to believe in it, even when the sovereign's decisions appear to be guided by the interests of the monarchy and the social categories closest to it' (Hammoudi, 1997, p.23). However, the analysis is silent on whether, in the particular case of civil service reform, that intervention will materialize or, rather, will resemble the 'Godot' character in Beckett's play (1952) for whom the other characters are doomed to wait in vain.

Stability and change

Now some would object that while our account might have been true for most of the late king's reign, his last few years, when he deliberately smoothed the way for his son, and the first few years of his son's reign itself have changed everything. This brings us to the stability verging on sclerosis which is the second relevant feature of Morocco's governance.

At issue here are the degree and scope of the changes. No one disputes that there have been real changes. Already in 1997 the general election had ushered in Morocco's first centre-left government, popularly known as 'le gouvernement de l'alternance' (the government of the changeover), and the old king had appointed respected opposition leader Abderrahmane Youssoufi as his prime minister. The new king continued the trend through symbolic actions like dismissing the powerful Minister of the Interior, Driss Basri, and allowing longstanding opponents to return from exile. In 2004 he took a further symbolic step by setting up an 'Equity and Reconciliation Council' (Instance Equité et Réconciliation), modelled on South Africa's Truth and Reconciliation Commission, which inevitably would expose the torture and other abuses which had disfigured his late father's reign (Mirguet, 2005). Even Amnesty International, previously scathing about Morocco's human rights record, welcomed the initial changes, and has continued to welcome ensuing measures such as the gradual release of political prisoners (Amnesty International, 1999 and 2002). Outside government, civil society groups have mushroomed (Sater, 2002). At the start of the new century, Morocco's semi-absolute monarchy was still one of the most democratic régimes to be found between the Atlantic and the Persian Gulf.[4]

But how profound have all the changes been? After three years in office, the 'gouvernement de l'alternance' represented 'a kind of continuity rather than a break with the past' (Bouachrine, 2001, p.10). Following the 2002 elections, as well as his usual quota of five key ministers, the king appointed an unelected businessman and political neophyte as his prime minister, picked *faute de mieux* when the squabbling political parties failed to yield up a credible candidate. (It is important to note that recent governments have been coalitions drawn from the plethora of political parties, with all the problems of agreeing a common programme that bedevil coalitions everywhere.) The new prime minister was even more the creature of the palace than his predecessor, who at least had an independent political base. The king continues to chair the meetings of his 'inner cabinet' of appointed ministers, at which all the big decisions are taken (Economist, 2002). According to one critic, even the government's privatization pro-gramme, which was proceeding and even accelerating (Al-Hayat, 2002), has become ensnared in the patronage game so as to strengthen the state's links with the commercial élite (Najem, 2001). Thus while we do not accept the cynical view of one of our interviewees that the 'gouvernement de l'alternance' was no more than a device *'to facilitate the transfer of power from the old king to his son'*, we consider that recent changes have been real, but not fundamental.

Every manager will recognize the king's dilemma in this some-what changed context: should I facilitate, 'empowering' and build-ing up long-term capacity, or command, getting things done today? Morocco's segmentary political system gives him the abiding temp-tation to use his power to break the stalemate; the more so because the public, whose confidence in its bickering and historically corrupt politicians is scant, has mostly been happy for him to use it, even when it has served a particular royal interest. But each time he does, he confirms other political actors in their passivity and negates his espoused commitment to democracy and a strong civil society. His uneasy solution, one that in the Waterbury tradition is typical of the timidity of Moroccan political actors, is to use his power sparingly and hesitantly, with the result that areas that are not vital, or that are simply outside his field of vision (this is the issue of the scope of change), have been left to stagnate. We shall suggest that government effectiveness, including staff management, is one such area.

Interview findings

Interview details

Seven government officials were identified for interview in April 2003 by the first-named author, who as a former civil servant is familiar with the structure of the Moroccan civil service. They were as follow:

- The secretary-general (i.e. the most senior official) of a central min-istry
- A senior official with a central responsibility for civil service reform
- A senior official in the Ministry of Finance
- The Human Resource Directors of four Ministries
- The director of the civil service training academy

In addition, we interviewed a member of the national executive of one of the largest trade unions representing civil servants, and an international consultant based in Morocco who has conducted HRM projects with several Ministries. We also conducted a mixed gender focus group of junior civil servants from different Ministries.

All but one of the interviews, and also the focus group meeting, were conducted in French.[5] The data generated were analysed in the same way as in the other case studies in this book.

The civil service

The picture that we hope to paint is of a government, recently elected when we conducted our interviews, inheriting a stagnant, partly corrupt administration leavened by some able technocrats in senior positions, and relying on weak central authority and a standard but very slow-moving reform model as a vehicle for change. On the margins of the picture, a few technical ministries were moving ahead with HRM initiatives of their own whose sustainability and transferability, however, were in doubt. We will fill in this picture with some additional information about developments between the date of our original research and the time of writing.

The civil service partakes of the 'disparate centralism' of government as a whole. Hourani (1991) has observed how different branches of government in Arab countries tend to become separate centres of power, a tendency strengthened in Morocco by the French administrative heritage, ironically consolidated by Morocco's haste to develop its own administrative procedures after independence when the French model was the only one available (Moussa, 1988; Snoussi, 2001). Morocco has reproduced intact the French system of powerful professional *corps*, the groups of engineers, lawyers etc., each with its own *statut particulier*, to which every senior civil servant belongs (Rouban, 1999).

Thus the *corps* of engineers, with its graduates from élite institutions like the Ecole des Ponts et Chaussées (School of Bridges and Highways) in France, has its own favourable pay and benefits which reinforce the separateness of the Public Works Ministry where most of them work. This has created a rather divisive 'administrative feudalism' (Marais, 1973) but it does give ministries some real autonomy. A second desirable consequence, augmented by the monarchy's technocratic bent, is that the senior civil service is competent, as Evans and Rauch's (1999) informants and Nsouli *et al.* (1995, p.55) agree.

Another aspect of the French influence is that Anglo-Saxon models of strategic management and SHRM are not widely disseminated or practised in Francophone countries (Barsoux and Lawrence, 1990). Moreover, a system where officials identify with a technical *corps* undervalues management. One of our interviewees noted that line managers tend to see themselves as technical experts rather than managers.

The French legacy also affects the role of the Ministry of Finance and the Ministry of Public Service Modernization (MPSM),[6] the relevant central agencies. As throughout the political system, they have more power to block than to initiate. Budget approval for staffing decisions has to come from Finance. MPSM, the gatekeeper of administrative law – its legal remit charges it with 'ensuring the application of the *statut général* of the public service' (Sbih, 1977) – is there mainly to confirm that decisions conform with law and regulations, just as one would expect in a society where what Hofstede (1980) called 'uncertainty avoidance' is high. Despite this cultural appropriateness, few readers will be surprised to hear that line ministries do not particularly appreciate MPSM's 'finicky'[7] role (*'All that MPSM and Finance are interested in is following the regulations'*), and we shall see that the decision to locate the civil service reform programme in MPSM has in fact undermined its credibility and contributed to the inertia of reform.

Civil service reform

Improvements to HRM stand or fall with the national administrative reform programme which has been the vehicle for introducing them. The 'gouvernement de l'alternance' wanted to turn over a new administrative leaf, aware that despite able technocrats in senior positions, the emphasis on patronage and security during most of the late king's reign, when the Ministry of the Interior was paramount, meant that the civil service had stagnated. A critical report from the World Bank (1996a) corroborated this view. So the government placed a small reform team in MPSM which, following the usual diagnosis and consultation, launched a 'Good Management Charter' with three elements: action against corruption, budget rationalization and improved communication. The latter included HRM initiatives designed to promote merit selection, fair pay and productivity.

Some actions duly followed. Civil servants had to declare their property in order to identify people whose wealth had corruptly increased. The government sold off official vehicles and stopped paying water, electricity and telephone charges in senior officials' homes. It also changed public procurement law and asked Ministries to take heed of press criticisms and respond to citizens' requests and complaints.

As for the Charter, its aim was as much to raise awareness as to bring about concrete changes. MPSM organized workshops at which the Charter was presented, and ministries and representatives of overseas governments which had introduced things like performance appraisal were invited to present to ministries at large, the hope being that the latter would recognize the value of the innovations and spontaneously adopt them. *'Our only power,'* said a central official, *'Is the power to persuade.'*

All these were definitely steps in the right direction. *'This is the first time that we are talking about corruption in Morocco,'* said one senior official. Another declared that *'Until now we've been thinking that administration represents authority and power, but now we think that it should serve people and resolve their problems.'* Moreover, rather than resent the endless workshops, *'tables rondes'* and the like, some of our interviewees appreciated the attempt to consult. But there were still difficulties. A central official closely involved in the Charter urged us to *'Go now and ask about the destiny of this Charter. People don't even know what it is'*. When we took him at his word, we found that junior civil servants did know about it but saw no sign of it being implemented: *'We are good at studying problems and proposing solutions, but they are rarely implemented. That's why I haven't even bothered to see what's in the Charter.'*

Strategic integration

We turn now to the first of the HRM elements on which this book concentrates. In a word, there is virtually no evidence of SHRM-style strategic integration in the civil service. There are favourable factors: the policies of the new government could be the basis for strategy, piecemeal though they are; there is some awareness of strategic management among central officials and in some technical line ministries; and the relative autonomy of line ministries makes it possible for them to develop their own strategies, as one of them was at pains to point out. But one looks in vain for the strategic elements: there is no HR strategy, and no conscious attempt to link individual HR activities such as employee selection to an overall strategic plan which in any case does not exist (vertical integration) or to each other (horizontal integration).

What goes on instead is what ministries call 'gestion courante' or day-to-day management, pretty much what we called the 'clerk of works' model in Chapter 1. The more able technical ministries like Finance, Housing and Public Works have taken professional initiatives, introducing computerized HR information systems or performance appraisal. The less able ministries see themselves as fighting, and sometimes losing, a battle to maintain basic integrity, with a demoralized, partly corrupt HR function which competent staff make it their business to get out of. Able and unable alike are pinned down by personnel files. To get a civil servant promoted, a ministry has to satisfy itself that there is a case, before referring it first to MPSM and then to Finance. The whole thing takes up to three months, during which the anxious civil servant bombards the ministry with requests for an update (*'you might have a couple of hundred a day'* said one official, using dramatic exaggeration to make his point).

Line manager ownership

Are managers free to manage? Yes and no. At the top, Morocco's 'administrative feudalism' means that line ministries have more autonomy than in Commonwealth countries like Mauritius (Chapter 3), and some of them have taken advantage of it. But delegation to lower levels within ministries is constrained by the central controls that we have already discussed, and also by both a tangible barrier – the high pay and education differential between senior and junior staff in this relatively unequal society – and an intangible one: Morocco is very high in what Hofstede called 'power distance', just like other Middle Eastern countries and also France (Hofstede, 1980; House *et al.*, 2004). It is symptomatic that one of our informants said that *'Your relationship with your boss determines everything.'* The same officials who grumble about petty central controls impose them on their own subordinates. Junior officials complained that even a simple decision about going on a training course might go all the way up to the ministry's secretary-general.

Employee selection

The Moroccan constitution stipulates that 'each Moroccan has the right of access, in equal conditions, to civil service jobs'. Article Six of the *Dahir*, or royal decree, of February 24 which fleshes this out, states that the king, acting on the Minister's recommendation, appoints senior civil servants such as secretaries-general and Chiefs of Police. The king and his ministers have a great deal of discretion in how they do so, while ministers are free to appoint anyone they like to their personal Cabinets.[8] Moreover, while the Palace and Ministers influence official appointments, there is movement in the other direction too: the post of minister can turn out to be the next rung on an official's promotion ladder (El-Messaoudi, 1996). At less exalted levels, appointments have been regulated since 1976 by a legal text which specifies some criteria to which all but the most senior appointments are supposed to conform. That is why Claisse (1987, p.53) says that 'The highest and lowest levels of administration reflect the most traditional forms of patrimonialism whereas the intermediate level is evolving towards modernization.'

Moreover, just as patronage appointees can be competent, 'merit' appointees can be the opposite. *'Someone with a Master's degree in nuclear studies may be recruited as an administrator.'* The state still plays the role of employer of last resort to an extent, even though *'Recruitment and promotion of people without the required qualifications and training does not reflect commitment to reform. It is not with these practices that we are going to reach performance and quality.'*

In October 2000, the former Prime Minister exhorted his Ministers in a circular to make key appointments on merit. How much notice did they take? These days, vacancies do get advertised, examinations are administered, private recruitment agencies are engaged, eventual appointments are made by a selection panel – sometimes. Such initiatives by individual ministries taking advantage of the freer climate of government are sporadic and not institutionalized,[9] and Ministers and senior officials continue to use and abuse their discretion. We certainly do not have the monolithic central civil service recruitment examination hankered after by Evans and Rauch and by the World Bank (1997), which recently advised the government to emulate the Commonwealth Public Service Commission model by centralizing recruitment.

Performance management

The civil service law stipulates that civil servants should be appraised and graded every year on their 'professional knowledge, effectiveness and performance, and behaviour', criteria vague enough to leave appraisers plenty of room to manoeuvre. The grade can affect salary, but only at the margins. Reports, which supervisors have no obligation to discuss with subordinates, have to go to MPSM and Finance, like most things. Our interviewees agreed that there is much effort for little return.

In other developing countries like Tanzania or Mauritius, whose experience we have discussed already in this book, that is where things have been left. But in Morocco the Ministries of Agriculture, Housing and Public Works have taken the initiative by introducing a version of performance appraisal which has the modest objective of getting managers to take responsibility for staff performance. The reform team in MPSM has pounced on this and, in its reform broker role (see below), disseminated it to other ministries. But the initiative has two limitations. The first is that it is not linked to any overall strategy, which in HRM practice is essentially what distinguishes performance appraisal from performance management. (However, and by way of compensation, the scheme is consequently not over-ambitious.) The second limitation is that the scheme is not fully owned by government, reducing its chances of spreading to other ministries or even of being sustained by the ministries that have introduced it. Several informants said that initiatives depended largely on individuals, so that progress could come to a halt if that individual moved elsewhere, as happened when the dynamic secretary-general of one ministry was transferred.

Civil service pay and employment

There is one other important HRM issue which is outside our case research framework, but which was the subject of Chapter 2. Observing that public sector wage bills represent 12 per cent of GDP (and 30 per cent of government spending, as the Minister for the Civil Service admitted in a TV interview), the World Bank (2000b) called for 'resizing' of the civil service to free resources for productive investment. As so often, a comparison with other countries in the region muddies the waters (Schiavo-Campo *et al.*, 1997), yet none of our informants disputed the need to do something. At the time of our interviews, action was incoherent: the former Prime Minister had frozen senior salaries pending a general pay review which failed to materialize. The pay freeze built up pressure, especially from the *grands corps*, to which the government eventually capitulated, at some cost to its credibility.

Changes since 2003

What changes took place in the two years between our interviews and the time of writing? The main one, in fact, relates to the size of the civil service. On January 1 2005 the government announced a scheme, to be open only until June 30, for 'rightsizing' the civil service through a programme of voluntary retirement entitled 'Fresh Start' ('Intelaraka' in Arabic). According to the Minister for the civil service, 32,500 applications had been received, 62 per cent of them from civil servants in the upper echelons. While this might appear to make the scheme top-heavy, the Minister declared that the government was hoping that these highly skilled people would create businesses and jobs in the private sector.

Behind the announcement was the perceived need to reduce the public sector wage bill, and to distribute public servants more evenly across the country; an initiative to address the latter was in the pipeline. The government was also keen to change the age profile of the civil service by allowing young civil servants to rise into the posts that their senior colleagues had voluntarily abandoned. Finally, the government was proposing to tackle the imbalance between allowances and base salary.

As we completed this chapter, 13,600 of the 32,500 applications had already been approved – apparently the say-so of the employee's immediate supervisor was all that was needed. The government had also rooted out 450 'fonctionnaires fantômes', or 'ghost workers' as we called them in Chapter 2. The effects of all this were still in the future when we wrote. However it is difficult to be optimistic in the light of our discussion of downsizing in Chapter 2. The severance package was generous enough to elicit the enthusiastic response we have reported. Making senior employees redundant would be proportionately expensive, since their severance packages would be based on their final salaries, and they might also be the very employees that the government could least afford to lose. A voluntary scheme of this kind avoids political pain, but at the expense of a real financial cost, as countries like Ghana and the UK have found. The government appeared to be continuing its favourite approach of entering the reform waters one toe at a time.

Discussion: the politics of HRM

The inadequacy of a management explanation

How can we make sense of our findings? A parsimonious explanation would be to see them through a management lens as an instance of generic resistance to change (Kotter, 1979), a view which duly emerged in our focus group discussion, one lending itself to the use of standard techniques like force-field analysis to analyse change, as one of us has done already (Alarkoubi, 1999). Moreover, there is a simple dissemination issue: it was clear that current normative management approaches, including the SHRM model which we focused on in our interviews, are not widely known. There was also scope for a management restructuring, whether to delegate stifling administrative controls from Finance and MPSM to line ministries or even, moving in the opposite direction, to centralize employee selection as the World Bank has recommended.

But pondering the role of MPSM shows why a management explanation is inadequate. As one of our interviewees said, *'We need to diagnose the Civil Service Ministry itself ... this Ministry is not appropriate to conduct reform.'* MPSM is expected to drive reform, but we have seen three reasons why it is weak. The first is its role in the French tradition as the gatekeeper of civil service law, which disposes it to assume that reform can proceed by administrative *fiat* (Proulx, 1999), and which makes it all but despised by the line ministries and the *grands corps*, who tend to look down on their administrative brethren, just like in France (Rouban, 1999). The second is the strength of the line ministries, organized around their *corps* and centres of power in their own right. The third is the deep-seated inclination of political actors to hold the ring between opposing factions rather than to initiate, with the related preference for keeping every option open without committing oneself irrevocably to any of them.

All this is reflected in how the government has handled reform. Putting it in MPSM was its first mistake, as reform got tarred with MPSM's legalistic brush.[10] The government then mitigated its mistake by placing typically able technocrats in charge of the reform. The technocrats played a weak hand skilfully, but also characteristically. The Good Management Charter raised awareness of new but not over-ambitious approaches to reform, which some ministries, who wield the real power in staff management, moved to exploit. MPSM then used its central position to act as a broker of good practice, organizing workshops, circulating newsletters and so on: *'To those who are lagging behind we say: Look what others are doing, try and imitate them.'*

But in doing all this they lowered their own expectations of reform – *'there are some modest reforms which are also necessary'*, as one of them put it. Officials whom one might have expected to be champions of change talked about *'trying to be neutral, open to all experiences'*, and of *'facilitating, not saying: C'est moi, la réforme'*. This was sensible in a way, but also allowed them to keep their heads down in the way political actors in Morocco like to do. It provoked the observation from one of our interviewees that *'the dossier of civil service reform has been opened, but very timidly.'* Crucially, the observation was echoed in a UNDP evaluation report which regretted that the programme 'seems a little timid to us' and, since 'concrete results remain(ed) some way off', which led to the termination of UNDP's support (Proulx, 1999, p.8 and p.41). It all boils down to that classic reform black box, 'political will': *it is not so much (a problem of) having models to apply but having capacity to change'* or, as another interviewee put it neatly, not so much of 'savoir faire' as of 'vouloir faire'.

In a way, SHRM-style strategic integration is well suited to an assault on Morocco's 'administrative feudalism'. Surprisingly enough, it was a trade union official who was most emphatic that a *'holistic and global'* approach to HRM would be an antidote to the multiplicity of *corps* and the piecemeal character of reform initiatives to date. Moreover, the fact that Morocco's ministries have greater control over their staff than their Commonwealth counterparts facilitates line manager ownership. But the sheer unfamiliarity of SHRM means that introducing it would require a considerable slice of the government's limited political resources; and even then the underlying problem of political will would remain.

Thus we judge that it is actually beside the point to recommend that Morocco should adopt SHRM or indeed any specific management approach at the moment, because any and every approach is likely to fall prey to the same timidity that has put paid to attempts at reform in recent years, with the danger of each successive reform failure eroding the will of political actors, which was weak to begin with. There is no harm in carrying on with modest awareness-raising exercises which may bear fruit later on, but it is the underlying political problem that needs to be solved before progress at the management level will be feasible. Thus at this point we make a clean break with the assumption of Chapters 2, 3 and 4 that we can discuss public staff management exclusively in management terms.

Political action as a prerequisite for management change

How to proceed in a system where no one wants to be the first to jump? We suggest that the problem should be reframed as one of overcoming political timidity and taking purposeful action, rather than of adopting this or that management model. Following that, any action to address the problem must take account of the need to recognize the fundamental reality of the primacy of the palace while not reinforcing the timidity of other political actors by an arbitrary royal decree, something that we have seen the present king is in any case reluctant to impose. A number of approaches are possible. A first, low-key approach might be to enhance the Civil Service Council, envisaged in the *Statut*

Général of the Civil Service as long ago as 1958 but only convened for the first time in 2002. However, it follows from our analysis that such an approach, which would not involve the Palace, would fail to overcome the inertia in the political system.

A more ambitious approach would be for reform advocates to persuade the king to make a keynote speech setting up something like a British Royal Commission, a committee of eminent people which would take submissions, including possibly from abroad. Just as we saw that South Africa's Truth and Reconciliation Commission has been adopted as a human rights model, so South Africa's Presidential Commission for the Transformation of the Public Service (Government of South Africa, 1998), set up after the first democratic election, might be a model in our area. The Secretariat for such a Commission, which would need to be in the Office of the Prime Minister or possibly even the Palace itself rather than in MPSM, might over time evolve into an Office of Public Service Reform, which while small should have greater resources than those available to recent reform efforts.

The advantages of such an arrangement are that it would harness the authority of the Palace while not disempowering politicians and officials; it would allow the preferred consultative style to continue, in fact extending it to Morocco's energetic civil society, which could be represented on the Commission and might supply a director of reform who was untainted by the ingrained timidity of the civil service; and it might be possible to interest an international donor in providing technical support. Moreover, one central official volunteered something very like our Office of Reform proposal in an interview, though without the Palace dimension. There is also an analogy with a similar body which the king set up to revise family law: its recommendations were already being acted on when we wrote.

The danger, however, is that our arrangement could degenerate into merely the latest in a line of talking shops: reform commissions have had a chequered history elsewhere (Polidano, 1995). Granted, a suitable head and secretary for the Commission and progress-chasing arrangements would reduce this danger, but essentially one would be relying on the king to act in his role of arbiter, for which Morocco's history provides strong precedents, reconciling the different views and deciding the way forward. This scenario would give us a political drama which has a happy ending, contrary to all expectations (and unlike Beckett's play!), with Godot turning up in the final act in the form of a royal resolution of the reform stalemate. However, the danger of vesting so much in the whim of an individual with a finite attention span, albeit a royal one, will be obvious to most readers.

Lessons of the Morocco study

In the face of those like Pfeffer (1998) whose suggestion that favoured HRM practices are universally valid we reported in our opening chapter, our study has found that they are not widely known let alone widely practised in the government of Morocco, despite it being overwhelmingly Morocco's biggest employer and despite the abundance of able technocrats in senior positions. This amplifies the finding of our Mauritius chapter, since moving from the Anglophone Commonwealth world of Mauritius to the Francophone world of Morocco increases the intellectual distance from HRM practices, including of course from the SHRM model on which our research interviews focused. Moreover, while we noted that such practices would address real problems that at least some officials recognize, the effort required to implant them would be misplaced, as it would be at the expense of addressing the underlying problem of political timidity.

Every country is *sui generis* to a degree. When we get to the Malaysia chapter in this book, we will see a country whose administrative style is as decisive as Morocco's is timid. But we suggest that the importance of the relationship between HRM and the underlying political dispensation is an intrinsic feature of HRM in the public sector, even if its particular terms vary from country to country. Evidence for this comes, as we shall see in Chapter 6, in the ubiquity of 'political will' in World Bank evaluation reports as an explanation for the failure of so many of the Bank's civil service reform efforts, and in public administration sources going all the way back to Caiden (1970).

Now of course a political view of organizations is quite well established in the management literature through work such as Child's (1972) or, slightly ironically, even that of Pfeffer (1992) himself. But such work applies the notion of politics metaphorically to organizations, treating them *as if* they were political systems (Morgan, 1986). By tracing a direct connection between a nation's politics and the way its government manages its staff, we are talking about politics in the literal sense. Organizational politics, with all the shifting alliances and conflicts of interests that Pfeffer and Morgan discuss, is still only as big as the organization itself. The politics that influences HRM in a government is as big as the society that the government presides over, and can encompass, as in Morocco, a monarchy, a democratically elected government and civil society. The implication is that anyone hoping to influence HRM in the public sector necessarily becomes a political analyst. To make a difference, an understanding of politics is every bit as important as an understanding of HRM itself.

Conclusion: adding the political dimension

In this chapter we have tried to understand why one developing country, Morocco, has made so little progress in improving the way it manages its public servants. We have suggested that while the SHRM model has some relevance to its problems, ignorance of the model means that the effort of introducing it would be disproportionate, and would be at the expense of tackling Morocco's fundamental problem, the institutional timidity of political actors which is not a personal failing but is a consequence of the way in which Moroccan politics has evolved. Rejecting the Beckett-like fatalism into which an analysis like ours might easily slide, we have suggested practical steps that political actors might take in this unpromising situation.

Ultimately, our analysis suggests that the elusive Monsieur Godot of civil service reform and improvements in public human resource management is most likely to be found lurking in the political undergrowth of reform. If we want staff management to contribute to overall government objectives such as economic development and poverty alleviation, as Evans and Rauch and Kaufmann *et al.* (2005) have shown that it can do, then those of us whose disciplinary expertise is in HRM will need to look beyond 'universal' models of HRM and engage with political issues, both the metaphorical ones that we find in private companies and the literal and very complex ones that we find in governments. This is an insight that we will develop in later chapters in this book.

6
Swaziland: Political Commitment

Introduction: commitment and the failure of reform

We now move from the Mediterranean state of Morocco to a small landlocked country in Africa's southern cone: by a quirk of colonial cartography, Swaziland's eastern border stops a tantalizing hundred kilometres short of the Indian Ocean, so that it finds itself hemmed in on three sides by South Africa and on its eastern frontier by Mozambique. Swaziland had a population of roughly 1.1 million in 2003, projected to reach 1.5 million by 2015. Having been ranked 112th in 2000, by 2003 it had slipped to 137th out of 177 countries on UNDP's Human Development Index, as we saw in Chapter 1, mainly owing to the HIV/AIDS pandemic. Unusually for Africa, it is a virtually monoethnic state. That, together with its monarchy, an institution that straddles the colonial period, and its relative prosperity have given it considerable stability: its ranking on this factor is higher than on any of the other factors in the World Bank's governance index (again, see Chapter 1).

Swaziland is a lower middle-income country. However, with no significant GDP growth since 1990 and a highly skewed income distribution, the IMF (2004c) has described its situation as 'serious'. Despite this, dependence on donor assistance is low and the debt service ratio is light (Table 1.4), including in relation to Swaziland's nearest neighbours. Swaziland has managed to avoid seeking loans from the IMF and the World Bank. The European Union, the UK government's Department for International Development (DFID) and UNDP were active in Swaziland in the period of our research, but had little role in economic management and only a small role even in civil service reform, as we shall see. This allows us to concentrate on

113

the domestic determinants of reform, largely uncontaminated by donor influence.

Commitment and the failure of reform

The theme of this chapter is political commitment to reform. We argued in Chapter 5 that we needed a political explanation to make sense of management reform in Morocco, where staffing reforms had been conditioned by government's political commitment or lack of commitment. It was a question of what one of our Moroccan interviewees called 'vouloir faire' as much as 'savoir faire'. This, as we will try to demonstrate, is also true of the quite similar reforms that Swaziland has attempted.

We begin by showing how political commitment as an aspect of the wider system of politics is central not only to staff management in developing countries, but also to the broader project of governance, and indeed international development as a whole, of which staffing reform is a sub-set. The tradition of emphasizing it, along with its presumed synonyms of 'will' and 'ownership', is very well established (Caiden, 1970), widespread (Ahmed, 1988; Barnes, 1997; Kitchen, 1989; Regulska, 1997) and supported by the World Bank's evaluation reports of its own civil service reform projects. In the mid-1990s, the Bank's evaluators blamed the failure of 40 per cent of those projects on the failure of national governments to commit themselves (Nunberg, 1997).

But 'commitment' is also one of the latest of international development's many holy grails, found in discussions of rural development (Clay and Schaffer, 1984; Hulme, 1995); macroeconomic management (Killick, 1998; Tsikata, 2001) and public enterprise reform (Campos and Esfahani, 2000). It pervades donor documents. An early World Bank study claimed that degree of country commitment was 'almost universally recognized as one of the main factors explaining success ... (and) is one of the most commonly quoted causes of unsatisfactory project completion' (Heaver and Israel, 1986, p.1). A later World Bank study found that 'ownership' explained overall programme outcomes in no fewer than 73 per cent of 81 World Bank operations completed in the 1980s, with exogenous shocks explaining many of the remainder (Johnson and Wasty, 1993; see also Jayarajah and Branson, 1995).[1]

This evidence has propelled commitment into the mainstream policy discourse. The World Bank's president in the late 1990s, James Wolfensohn, declared that

It is clear to all of us that ownership is essential. Countries must be in the driver's seat and set the course. They must determine goals and the phasing, timing and sequencing of programmes (1999, p.9)

and the UK's Secretary of State for International Development quoted with approval the belief of Tanzania's President Mkapa that 'Development cannot be imposed. It can only be facilitated. It requires ownership, participation and empowerment, not harangues and dictates' (Benn, 2005, p.iii; see also Camdessus, 1999).

Its importance is reflected in the design of the World Bank's (1999) poverty reduction strategy papers (PRSPs), the *sine qua non* for debt relief under the Highly Indebted Poor Countries (HIPC) initiative. Quite properly so: if structural adjustment programmes failed as much because of the 'process' issue of commitment as because of their content, the new poverty approach is likely to fare no better unless commitment is built into it.

The emphasis on commitment has also led to a new 'selectivity' view of the role of aid. In an admirably self-critical, though damning, critique of what was arguably the central assumption of conditionality-based structural adjustment lending in the 1980s and 1990s, the World Bank (1998a, p.58) now admits that 'In the past donor agencies have tried to 'buy reform' by offering assistance to governments that were not otherwise inclined to reform. This approach failed.' Since donors will only know that governments are really committed once they have actually implemented reform, substantial aid should only be forthcoming after implementation: donors should back winners. This is notwithstanding the recognition, inopportune given the return of poverty to the top of the development agenda, that the implied change in aid allocation would have a severe impact on poor countries, since they are the very countries likeliest to have bad policies. Until then, donor engagement should largely be confined to low-cost awareness-raising measures like overseas scholarships and dissemination of ideas (World Bank, 1998a).

The evidence on commitment is compelling, and it would be pointless to support initiatives in staffing reform or anywhere else that have little chance of success because commitment does not exist. But there are still two objections to the selectivity view. The first is its lack of curiosity about why so many governments stubbornly refuse to implement staffing or other reforms, given all their presumed benefits. The second is that although it relieves donors of the temptation of meddling in domestic politics, it is not clear where the motivation to reform is now going to come from. If 'jam today' in the form of conditionality was an inadequate incentive, 'jam tomorrow, after implementation' in the form of selectivity is no incentive at all. 'National transformations often catch observers by surprise', says the World Bank (1998a, p.116), a disarming admission in view of its widely scattered network of country representatives, but one that leaves it and other observers in the Micawber-like posture of waiting for something to turn up.

Thus on one hand we can admit the futility of donors throwing money at, or activists wasting their time lobbying, governments that have no commitment to reform, while on the other hand still seeking for a way to engage with those very governments, often among the poorest. In the first place that means trying to identify as early in the policy process as possible whether commitment is genuine and will lead to implementation: it is child's play to back a winner when the race is over. In the second place it means trying to understand those cases where commitment does not exist, even though a government may have flirted with reform, with a view to suggesting how it might be generated. Such a two-pronged approach will allow donors, indigenous development activists and citizens at large to distinguish between governments where the intention to reform exists and deserves support, and governments that have no such intention, where an effort of understanding and agenda-setting will usefully augment minimal forms of engagement like scholarship programmes. This chapter aims to lay the groundwork for that approach by creating a more robust understanding of commitment and applying it to a case study of staffing reform in Swaziland.

Identifying political commitment

While the invocation of commitment is ubiquitous, the concept itself is a classic 'black box', habitually invoked in reform *post-mortems* in these terms: there was a reform programme, we tried to implement it, but we failed because 'commitment' was not forthcoming. Heaver and Israel pointed out in 1986 that, 'in spite of its importance ... (commitment) has seen little systematic treatment or research' (1986, p.13), and there have been few serious attempts to come to terms with it subsequently, even by those writers who use it most. Everyone finds it 'conceptually difficult' (Heaver and Israel, 1986, p.1) or 'elusive' (Johnson and Wasty, 1993, p.2; Jayarajah and Branson, 1995, p.233), if not *'ad hoc'* (Killick, 1998, p.91; see also Thomas and Grindle, 1990, p.1164).

We suggest that the problem is not so much one of definition – we can rub along with the dictionary definition of 'pledge or undertaking' or, more formally, 'a binding of the individual to behavioral acts' (Kiesler and Sakamura, 1966, p.349) – as of identifying it and, even more, predicting what it will lead to. How will we know it when we see it? And how can we tell if a government will follow through from commitment to implementation?

Numerous studies have tried to answer the question of what makes governments implement an espoused policy, including Gulhati (1990), Heaver and Israel (1986), Mosley *et al.* (1991), Rodrik (1996), Thomas and Grindle (1990), Waterbury (1993) and Whitehead (1990). Table 6.1 confines itself to studies that have successfully tested individual factors that are associated with successful reform implementation.[2]

It is also instructive to look at commitment from a psychological point of view, since it is by definition a psychological concept, though we must take care when we apply individual-level concepts to the behaviour of complex political coalitions. The pioneering theoretical and experimental work of Kiesler (1971) and his colleagues, taken up

Table 6.1   Factors associated with reform success

Study	Sample[1]	Factors identified
Nelson (1990, pp. 335–44)	12 countries	• Evolving economic trends • Administrative capacity, notably a united economic team • Executive authority
Johnson and Wasty (1993)	81 World Bank programmes in 38 countries	• 'Ownership', in which 'expression of political will by top leadership' was the most important component
Levy (1993)	8 countries	• Administrative load imposed by reform • Political constraints
Williamson (1994)	11 countries	• Coherent economic team • Strong political base • Visionary leadership
Campos and Esfahani (2000)	7 countries	• 'Reform readiness' (ratio of expected gains to costs in reform proposal) • Trust between government and entrepreneurs • Political turnover

[1] Based on countries whose attempt to implement reform is assessed.

by Salancik (1977) in an organizational setting, found that personal commitment is strong to the extent that it is explicit, irrevocable, voluntary and public. However, Kiesler's experiments were conducted in laboratory settings, typically using student subjects, so the commitments that he was testing were inevitably trivial ones. Drawing on goal-setting theory (Latham and Locke, 1991) allows us to add that a commitment should also be challenging.[3]

Although research on commitment has fragmented, we suggest that the structure shared by two recent organizational models is relevant to us, even if their content is not. Both view commitment as having antecedents, such as organization size and the individual's socialization experiences, which lead to commitment proper, which leads in turn to organizational outcomes, such as staff turnover and individual productivity (see Mowday *et al.*, 1982, p.30, Figure 2.1; and Meyer and Allen, 1997, p.106, Figure 7.1).

From all this we derive the following model of political commitment to reform, in which the 'antecedents' correspond to major factors identified in at least two of the reform studies that we have reviewed,[4] and the 'elements' correspond to factors identified in the psychological literature; the 'voluntary' element also corresponds to 'ownership' as discussed by Johnson and Wasty and Killick. The model hypothesizes that when the antecedents are sufficiently present, commitment will emerge, strong to the extent that it is voluntary, explicit, challenging, public and irrevocable, and that strong commitment will in turn lead to successful reform implementation, see Figure 6.1.

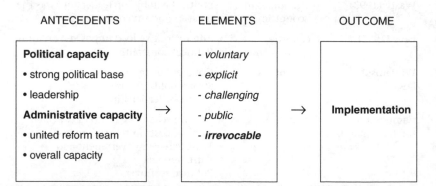

Figure 6.1   A model of political commitment to reform

This is a behavioural model (Mowday *et al.*, 1982, p.26), in which commitment is viewed as an intention which predicts whether a government will implement a policy proposal or not (Ajzen, 1988). Prediction is crucial in terms of our earlier discussion. Moreover, we have a tautology unless we can separate commitment from the later action that commitment elicits (Becker, 1960, p.35; see also Johnson and Wasty, 1993, p.2).

Although the model's elements come from the psychological literature, the reform literature echoes them. Most notably, there is the equation of the 'voluntary' element with ownership by policymakers like James Wolfensohn, and also by scholars (Nelson, 1990, p.344 and Killick, 1998). The 'explicit', 'irrevocable' and 'public' elements are present in Campos and Esfahani (2000, p.226), Heaver and Israel (1986, p.11 and p.28) and Johnson and Wasty (1993).

We need to make three qualifications about our model. First, it gives us no formula for predicting the strength of the different antecedents and elements. Second, we lack a sense of whether antecedents or elements might interact, and in what way. Third, while our model may be at a high enough level of abstraction to avoid the trap of merely listing the idiosyncratic characteristics of individual governments, 'Almost none (of the many identified factors affecting commitment to economic reform) seems to have a uniform effect across countries ... Reform outcomes depend on complex combinations of a variety of factors' (Campos and Esfahani, 2000, p.222). It remains likely that 'Answers must be invented for each country individually' (Nelson, 1990, p.361).

We had better be careful to emphasize that we are not trying to give donors a stick to beat governments with. While we do hope that our model will aid the analysis of government reform initiatives, governments could equally turn the tables on donors, using our model to evaluate the seriousness of donors' commitment to, say, debt write-offs, or South African President Thabo Mbeki's 'New Partnership for African Development' initiative, both bones of contention in the development community at the time of writing.

Interview findings

Interview details

In this chapter we concentrate on one element of staff management, employee selection, which is central to Evans and Rauch's staffing model (1999; see also Chapter 1). Primary data gathering in the first half of 2000 took the form of interviews with the following stakeholders identified jointly by the author and relevant Swazi officials:

- 25 senior officials in central and line departments and agencies
- a past president of the Swaziland National Association of Civil Servants
- a judge
- an academic observer
- representatives of three donor agencies.

It was not possible to arrange meetings with ministers or with representatives of the 'traditional' side of government (see below). Interviews were conducted face-to-face, except for telephone interviews with two donor officials.

Since we will be concentrating on selection, we will first briefly review the position in relation to the other HR issues which we focus on in this book. Strategic integration goes no further than the mission statement which each ministry had at the time of writing. Swaziland has what readers should be starting to recognize as the standard Commonwealth 'balkanized' model, in which there is a central civil service ministry (in Swaziland's case, the Ministry of Public Service and Information) with freestanding agencies responsible for training (the Swaziland Institute of Management and Public Administration) and employee selection (the Civil Service Board, which we will be discussing in detail). A performance management scheme was drawn up in 1999, but at the time of writing had still not been implemented. In theory, employees were still subject to the pre-independence system of 'annual confidential reports'.

The history of reform

To understand the current state of affairs, we have to take account of the past, and in particular of attempts at reform.[5] An account of Swaziland's experience of reform is necessarily an account of failure. It is not as if no one knows what the problem is. Shortly after independence, the Wamalwa Commission produced a comprehensive report, a quotation from which gives its flavour: 'Most of those in leadership positions in government considered the Civil Service as a "milking cow" for friends and relations. And worse still, they wanted to do the "milking" in the shortest time possible' (1976, para. 104). But Wamalwa's was to be the first in a long line of reports whose recommendations were only ever partially implemented at best. Joubert and

Table 6.2   Implementation of reform recommendations in Swaziland

Report	Not implemented	Implemented
Wamalwa (1976)	14	5
Hlophe (1986) (excluding salaries)	7	0
Richards (1988)	14	0 (though 10 of 14 accepted in principle)
Steyn (1993)[1]	New salary structure implemented	Recommendations on performance and productivity not implemented

Source: Joubert and Zoubi (1995).
[1]Publication details for the latter three reports appear in Joubert and Zoubi (1995). The reports themselves can be obtained from the Government of Swaziland.

Zoubi (1995), the authors of a study conducted on behalf of the United Nations Development Programme (UNDP), looked at what happened to four major reports. Their findings are summarized in Table 6.2.

Joubert and Zoubi recount how the major brief of the Richards report was 'to examine, enquire and make recommendations on the Hlophe Committee report' (35), and how the Steyn Commission in its turn used Richards as a major source. Not surprisingly, they comment that 'There is an important need for the government to adopt the practice of taking the recommendations of such reports, accepting, modifying or rejecting them, and then implementing a follow-up plan' (6). One of their own recommendations, significantly, is that 'We believe that the government could do no better than to implement the recommendations of the Steyn report' (34).

Alas, Joubert and Zoubi's own report was to share the fate of its predecessors. In an initial flurry of enthusiasm, a workshop at which they presented their findings on May 24 1995 was attended by ministers and senior officials, and also by the new Prime Minister, an economist whom the king had recalled from the IMF: he proceeded to present his reformist credentials in a National Development Strategy (Government of Swaziland, 1999a), in which a Public Sector Management Programme (PSMP) had pride of place. But PSMP soon ran into problems. A Public Service bill drafted in 1996 was stalled. PSMP's first director, appointed after a long delay, resigned after only 18 months in post, and with his resignation, activity ground to a halt. A relaunched PSMP with a new, though acting director, appointed internally and below the level of Permanent Secretary, found it hard to regain momentum. Of eight organizational reviews of government ministries started in 1999, only one was complete by March 2000, with no sign of follow-up. As these were PSMP's only concrete achievements up to that point, it was hardly surprising that, as one official drew to our attention, this flagship of the government's reform intentions had dwindled to a single line in the prime minister's budget statement for 2000.

Government officials in other agencies pronounced the obsequies on the government's attempts at reform: *'I don't understand the relaunching (of PSMP). What can they say that hasn't been said before? I have given up on PSMP. They produced reports that disappeared,'* said one. Another dismissed PSMP laconically as *'A headless chicken.'*

The picture is no different when we look narrowly at attempts to strengthen merit-based selection. Following what has been styled as the 'king's coup' in 1973 (see below), a 1973 Order in Council downgraded the Public Service Commission, whose autonomy had been enshrined in the 1968 Independence constitution, turning it into a Civil Service Board whose status was merely advisory. A 1981 Order asserted the 'continuing independence' of the Board, but in an equivocal fashion that did not restore features that would have made the assertion a reality, notably the independent appointment of its members. Both a Civil Service Commission Bill, complementary to the Public Service bill and also drafted in 1996, and a more limited 'Order' drafted in 2000, would have restored at least some of the independence of the Civil Service Board; both alike failed to reach the statute book. A promised review of CSB and of civil service staffing was duly carried out, leading to another enthusiastic workshop in July 2000 but not, at the time of writing, to action.

UNDP's final involvement had been to support an ineffectual retirement options study in 1997. DFID had completely withdrawn from governance, having found very little to spend its money on, and at the time of writing was allocating only 1.5 million dollars annually to Swaziland as a whole. The European Union, which had funded the review of CSB, closed down its assistance in this area in September 2001, frustrated that 'half of the project resources had been utilised with little discernible impact'. Government found it hard to revive the interest of donors – the EU rejected the government's renewal request in 2002 – leaving PSMP's already modest projects either in limbo or proceeding on what one official called a *'shoestring basis'*, the training of 400 secretarial staff in customer care in 2002 being one of very few concrete achievements (Government of Swaziland, 2005).

In short, the verdict of the leading Swazi scholar of administrative reform is surely correct:

An examination of the country's administrative reform record shows that the implementation process was weak and tardy and that ... reforms rarely go beyond the level of rhetoric (Dlamini, 1992, p.176).

Using the commitment model to explain reform failure

In this section we discuss to what extent our model explains – and to what extent it could have predicted – the failure of reform, by exploring whether the 'antecedents' and 'elements' of commitment were present in 1995, the point where the latest reform programme began.

Antecedents of commitment: political, institutional and administrative capacity

As we saw, the Prime Minister appointed by the king in 1995 had given every indication of strong *leadership*, with his personal involvement in reform. As we shall see a little later, however, in terms of Swazi political culture this was almost beside the point. Additionally, there was a *strong political base* in the form of the well-established monarchy and the absence of coherent opposition to reform from outside the executive.

In terms of administrative capacity, the *reform team* was united, but it was also weak: the unity that Nelson and Williamson set such store by is probably not more important than competence, momentum and credibility with stakeholders. In terms of *overall capacity* of administration, the evidence is mixed. In money terms, although PSMP activities were on a *'shoestring basis'* following donor withdrawal, the budget situation in Swaziland was healthier than in many other African countries, with only modest levels of donor assistance and debt. Moreover, *'several donors were ready to disburse'*, as one of them said; and, as we saw, DFID was unable to spend the money it had already allocated. Finally, the types of reform actually canvassed in Swaziland would have been cheap to implement.

Where the capacity to implement policy is concerned (Pressman and Wildavsky, 1979; Thomas and Grindle, 1990), there is also some positive evidence. Although we saw that most recommendations from earlier reports were not implemented, there is a systematic exception to this: the government usually acted on recommendations to improve civil servants' pay and conditions right up to the time of writing, increasing the overall deficit and incurring the IMF's (2004c) disapproval. 'If you go through all the reports, upward salary recommendations and conditions of service improvements have always been implemented. But if there are unpopular elements, those remain undone', said one well-placed official, corroborating the data summarized in Table 6.2.[6] Thus implementation appeared to be a question of commitment rather than capacity.

In other respects, however, administrative – and also institutional – capacity were weak. Two longstanding examples of poor administration of staffing decisions are relevant. First, CSB's main public function is to act as employer in employment cases that are brought with alarming frequency by aggrieved civil servants. A legal figure commented that *'Most of the time, when cases come before the courts, procedures have not been followed ... The accused's lawyers run rings round the CSB.'* Even government officials admitted that the government has applied the law wrongly on some occasions. There are basic institutional weaknesses of the kind that we have already discussed in Chapter 4 and which we need not dwell on here.

Second, less embarrassing but at least as damaging to the efficiency of government, there were complaints from several departments of delays going back two or more years in getting CSB to fill vacancies, leading one official to denounce CSB publicly at the workshop in 2000 as *'an institution of delays'.*

Elements of commitment

Thus the 'antecedents' of commitment, including political leadership as we will show, were not sufficiently present in 1995. What about the 'elements'? There was certainly a general perception when we conducted our interviews in 2000 that commitment was lacking. Officials tended to see political leaders' commitment to reform as lukewarm,[7] and 'commitment to reform by government' was identified as a major issue at the workshop in 2000. Donors shared this opinion: one donor's plans had made little headway *'because of government's lack of commitment'*, and a second donor concurred: *'We didn't see at all the human element of it, the will element of it, political will as well as the personal will'.*

When we focus on the 'elements', we find that the government's commitment was largely *voluntary*: while, as we shall see, the international community has shown an occasional interest in the progress of reform, Swaziland does not depend on international loans or donor aid. The government proudly proclaimed that 'PSMP was launched as an internally conceived civil service reform programme. It is Swazi-owned and predominantly Swazi driven.' (Government of Swaziland, 1999b, p.2). Such statements also show that government's commitment was reasonably *public*: there was the National Development Strategy, and the prime minister routinely cited PSMP as one of the three planks in the government's economic growth strategy in public statements (Dlamini, 1999; Nevin, 1999).

But the other elements were absent. The reform programme was not *explicit* or *challenging*. The prime minister in the above interview described PSMP's aim as being 'to make the public sector more cost-effective and efficient', but the actions that would produce this desirable result were not specified. Government never committed itself to anything more than appointing commissions and carrying out reviews such as the review of CSB and the organizational reviews of several ministries. Nor were these actions *irrevocable*: the government had an easy line of retreat.

Thus commitment to reform, in terms of our model, was weak: the antecedents of commitment were not strong enough to generate a genuine commitment that would lead to reform implementation. Applying the model makes it reasonable to yield to the consensus among government and donor officials alike that reform has not proceeded mainly because the government's commitment has been inadequate.

Three comments arise from our analysis. First, the government's lack of commitment was identifiable, and its consequent failure to implement was predictable. All the salient information was available at the time of PSMP's original launch in 1995. The government did not renege on any commitment; it simply, and quite properly in a way, avoided making a promise it could not be sure of keeping.[8] The devil was in the detail. The government may have been happy for the expectation of reform to arise, but its undertakings were never explicit or challenging, it took no irrevocable steps, and there was always the danger that the underlying weakness of political, institutional and administrative capacity would bring action to a standstill.

Second, our analysis supports the view that 'ownership' is merely an element of commitment, rather than synonymous with it, *pace* Johnson and Wasty and Killick. The Swazi government 'owns' its programme; it has not carried it out under donor pressure; but commitment has still not emerged.

Third, we have evidence of interaction between the model's antecedents of political and administrative capacity. The administrative delays which we described earlier appeared to be a symptom of a deeper malaise. One senior official said, *'You hear of backlog all the time. Political factors come in.'* A second official specified that *'A tendency to refer things 'elsewhere' is what causes the problem.'* *'Even promotions have to be referred "elsewhere"'*, said a third. (*'Elsewhere'* was a coy reference to the political level of government.) This evidence corroborates Gulhati's (1990, p.1128) mordant comment that 'The quality of the civil service ... stems from political culture ... Countries get the bureaucracies they deserve and can use'.

Understanding commitment: Swazi political culture

We have been able to use our model with a couple of qualifications to explain the failure of reform in Swaziland. How should stakeholders have reacted if we had been able to present our analysis in 1995, the date when the latest reform exercise began? Certainly a donor would have been unwise to commit money to implementation that was unlikely to materialize. However, we argued at the start of this paper that even in such a case, stakeholders should still seek for a way to engage with governments like Swaziland's, as we should not wash our hands of precisely those poor countries where the problem of commitment is likely to be greatest. We suggested that an effort of understanding and agenda-setting could augment the minimal engagement that *Assessing Aid* proposes for recalcitrant cases. Let us now make that effort, examining the nature of political capacity in Swaziland, which is fundamental to the question of commitment to reform. In doing so, we will also explain why the political leadership of reform was weak, despite appearances to the contrary.

The dual system of government

At first glance Swaziland gives the impression of a standard British-style administration, with regular parliamentary elections. A prime minister presides over a cabinet of ministers who are supported by ministries staffed by appointed officials and headed by principal secretaries: these are the people that visiting donors, consultants and academics find themselves meeting. But the impression is false. While there was a short period following independence from Britain in 1968 when it had some limited validity, Swaziland's career as a constitutional monarchy on the British model came to an abrupt halt in 1973, when the late king Sobhuza II gave what has been styled the 'king's coup' as his riposte to the rather modest growth of the political opposition, which had merely won one constituency in the 1972 elections. When the king restored parliament after ruling by decree for five years, he put in place a system of elections where candidates are nominated in constituencies, *tinkhundla*, by a public show of hands, often under a chief's watchful eye; but he did not rescind the ban on political parties.

The significance of all this is that it effectively put in place a 'dual' system of government, comprising what Swazis call the 'traditional' side – the monarchy and the traditional chieftaincy – and the 'modern' apparatus of Westminster-style cabinet government.[9] We need not struggle with the 'elusive and opaque' (Russell, 1986, p.306) structure of the traditional side, on which readers may consult Booth (1983) or Kuper (1980). It is rather the traditional side's pre-eminence that is at issue. Despite his protestations to the contrary (The Namibian, 2005), the king is effectively an absolute monarch (Baloro, 1994), in sharp contrast with his counterpart in Lesotho. He appoints the prime minister and other ministers – there is no obligation for them to obtain an electoral mandate – allowing him to dismiss his entire government 'casually' in the run-up to the 2003 election (Economist, 2003, p.67). He also personally appoints ten of the 65 members of the House of Assembly, and 20 out of the 30 members of the senate. Informally, every prime minister, including the present incumbent, has come from the royal Dlamini clan; one government minister and royal prince went so far as to say that anything else 'would be against God' (quoted in Levin, 1991, p.16).

Our assessment is corroborated by the World Bank's governance index rating for 'voice' and accountability (Table 1.4). If even government ministers, ostensibly the pinnacle of the modern side, are actually the traditional side's subordinate appointees, then we must ask: What is the traditional side's attitude to staffing reform? The opaqueness of the traditional side precludes a straightforward answer. We suggest that we can approach the question obliquely *via* the somewhat similar operation of patron-client relations in land tenure.

Patron-client relations in land tenure

Land is the essence of power in Swaziland: 'The power that (rulers) wield over subjects is usually referred back to the control that they have over the distribution of land' (Kuper, 1980, p.149). Through an astute combination of purchase and legislation, the Swazi monarchy has largely succeeded in reversing the colonial alienation of land. From a low point in 1907 where approximately two-thirds of land was in foreign hands, by the early 1980s 'Swazi Nation Land', controlled by chiefs on behalf of the king, covered 60 per cent of the national territory, and about 70 per cent of the population lived on it (Booth, 1983).

It is essentially the chiefs' control over land that sustains the 'patron-client system upon which political control in Swaziland is based' (Sallinger-McBride and Picard, 1986, p.35), and chiefs tend to repel threats to their control. One such threat has come from the steady growth of a bureaucracy whose status derives from its members' education and from their jobs in the government; in other words, to use anthropologists' language, from achievement rather than ascriptive factors (Rose, 1992). That is why integrated rural development failed in Swaziland in the early 1980s, according to Sallinger-McBride and Picard: traditional leaders saw this technocratic, civil servant-led initiative as a threat to their control over land through its potential to empower entrepreneurial peasants, and as an exercise in bureaucratic self-aggrandizement.

Patron-client relations in civil service staffing

In this respect civil service reform is similar to rural development: it is another arena for the covert conflict between the traditional and bureaucratic elites. The opposition of interests was manifested at an important ritual ceremony in 1989 when the current king asked his audience of traditional supporters if he should take from them the money that civil servants were claiming in a pay dispute. As Levin (1991, p.18) comments, this was an attempt to drive a wedge between the king's traditional supporters and civil servants.

Jobs are the medium of exchange in the government, just as land is the medium of exchange in the countryside, and a traditional 'patron' is as likely to try to exercise patronage over one as over the other, prioritizing ascriptive rather than achievement factors in the face of the received wisdom about merit-based selection. A key instance is the quashing of the successive attempts to restore the pre-1973 independence of the CSB, which would have returned power over appointments to bureaucrats, an independence that one CSB official gloomily predicted that the government would never let his agency recover. A second instance is the reluctance of the prime minister to give up his rather unusual personal power to transfer civil servants. While some officials claimed that the power resulted from a mere *'clerical error'* in the drafting of a legal instrument, others were suspicious. Certainly Wade's (1989) analysis of India shows how power over senior officials' transfer can be a potent form of patronage, and it is hard to see why a simple 'error' should persist uncorrected for over a quarter of a century. Some officials also claimed that, at a petty level, members of the very numerous royal family (the late polygamous king had over 100 children) have tried to intervene in individual staffing decisions.

It turns out that the traditional elite perceives merit-based selection, that unquestioned good of the governance agenda, as a threat to its patronage prerogative because of the shift that it represents from ascriptive criteria, which support the interests of the traditional elite, to achievement criteria, which support the interests of the modern elite. Thus 'political leadership' of reform is actually weak, despite the Prime Minister's personal involvement. There is no real consensus among policymakers about the direction of reform: based on how they perceive their interests, bureaucratic and traditional elites have diametrically opposed views.

So why doesn't the traditional elite just dispense with the charade of reform once and for all? It is because the forces of reform are too powerful to be defeated in open battle. First, even the traditional elite, headed by its English public school-educated king, is probably susceptible to the attraction of 'modern' reform. Second, the Swazi bureaucratic elite, like its counterparts elsewhere, has some power of its own, for instance in its control of the rhetorical resources of reform. Third, there is a growing internal political opposition (see below) which is sympathetic to reform. Fourth, the international community has expected Swaziland to show some commitment: US President Bush senior sent a message of encouragement in the middle of one reform exercise (Levin, 1991), and President Mandela of South Africa made it clear in 1996 that he supported the king precisely because the king was committed to reform (Matlosa, 1998).

Thus the traditional elite uses lip service to neutralize reform and to deflect internal and external criticism. In the words of a donor representative, *'What people won't say is that they'll say yes, yes, but when it comes to actually implementing they will sense that they will not be the beneficiaries, because they are the beneficiaries of the present system.'* This evasiveness is arguably compounded by a national determination to avoid confrontation in the interests of maintaining social harmony (Rose, 1992). At the same time, the ubiquitous employment cases brought by disgruntled civil servants in the 'modern' courts, fielding which takes up so much of CSB's energy, are a safety valve for civil servants' dissatisfaction, just as the customary jurisdiction of chiefs over land disputes is a safety valve for dissatisfaction in the countryside.

Hence the impression of a civil service addicted to litigation. Hence also the endlessly repeated reports and recommendations, one of the ways in which 'a highly stable political system (is) able to accommodate and control innovations' (Radipati, 1993): the Swazi government seems to have adopted as its watchword the *leitmotif* of Lampedusa's great novel of the Sicilian aristocracy: 'If we want everything to stay as it is, everything will have to change' (Lampedusa, 1963, p.41). Hence, in the end, Swaziland's dismal history of reform failure, despite the best efforts of many of its officials.

Generating commitment to civil service reform in Swaziland

So while 'political capacity' is every bit as important as our model suggests, in Swaziland's unusual political culture it has a particular meaning. It is the traditional side that needs to demonstrate 'political leadership', acting in concert with the modern side. Up to now, the traditional side has equivocated at best, and has undermined the leadership and administrative capacity of the modern side by intervening in staffing decisions.

In such a setting, how can commitment be generated? We must beware of voluntarism: it is certainly possible that the *status quo* will continue. With hope triumphing over experience, the modern side may continue to take initiatives and commission reports which the traditional side will continue to quash. The monarchy appears unwilling to engage with the internal political opposition: the Constitution belatedly unveiled in 2003 did not legalize political parties, and left effective power in the king's hands. One observer has suggested that 'the Swazi monarchy ... perceives politics as a zero-sum game wherein the winner takes all' (Matlosa, 1998, p.336). Even the modest reform discussed here could be seen by the traditional side as the thin end of a wedge.

Looking more positively, the first possibility is of a *deus ex machina*, of matters being taken out of the current rulers' hands. Kings are subject to mortality and infirmity, of course, but also to political challenges. There is an opposition movement which organizes openly, despite the formal ban on political parties (The Courier, 1999). Acting in concert with trade unions, it has called several national strikes (McGreal, 2000; Mail and Guardian, 2005). However, the balance of opinion predicts continuing stability, and there are many who are glad of that (see Booth, 1983; Kuper, 1980; Rose, 1992; and Sonko, 1994). Even a donor who was frustrated by the absence of reform still insisted:

'I'm not saying dualism is bad or not working. I would say that Swaziland should retain it. That's why Swaziland is so peaceful. It's a well-managed country, which I attribute to the traditional system.' Moreover, the death-knell of the dual system has been sounded prematurely before (Daniel and Vilane, 1986; Levin, 1991), and it is clearly impossible to predict what would be the commitment to reform of a government coming to power through a multi-party election.

Failing such a fundamental change, the most intriguing possibility is that it will be possible to circumvent the resistance of the traditional elite by reconciling civil service reform with its interests. Arguably it could be persuaded to distinguish between its fundamental interest in the continuation of the present political system and its contingent interest in perpetuating a system of patron-client relations in the allo-cation of government jobs. How might that happen? It seems likely that stakeholders will need to engage with the political or meta-level in our model of governance, and particularly with the traditional side of government, dispensing with the useful fiction that key management decisions are taken at the management level. In the case of indigenous actors, some officials appear to have informal channels of communica-tion that they can use, while other activists can lobby the traditional side directly; the king is an absolute monarch, but there is also a tradi-tion of direct communication between the king and people. Stake-holders would not be going over old ground here: we could find no evidence of any explicit engagement having occurred on this issue in previous reform attempts. In the case of donor agencies, their relation-ship with governments means that they are not always well placed to engage at the political level. They might need to work with their diplo-matic colleagues, who have greater access and influence at that level: for example, DFID might need to work with the British High Com-mission. Admittedly, however, external pressure was not strong at the time of writing. South Africa, the key external actor, has shown no inclination to impose a political agenda on its neighbours, not even on President Mugabe's Zimbabwe, where at the time of writing there was a stronger justification. At the time of writing, there was no sign that the United States' government's interest in democracy in the Middle East would extend to Africa. Donors, given Swaziland's low levels of aid and debt, have even less financial leverage than they do elsewhere.

In engaging with government, stakeholders could deploy the man-agement argument that reform would increase the efficiency of govern-ment; and the political argument that evidence of reform action would address stakeholders' expectations of reform, and in particular would reduce disaffection among the bureaucratic elite from which the political opposition draws much of its support. Taking a first step towards reform in this way would represent an incremental approach which some observers are convinced is realistic in Swaziland's political climate (Rose, 1992; Sallinger-McBride and Picard, 1986): certainly it seems far-fetched to suppose that the patronage system in civil service staffing is the indispensable cement without which the current political system will come crashing down. Arguably the modern side of government, with discreet support from other stakeholders, could frame an institutional proposal that would address the essentials of staffing reform while reassuring the traditional side that its vital interests were not threatened. This would bear out the World Bank's opinion, which we quoted in Chapter 2, that commitment is partly a function of the quality of advice that officials offer to politicians.

If such an incremental approach did turn out to be viable – and the *quality* of engagement would be vital – our commitment model would help to frame a reform programme. We saw earlier that the government's commitment to reform was deficient because the antecedents of political and administrative capacity were insufficiently present, and because the reform programme itself was inexplicit and unchallenging, and no irrevocable action had been taken. With any new reform proposal, therefore, one could ask whether there is evidence that both traditional and bureaucratic elites are committed, whether it is more explicit and challenging than previous proposals, and whether irrevocable action has been taken as a token of intent.

The last of these is problematic: we must preserve the distinction between irrevocable action and full-blown implementation of reform, without which we lose the vital predictive aspect of our model. It is important to specify action that would be limited and yet decisive. We suggest that a binding commitment at the institutional level to restore the independence of the Civil Service Board and to take away the prime minister's power to transfer civil servants, sore points for many of our informants, would represent such an action. Given Swaziland's history of good faith dealings with donors over civil service reform (see endnote), one could reasonably expect such a commitment to be honoured.

One is entitled to be pessimistic about current prospects for civil service reform in Swaziland: the reform impetus, sluggish at the time of our interviews in 2000, seemed to have come to a complete standstill at the time of writing. Donors can walk away from a country with which they have lost patience: in that sense, their commitment is never irrevocable. For other stakeholders, the hope for worthwhile reform perhaps lies in the direction that we have outlined here.

Conclusion: lessons from the case

In this chapter we have found that staff management in Swaziland has stagnated, and we have presented our analysis that this is the result of a failure of political commitment to reform which in turn is rooted in Swaziland's unique dual system of government, in which the traditional side has precedence. We found it helpful to develop and apply a model of political commitment to make sense of the failure of reform.

While as always we must be cautious about generalizing from single cases, we suggest that our study provides the following tentative lessons.

1 *It is possible to use our model to predict whether a government will in fact implement a proposal to reform staff management to which they are ostensibly committed.* 'International institutions,' says the World Bank (1998a, p.59), unconsciously echoing Rodrik's (1989) language, 'Should learn to read the signals about whether governments are serious or not'. The model proposed here may be seen as a signals codebook. It allowed us to identify not only that adequate commitment to civil service reform did not exist at the time of our interviews in 2000, by which time donors had withdrawn, but that it would have been possible to identify that it did not exist in 1995, the date of the last major initiative, when donors were making significant new commitments.

2 *An analysis of political commitment entails a political analysis,* echoing our account of reform in Morocco in Chapter 5. This may seem a tautology, but would-be reformers seldom recognize it. There are particular reasons for this. For government officials, the doctrinal separation between politics and administration is an obstacle to a political assessment, as is all too clear from treatments of the subject in the public administration literature which have been referenced here. For donors, and especially the World Bank and the IMF whose charters prohibit it, there is the wholly proper reluctance to interfere in domestic politics, and the professional discomfort that staff with a technical training may feel in conducting a political analysis (Heaver and Israel, 1986, p.1). Clearly indigenous activists need feel no such reluctance, but both they and donors need to distinguish between political analysis and political agitation. For academics,

finally, action-orientated political analysis is still not well developed, with distinguished exceptions, some of which have been referenced here (see also Moore, 2000).

3 *'Ownership', meaning a programme where the government and not a donor is in the driving seat (Killick, 1998), is not a synonym for commitment.* The case study shows that a government may lack commitment to a programme that it indisputably owns. Ownership may be a necessary condition, but it is not a sufficient one.

4 *The five elements of our model arguably represent a sequence that culminates in irrevocable action as a precursor to full-blown implementation.* It is possible that 'irrevocable action' is the crucial litmus test of commitment: a replication study will be valuable here. In contrast to the 'selectivity' approach to aid allocation, moreover, it was possible to distinguish between such action and full-blown implementation: we suggested that in Swaziland, a binding undertaking to restore the independence of the Civil Service Board would be an irrevocable step.[10]

The overall lesson, however, is that those of us who would like to see more effective staff management in developing countries need to take a step back and consider whether the political base is firm enough to bear the weight of reform. Moreover, reforms that seem rational from a HR point of view can be politically very contentious, if as in this case they are perceived to threaten vital political interests. That is clearly true of the 'downsizing' reforms that we have already discussed in this book, but it is also true of the more modest reforms canvassed in Mauritius in the 1990s, and likewise in Morocco. Even readers who have followed our analysis up to this point may still think it absurd that the Swazi government could equate the circumscribed reform of staffing arrangements with its stranglehold of rural land tenure, yet that is the case. In a country like Swaziland where there are political obstacles to reform, it is only by understanding what they are, and what will be necessary to generate commitment to overcoming them, that there will be a realistic hope of improvement. Stakeholders need to be able to read the warning 'signals' of failure in time to do something about them.

7
Sri Lanka: Political Patronage

Patronage in civil service staffing and politics

A candidate appointed as a lorry driver following an 'interview', according to the official records, on a day when he was actually serving abroad in his country's armed forces; another appointed as an equipment dispatcher after he had already died. These things happened not in Chittagong's local authority but in Chicago's, and not in the nineteenth-century heyday of America's 'spoils system' but in the era of supposedly 'reinvented government' in the twenty-first century (the armed forces in question being the US army of occupation in Iraq). Patronage is not confined to poor countries, and is not in inexorable decline even in rich ones (Younge, 2005).

However, this is not to say that it is not widespread in developing countries. In fact readers may have noticed that patronage has been a thread running through our discussion of the influence of politics on HRM in this book. We have noted claims that political parties operate primarily as patronage machines (Mauritius); that the highest and lowest levels of the bureaucracy are subject to patrimonialism (Morocco); and that civil service staffing is one of the ways in which broader patron-client relations in society manifest themselves (Swaziland). Those claims now move to the middle of the stage in this chapter. For, as we shall see, many observers, including some of our research interviewees, see patronage in Sri Lanka as a major determinant of staffing decisions, and indeed of politics at large.

Of course the meritocratic consensus that crystallized in the 1997 World Development Report (World Bank, 1997) deplores patronage, seeing it as one aspect of 'the abuse of public roles or resources for private benefit' (Johnston, 1998) which constitutes political corruption.

The predominant view is that it should be tackled through institutional strengthening (the focus of Chapter 4), although opinion is divided on whether that should take the form of Weberian adherence to impersonal rules (Schick, 1998), devolved arrangements that let managers manage (Bale and Dale, 1998) or decentralized government that is closer to poor people (World Bank, 2003). Yet patronage persists unabated in many countries, including Sri Lanka, a country where all the above remedies have been canvassed at one time or another. Sri Lanka has the highest life expectancy of any South Asian country (Isenman, 1980; World Bank, 2004c), but is saddled with a public sector that has sometimes seemed to be not so much unreformed as unreformable. Nevertheless, against the odds it has introduced a fundamental civil service reform in recent years. As we discuss that reform we will be exploring the nature of patronage and the viability of remedies to it, shedding light on the problems of other countries which have public sectors that are as seemingly intractable as Sri Lanka's.

The history of reform

Three phases of reform

Sri Lanka follows an amended Westminster model of cabinet government with a French-style executive president on top, and a system of provincial councils underneath that was introduced without taking proper root in the 1990s. The important stages in the reform experience up to 1998 are summarized by McCourt (2001a). The earliest was when the Cabinet brought the Public Service Commission (PSC) under its control in 1972. The rationale was very similar to the one that inspired Tanzania's reforms at roughly the same time. Finding a civil service 'designed for the administration of a nation, not its development', in Nyerere's words, this was a *de jure* politicization whose ostensible goal was to break down the elitism of the civil service and to harness it to national developmental objectives. Unfortunately it resulted in the political capture of civil service appointments (ADB, 2004, p.3; De Silva, 1993b).

Starting in the mid-1980s there were three phases of reform, supported at different times by the United Nations Development Programme (UNDP), the World Bank and the Asian Development Bank (ADB), the first two of which 'unfortunately, like waves in the ocean ... have receded as fast as they came', as even the Cabinet Secretary at the time of writing believed (Wijesinghe, 1997, p.15).

The first was the very comprehensive report of the Administrative Reforms Committee (1987–88). Its chairman subsequently exclaimed that 'The recommendations concerning the increase of salaries were embraced with glee! But ... more important recommendations were glossed over ... When it came to biting the bullet, the political will evaporated' (quoted in Wijesinghe, 1997, p.21). The second was a structural adjustment-era downsizing programme. When it ended, the government had more employees than when it began, and had also, according to an official, mistakenly offered the generous Voluntary Retirement package to all its surprised but grateful regular retirees.

The third phase, triggered by an ADB report in 1996 but implemented with UNDP rather than ADB support (*'probably because [UNDP] can't impose conditionalities'* was a relevant donor's explanation), was managerialist, and featured mission statements and strategic objectives, management restructuring and performance appraisal. The plans, which included a proposal to restore the independence of the PSC, were subtle and incremental, but by 1998 had produced few concrete results (McCourt, 2001a). Several interviewees in 1998 attributed this to 'patronage'. A donor's explanation was that *'Politicians had a vested interest in maintaining a patronage system.'* A very senior official suggested that *'The expectation that the public sector should provide jobs is the root ... This is exacerbated by changes of government'*, following each of which a fresh crop of patronage appointments sprouts. Even a civil service trade union leader said that *'From time to time politicians have recruited without considering the need to recruit ... Politicians consider that government exists to provide jobs for their supporters'* (see also ADB, 2004, p.7). It is this attribution that we will explore in this chapter.

Even as we focus on patronage, we should recognize that it isn't the whole story, any more than most single-factor explanations ever are. First, steady, albeit modest growth has made state inefficiency affordable, despite relatively high public spending and low tax revenue (IMF, 2004a, p.23 and p.27). Fiscal necessity has been at best a weak countervailing force, unlike, say, in Ghana or Uganda in the 1980s. Second, the violent uprisings of the 1980s and 90s have played their part: in 1998 a donor official explained the failure of the 'second phase' like this: *'Momentum was lost, conflict sprang up, more people were killed in the south.'* Third, we should reckon with Sri Lanka's deeply ingrained ideology of 'welfarism'. We say more below about both the uprisings and welfarism.[1]

Patrons and patronage brokers

Patronage is a term that is more widely invoked than understood. It became the subject of scholarly attention once scholars realized that it was thriving in modern societies, and not just an episode in histories of ancient Rome or feudal society (Clapham, 1982; Eisenstadt and Roniger, 1984; Gellner and Waterbury, 1977; Roniger and Güneş-Ayata, 1994; Schmidt *et al.*, 1977[2]). It is the emergence of *brokers of political patronage* (Allum, 1973), that is relevant to us.[3] Alongside the 'traditional' patron who may provide informal insurance against crop failure from his (very rarely 'her') own resources, the broker, whether a politician or a bureaucrat, is not spending his own money but setting up as a conduit for the State's resources. Indeed as the State penetrated into all but the remotest areas, broking developed as a parallel track alongside the 'official channels' for managing the new relationship between the State and local people. That is true even in Campbell's (1964) early study of patronage in a Greek mountain community, where families attached themselves to an official who could *intercede* (the etymology is worth dwelling on) in matters like shortening a son's military service. This is not the 'old patronage' of Maecenas or the Medicis – or Bill and Melinda Gates. Part and parcel of the growth of the State, the patronage broker is a modern phenomenon and not an archaic survival.

But why manage the relationship like this? We need to remind ourselves that such brokerage is illicit: only the 'official channels' have an official sanction. It is because the citizen, whose daily dealings are local and individual, will appreciate the services of a 'selective, flexible, intermittent and emotional' flesh-and-blood broker when obliged to engage with 'the centrally imposed, cold, impersonal, even alien political system' (Landé, 1977, p.xvii; Güneş-Ayata, 1994, p.24; see also Eisenstadt and Roniger, 1984, chapter 5). The same citizen who seeks a loan from a moneylender rather than a bank may call on a local politician rather than a shadowy bureaucrat, and for the same reason.

Both citizen or 'client' on one hand and patron or broker on the other are after something: brokerage, like patronage in general, is a voluntary exchange relationship, albeit an unequal one (Blau, 1964; Scott, 1972). The patron or broker seeks a material or moral reward. The 'traditional' patron's reward may be the client's labour or produce, or even just his or her gratitude; the bureaucrat-broker's may be money, as in the elaborate market for transfer posts in an Indian irrigation agency which Wade (1985) has described. For the politician-broker, the reward is likely to be political support: the client's vote, or participation in electioneering. In return the broker, as opposed to the patron, offers what he can of the State's resources: information, as in Ireland

(Higgins, 1982); land, as we saw in Swaziland (Chapter 6); in other places, a trading licence, a place at a popular school or, crucially for us, a job, as in Chicago under Mayor Richard Daley Senior in the 1960s (Clark, 1994) and, as it seems we must accept, under his son, Mayor Richard Daley Junior in the first decade of the new century. Information, land, licences and jobs are all valid patronage currency: we must see job allocation as part of a broader patronage broking system.

How much must the broker offer? The bureaucrat-broker's schedule of prices may be semi-public knowledge, as in Wade's Indian irrigation agency. But it is hard to put a price on a vote, given the asymmetry of information in this particular market. What is the value of a politician telling you that you have been allocated a council house that was going to be yours anyway, as the politician neglected to say (Higgins, 1982)? The parties to the exchange collude in disguising this mercenary aspect of their relationship. However, a rough law of supply and demand will probably operate: the greater the competition for the client's support, the more the broker will have to offer to get it.

Brokerage as a mode of exchange

So far we have talked as if brokerage is a relationship between an individual public broker and an individual citizen-client. Can we apply the same model to a relationship between groups? When, for example, the British Labour Party promised in 1997 to sign up to the 'Social Chapter' of the European Union's Maastricht Treaty if elected, was its manifesto a 'dyadic contract' with the trade union movement? Eisenstadt and Roniger's definition of patronage is helpful here: 'not a distinct type of social organization, but different modes of structuring the flow of resources and of interpersonal interaction and exchange in society: different modes of generalised exchange' (1984, p.164). Arguably we have patronage or brokerage whenever the sense of *quid pro quo* enters a vertical relationship (that is, not merely a relationship between friends or groups of equal status), whether the relationship is between local individuals or between formal national groups, such as a political party and a trade union.

Why do we find brokering more in some places and at some times than others – more in Sicily than in Milan, and more in eighteenth- than in twentieth-century England (Tarrow, 1967; Namier, 1929[4])? There are 'countervailing forces' whose strength varies in different places and at different times (Eisenstadt and Roniger, 1984). The political system might be cohesive rather than diffuse, with autonomous

Weberian bureaucrats making rule-based and predictable decisions and resisting capture by would-be brokers – the official can only be a broker if he has something to broke. Alternatively, the 'system' might be accessible, either geographically close at hand or staffed by bureaucrats who are welcoming rather than aloof, so that using 'official channels' costs less than coaxing a broker to act as your middleman. Further, public resources may lose their appeal as private resources come on stream. Eisenstadt and Roniger's (1984, p.193) explanation for the recent decline of machine politics in US cities is that

> Socio-economic changes reduced the appeal of unskilled jobs available to be given as a patronage grant. Patronage jobs such as those, for instance, in federal censuses, in street repair or in custodial work in municipal buildings were increasingly considered as a short-term, last-resort alternative.[5]

Finally, citizens may come to see their interests in horizontal or group terms rather than 'vertical' individual or family terms, and feel they are best served by taking collective action to nullify the broker-client relationship, through class-based politics or even outright rebellion (Hobsbawm and Rudé, 1969; Scott, 1985).

Our account gives brokerage a clean trajectory: waxing with the growth of the State, then waning with the growth of alternative resources, such as private sector jobs, or of horizontal associations. But this is too neat and too Whiggish. Brokerage may equally decline and then grow, as in Turkey following the arrival of competitive multiparty democracy in 1946, and in Russia following the collapse of communism (Güneş-Ayata, 1994; Vorozheikina, 1994). Progress is not inexorable.

A good or a bad thing?

'One thing impresses above all,' insists Michael Higgins (1982, p.133), himself a practising Irish politician, 'Clientelism is exploitative in source and intent.' Weingrod (1977), however, suggests that it has had the positive function of inducting new groups into the political arena, and we shall see that his suggestion is echoed in Sri Lanka. Perhaps its status depends on the legitimacy of the benefit that the client receives: there will be cases where the broker's intervention rights a palpable bureaucratic wrong, as in Campbell's Greek village. But Eisenstadt and Roniger say about the allocation of public jobs in American cities that 'Public opinion became increasingly critical of inefficiency in the name of party loyalty. Patronage was seen as an outright political pay-off, and discredited as such' (1984, p.194). The onus is always on the broker to show that the private or the social gain is real, and not at the expense of other citizens or of government efficiency.

Patronage broking in Sri Lanka

Southern Italy has long been a by-word for poor governance, with patronage at the centre of many accounts (Allum, 1973; Banfield, 1958; Putnam, 1993; Tarrow, 1967). Yet as long ago as the late 1960s, twice as many citizens in the south as in the north said they paid a lot of attention to politics. 'Nothing,' comments Tarrow, 'Is more corrective of the vision of the South as a traditional society full of "parochials" who pay no attention to politics'. However, far from forming an opinion on Italy's role in the Common Market or other great issues of the day, 'Politics ... is a matter of patronage interest: interest in being able to control jobs such as town doctor, cemetery attendant, town guards and street cleaners' (Tarrow, 1967, p.77 and 78).[6]

Likewise in Sri Lanka, where politics is 'a consuming passion', the exact opposite of the 'anti-politics machine' which Ferguson (1990) identified in his well known study of Lesotho; but a passion that, according to one observer (Moore, 1985, p.224), boils down to the question of 'Who will be employed by the Ceylon Transport Board as bus conductors' (see also Jupp, 1978, p.162 and Spencer, 1990), allowing Jayanntha to explain political allegiance exclusively in terms of patronage networks (1992, p.206). That is why 'the outcome of parliamentary elections mattered in a personal way. This was one of the main reasons for the exceptionally high voter turnout ... and, in a sense, it has been at least a complementary cause for the apparent viability of the parliamentary system itself in Sri Lanka,' according to Sri Lanka's leading historian, echoing Weingrod and Tarrow (De Silva, 1993b).

Where does Sri Lanka's version of patronage broking come from? Again, the central fact is the growth of the State, and particularly its role as distributor of resources. This got seriously under way after the first universal suffrage election in 1931, still under colonial rule, when the state began to distribute Crown land on a large scale and to construct a British-style welfare state, including free medicine and education and subsidies on rice and wheat flour. As early as 1947, welfare spending was absorbing 56 per cent of government expenditure. With 'individual welfare to a very large degree shaped by administrative decisions', people came to expect that the State would provide (Moore, 1985, p.226).

Yet brokerage did not develop at the same pace as the State itself. At first, as in Turkey before 1946, distribution was in the hands of bureaucrats (Brow, 1996, p.73), something bureaucratic authors recall nostalgically (Root *et al.*, 2001; Wijesinghe, 1997; Wijeweera, 1989). The crucial change came in 1956 with the first of six successive defeats for the sitting government, ushering in knife-edge competition that was intense in proportion to the scale of the public spoils available to the winner.

In this electoral buyer's market, in accordance with the law of patronage supply and demand and replaying Turkey's experience, the 'traditional' patrons, those reliable vote-deliverers who were the core of the first generation of indigenous politicians (Jayanntha, 1992), had to make themselves attractive: in an electoral buyer's market, brokerage is only barely weighted in the broker's favour. With the public expectation that the State would provide in full swing, they did their best to interpose themselves as conduits for the State's resources, whether land or grants or (in our case) jobs. In one southern village, where all but 23 out of 173 households qualified for food stamps, and with 23 government employees resident in 1982 (as opposed to one in 1963), 'In virtually every case it is the spoils of politics that have done most to make (better-off villagers) better off in the first place'. So while senior politicians would discuss national issues at election rallies,

> Virtually all the village leaders' talk would be of the water supply we got for you, the school we built here ... The consistent aim of political discourse ... was to personalize the blessings of the State, to make 'us' the channel and 'you' the recipient (Spencer, 1990, p.214, p.217).

Altruism, welfarism and responsiveness

Politics might be a wholly negative affair in the Mezzogiorno, as Putnam implies, but not in Sri Lanka. Certainly political families were the disproportionate recipients of government jobs in Spencer's village, but examples of patron or broker altruism were common. One of the two UNP office holders in that village was 'a very poor Sinhala Christian ... popular for his willingness to help his neighbours in times of need' (1990, p.213). Elsewhere, a patron's standing derived from his grandfather having been a noted philanthropist in two out of three villages studied by Jayanntha (1992). Similarly, nationalist leaders in the 1920s lobbied for peasants to have priority over capitalists in distribution of Crown lands, 'An extraordinary move ... because many ...

had themselves greatly prospered from their involvement in the plantation sector' (Brow, 1996, p.82).

And anyway, there is more to local politics than clientelism. While politicians were hyper-sensitive to their fickle constituents' needs, bureaucrats tended to be remote from them, given the highly centralized nature of administration in an island comparable in size and population (18.8 million in 2001) to a single, not very large state in neighbouring India, and given the bureaucratic structure and 'arrogance and lethargy' (Wijeweera, 1989, p.291) which carried over from the colonial period. In what Oberst (1986, pp.172–3) describes as a typical response, one politician interviewee complained that

> The administrative secretary is living in a different world. There is no connection with the ordinary people. They are ... only trying to follow the rules and regulations.

So the politicians decided to bring the bureaucrats to heel. This was no 'creeping politicization', for the attitude had an unabashed formal expression. In 1978, a Decentralized Budget system gave every MP a million rupees to spend on local development: the dawn of 'MPs' Raj' had arrived (Wijeweera, 1989). The PSC had already come under Cabinet control in 1972. This largely legitimated the existing informal practice, to be sure, but it was only possible and defensible (Fernando, 1982) because the critics of bureaucratic remoteness had a point, even if the bureaucrats were loath to recognize it. The otherwise authoritative reports of the Administrative Reforms Committee (ARC) (1987–88), cleaving to the pure doctrine of political/administrative separation, do not even entertain it as a possibility, although at least one former senior bureaucrat was able to (Wijeweera, 1989).

Moreover, Brow's study of one village identified a profound belief in 'The vision of a just society in which the ruler ... provides for the material welfare of the common people' (1996, p.85). It seems plausible to suggest that this belief combined with the ideology of Fabian socialism which dominated the Indian sub-continent in the formative independence period to produce a not wholly self-serving welfarist conviction that the State *should* provide, irrespective of the electoral benefit of so doing, which has at least contributed to the impressive basic human development statistics, such as for life expectancy. We should also recall De Silva's insight that welfarism/patronage has contributed to the stability of democracy. All in all, we do the political class an injustice if we accept the jaundiced view that welfarism is nothing more than a polite term for the 'mass distribution of patronage measures to individuals' (Moore, 1994, p.25; see also Brow, 1996); just as well, as these are the very people from whom any change will have to come.

Patronage, growth and insurrection

There are two reasons why patronage broking in job allocation should not be a matter only for the civil servants whom it personally affects. The first is the negative impact which dependence on the public sector for the creation of jobs has had on economic growth, according to the World Bank (2004c). The second is that patronage has been a demonstrable cause of the two salient events of recent history, the civil war in the north and east fought on the rebel side by the 'Tamil Tigers' (the Liberation Tigers of Tamil Eelam, or LTTE) and the insurrection of the Janatha Vimukthi Peramuna or 'People's Liberation Front' (JVP) in the South that began in 1971, an uprising that killed almost as many people as the Tamil war (De Silva, 1993a; Shastri, 1997). We demonstrate that as follows.

Quid pro quo in the form of 'ethnic outbidding' has been an aspect of Sri Lanka's competitive politics since the mid-1950s, with the two major political parties, the Sri Lanka Freedom Party (SLFP) and the United National Party (UNP), each claiming to do more for Sinhalese voters (Devotta, 2003). An early Tamil grievance, consequently, was the Official Language Act of 1956, which enshrined Sinhala as the single national language and which, by making Tamils 'official illiterates' (Nithiyanandam, 2000, p.294), all but excluded them from government jobs outside the Tamil areas. In 1956 Tamils had represented 60 per cent of professionals, 30 per cent of the Administrative Service and 40 per cent of the armed forces, but by 1970 their numbers had plummeted to 10, 5 and all of 1 per cent respectively – and this at a time when the public service was expanding, and when Tamils represented over 20 per cent of the population. Tamil applications were then virtually choked off at source by a so-called 'standardization' of exam marking across language groups: there was to be the same percentage of Sinhala and Tamil students obtaining the highest grades, irrespective of their actual performance. It led, among other things, to a drop from 35 per cent to 19 per cent in the number of Tamils doing science subjects at university between 1970 and 1975 (Shastri, 1997). On the other side of the island, the JVP drew initial support for its uprising from unemployed young people who were excluded from rural patronage networks (Coomaraswamy, 2003; Jayanntha, 1992). Without trivializing the causes of the two insurrections, and while recognizing the case for addressing the Tamil predominance left over from British rule, one can see how electorally-driven patronage in job allocation not only affected growth, but played its part in driving both Tamil and Sinhalese young people into the arms of the militants in an extreme form of 'horizontal association'.

Summary

We began this section by accepting the consensus that 'patronage' has a lot to do with the failure of administrative reform in Sri Lanka, even while giving due weight to other factors. We outlined 'brokerage' as a humane adjunct to sclerotic official channels of contact with the State. Brokers offer state resources, including but not confined to jobs, in return for votes or money or esteem: the element of *quid pro quo* is what distinguishes brokerage as a mode of exchange. It increases with political competition or the decay of the 'official channels' (as in Russia). It decreases with the rise of the private sector or class politics or the autonomy of the bureaucracy. It is negative in principle, although it may be benign in individual cases and may even contribute to the stability of democracy.

Sri Lanka's 'traditional' patrons turned brokers are significant because of the decisive impact of the State on individual welfare, and the electoral importance for politicians of being seen to be personally responsible for distributing the State's largesse. Brokerage in Sri Lanka is intertwined with politicization, itself a response to the perceived remoteness of bureaucrats, and with the ideology of welfarism. It matters, finally, because of its negative impact on State efficiency, economic growth and the catastrophic insurrections of the 1980s and 90s.

Interview findings

Interview details

Eleven serving and one retired government officials were interviewed, identified by a Ministry Secretary (i.e. the most senior official) familiar with the structure of the Sri Lankan civil service as carrying a key responsibility for the design of operation of HRM systems. They were:

- the Secretary to the Cabinet
- a retired official who had a senior responsibility for civil service reform
- the Chairman and Secretary of the PSC (the body responsible for appointment of civil servants)

- the Secretaries of three ministries
- the Secretary of a Provincial Council
- the Secretary of a government district (the 'government agent')
- the Deputy Inspector-General of Police
- two staff with a senior responsibility for HRM in the Ministry of General Administration and Home Affairs

We also interviewed the directors of the civil service training academy (SLIDA) and of a postgraduate training institute; and leaders of the All Ceylon Civil Servants' Union (junior staff) the Sri Lanka Administrative Staff Association (senior staff) and the General Medical Officers' Union (doctors).

Developments since 1998

What had become of the 'third phase' of reform, in progress at the time of the 1998 interviews? There were few concrete achievements. Relevant to strategic integration, at least some ministries, such as General Administration and Commerce, were still producing action plans flowing from their mission statements, though an official in one such ministry said *'I can't see any change other than paper work'*, while in another the job of producing the action plan was given to a single middle-ranking officer. The projected management restructuring, said a well-placed official, *'Couldn't be done! The new government actually increased the number of ministries.'*[7]

By now the major donors had drifted away, denied the results they believed they had been promised, and from outside the prospects looked bleak. Yet this was the very point at which the government took a new turn, gaining the two-thirds majority necessary to enact a major institutional reform in 2001 in the shape of the Seventeenth Amendment to the Constitution. It did not affect the Provincial Councils, which notably employ the country's teachers, and the top two levels in each ministry remained political appointments. But it restored the independence of the PSC and created parallel Police and Judicial Service Commissions, with the Leader of the Opposition having a real say in the appointment of their members, who would serve a three-year term separate from the electoral cycle. The PSC's first Chairman was a retired ambassador, forthright and politically unaligned.

In fact the Amendment had been part of the action plan for the 'third phase' of reform. The official was correct who claimed that the 'third phase' *'did prepare the ground'* for a further phase of reform, despite its lack of tangible results. Its realization seems to have been the initiative of the professional associations who represent government employees. In an example how a 'policy network' (Rhodes, 1997) operates, they enthused the JVP party, who in turn made it part of their price for participating in a 'probationary government'.

But having taken a step forward in 2001, the government now took half a step back. In the run-up to the general election of April 2004, the SLFP/JVP coalition which was to take power committed itself to providing training places for all the country's unemployed graduates (interviewees could not agree on how many of them there actually were). The commitment should come as no shock to readers who have persevered with our chapter, and neither should the increases in salaries and allowances paid to state employees by the outgoing government in the run-up to the election – nor, for that matter, the permanent jobs offered to thousands more in the run-up to the previous election in December 2001, despite this open breach of the government's agreement with the IMF.

In fact the SLFP/JVP coalition won only 105 out of 225 seats, so that interviews in June 2004 took place in the latest period of political uncertainty. The new government was preoccupied with its own survival, and our interviewees were divided on whether it would see out even a year in power.

Strategic human resource management

How did the political and institutional context affect the way government managed its staff? In this and the following sections, we will describe how the system works, and what had happened to the 'third phase' of reform which was in progress at the time of my earlier study.

We could find no evidence of a thoroughgoing strategic approach. As the Head of a Provincial Council said, *'Mostly it depends on the minister's desires, not in a strategic way.'* One Ministry had published a policy and accompanying strategies, but that may have been to satisfy the donors contributing substantially to that sector, and in any case its implications for HR were not addressed. At best the mission statement and action plan initiative of the 'third phase' had created awareness of what a strategic approach might look like.

In other respects the 'clerk of works' model was as much in evidence as it was in Morocco (Chapter 5): *'We don't have any freedom, every aspect comes under the Establishment Code'*, said one line agency head of the 'book of rules' which even a central custodian admitted *'Hasn't been amended for at least 15 years.'* A large part of the central staffing agency's work seemed to consist of sending out circulars, on insurance, leave entitlement and so on, for ministries to follow.

Line manager ownership

Contrary to HR fashion, the deliberate effect of the Seventeenth Amendment, which states that 'The appointment, promotion, transfer, functions of disciplinary control and dismissal of public officers shall be vested in the (Public Service) Commission,' had been to move power into the centre rather than away from it. In keeping with the view of the line agency head already quoted, this had some predictable consequences. A police officer who had mugged up for his or her promotion exam, possibly at the expense of his duties, could get promoted ahead of an officer whose boss's high opinion of his performance was now discounted as 'subjective'. Letters to the PSC had to be signed by Secretaries personally, meaning that one of them was signing letters about staff he had never met. Promotions that the Cabinet Office would have processed in a couple of weeks took a good deal longer to make their way through the PSC: *'When you go to the PSC office, it's like a storeroom.'*

Efficiency was suffering – and yet none of my interviewees opposed the reform, and most, including all the staff associations, welcomed it: *'PSC means we have justice,'* was one representative view. A line agency head who began by complaining about his lack of discretion still ended up saying: *'I'm not asking for any more powers ... The Establishment Code is there for our protection.'* An Oliver Twist among our interviewees who did ask for more still wanted flexibility in the existing centralized structure rather than proper delegation to himself and his line colleagues.

With the decision to centralize HR having been taken, horizontal integration became difficult if not impossible, given the structure of government. As elsewhere, the PSC is responsible for initial employee selection, Finance for pay, General Administration for promotion and employee relations, and SLIDA for training. Each has its own remit, with the PSC in particular deliberately distanced from the line structure to preserve its independence. One could envisage all the central stakeholders uniting around a single competence model which would be applied uniformly in all the HR activities, acting as selection criteria and then as a statement of training needs for example, but the size and rigidity of the ministerial 'silos' effectively precluded it.

Employee selection

As mentioned already, the PSC is the body responsible for employee selection, given that only junior appointments are delegated. The staple diet of selection is academic-style examinations and structured interviews conducted by untrained interviewers and not based on competence data, although decisions were at least based on scores. Apart from this last point, which reflects a steely resolve to leave no room for interviewers' 'gut feeling' to contaminate decisions, it is easy to see how this fell short of what research and textbooks such as Conway *et al.* (1995) and Cook (1998) regard as good practice. But good practice is not the PSC's priority. When asked if there might be a role for, say, Assessment Centres, an official's reply was:

> *Ours is a Third World country. Even the interview board, when you give that latitude we tend to listen to the political head and give marks to people who have no qualifications. To avoid that, even though we don't like it, we have to limit (ourselves) to very few marks for the interview. Otherwise that requirement (i.e. using Assessment Centres) is very necessary, I am in agreement with that.*

To paraphrase: we know about 'good practice', we would love to use it, but we see it as a luxury that we can't allow ourselves for fear of political interference. Whether it was necessary to see independence and good practice as opposed is not the point. The quotation reflects the fact that the PSC was focusing on maintaining its independence from politics – that, rather than improving the quality of civil service entrants, was the thrust of the Seventeenth Amendment – and good practice was the casualty of its otherwise admirable determination.

Performance management

In a career civil service with fixed pay scales and central bargaining between government and powerful trade unions, performance management does not work in the way it does in many private firms. Performance-related pay, for example, was used only exceptionally and experimentally. On the other hand, promotion was impossible unless the employee had crossed the performance management hurdle. However, that had traditionally taken the form of a supervisor's confidential report, ruling out the objective-setting and feedback which research indicates are crucial to performance improvement.

Performance appraisal had been one of the initiatives of the 'third phase' of reform. While it was continuing in one or two places, an interviewee who had introduced it in his department said, *'It slowly went down ... My personal opinion is that it wasn't popular with staff. At the start there was a good response, but ... now (it would be) hard to reintroduce, no one is interested.'* There was some political support: one interviewee claimed that the President had personally insisted that the minister as well as the Secretary in his department should attend a presentation on appraisal. Two interviewees blamed its atrophy on the absence of a management or performance culture, something that is of course not unique to developing countries or to the public sector. One specific constraint, however, was the lingering expectation that promotion would be based on seniority, which even the interviewee who was most personally committed to appraisal still believed in: *'If he is a senior and if promoted I cannot grumble. It is a natural process, your father you respect.'* Officials tracked the performance of their contemporaries very closely. The 'merit list', showing the status of officials at the time of their entry to the civil service, was posted on the Internet for all to see. One official was proud to have reached the rank of Secretary, but even more proud to have been the first member of his 'batch' to do so. A trade union leader, who had the typical union suspicion of appraisal, made clear his expectation that promotion should be based on seniority throughout the official's career.

Understanding HRM in Sri Lanka discussion: dealing with patronage in Sri Lanka

The problem

How can we make sense of the way staff are managed, and in particular the character and the fate of attempts to improve it, particularly the Seventeenth Amendment? The starting point for an explanation might be a simple lack of capacity, compounded by ignorance of current normative models. Certainly there were management weaknesses, stemming perhaps from the 'clerk of works' mentality: *'The Establishment Code was written 30, 40 or 50 years ago. The word performance does not appear there.'* Two central officials complained that line ministries very often referred decisions upwards, lacking confidence to make even the simple decisions that the system did allow them to make. Very few staff had had professional HR training; current topics like 'broadbanding' or even TQM were largely unknown.

Yet the official's explanation for the absence of Assessment Centres gives a clue, we suggest, to the existence of a problem at a more fundamental level; in a word, the problem of patronage. Interviewees were as

clear as in 1998 that the local discretion which the Amendment curtailed had been abused by ministers: *'I'm sure my minister will say:
appoint so-and-so'* if left to his own devices, said one; *'Influencing by the
local level, especially by the politicians, cannot be managed'*, said another.
A third claimed that placing supporters in government jobs had made
them available for electioneering. Everywhere the story was the same:
'push in and push up': get supporters appointed, possibly in temporary
jobs, get them confirmed and in due course promoted. This of course is
in line with our literature review, but it is worth remarking how different it is from the diagnosis underlying previous phases of reform: it
does not issue from the 1970s critique of bureaucratic remoteness, nor
the structural adjustment critique of overstaffing and overspending,
nor even the managerialist measures of the 'third phase' of reform.

But given the diagnosis, why did the government decide to treat the
disease with a dose of Weberian bureaucratic medicine rather than the
alternative cures alluded to at the start of this chapter; with centralized
rule-following à la Schick, in other words, rather than devolving management responsibility or strengthening citizen 'voice'? Devolving was
consciously rejected by all the interviewees, the reason being that at
ministry or local level, it is politicians who dominate administrative
decisions: *'Government officers' sound is very low, MPs' sound is very big.'*
Ministry Secretaries – the official Heads of the ministries – were political appointees, and could be removed if they fell foul of ministers. One
interviewee *'had a very, very difficult time with the Minister: he chased me
out!'* At that level, politicians had impunity to make staffing decisions
on political rather than merit grounds, and interviewees furnished
endless examples of why that was a bad thing: local staff or 'consultants' appointed on politicians' say-so; staff arbitrarily denied or
granted transfers into or out of Colombo, police constables promoted
over their sergeants' heads, and so on.[8]

No one mentioned the 'voice' alternative, and it is interesting to
speculate why that was. Could not the JVP, the reform's political
sponsor, have mobilized the unemployed young people excluded from
rural patronage networks who were its initial supporters? But in the
prevailing welfarist climate, citizens might well have sided instead with
the politicians who had 'personalized the blessings of the State', in
Spencer's words, rather than the 'centrally imposed, cold, impersonal,
even alien' bureaucrats. In the end, the thrust of the reform was to
stifle voice rather than amplify it.

However, the proposed solution in the shape of the Weberian rule-
following Seventeenth Amendment was not the default option. 'Rules

and regulations' have a sanctity in the eyes of Sri Lankan officials that is only a puzzle until one grasps how they prize them as the indispensable bulwark against political interference. Hence the paradoxical statement by one central custodian of the rules that *'The bureaucrat should be ... guided by the rules and regulations ... he should have the independence not to deviate from that.'* What she meant was independence from the politicians, not discretion to follow the spirit rather than the letter of the law.

The results of the reform

The Seventeenth Amendment was still bedding in at the time of my interviews, but it was indeed doing what it was meant to do. We have already noted the view that *'PSC means we have justice'.* In one uniformed service, political interference had gone down *'from 90–100% to 5–10%'.* The staff and staff associations who supported the reform included line ministry officials, because they knew that the reform was more about transfer of power from politicians to officials than from line to central agencies. Loss of local discretion was an acceptable price for the officials to pay, especially when it meant ministers' discretion rather than officials'. In any case, frequent transfers within an all-island service meant that today's line ministry civil servant could be tomorrow's central official.

An advantage of the adopted solution was that it was a genuine indigenous initiative. It is a remarkable fact that not once in my 16 interviews did anyone volunteer a reference to a donor agency, including to the vaunted and donor-sponsored Poverty Reduction Strategy Paper. Previous donor-sponsored reform was never fully 'owned': *'They pay lip-service, but it's not real,'* said a donor in 1998. And yet this reform, entailing a constitutional amendment, was more fundamental and harder to reverse than anything attempted under donor auspices, and it did have an indigenous power base in the officials and unions who had promoted it. Admittedly some credit is due to UNDP, under whose auspices the preparatory work was done in the 'third phase' of reform, but crucially the impetus came from within, given that the government had chosen to work with UNDP precisely because it could not impose conditionalities, and in any case the actual implementation took place after UNDP support had ended. Where donors had an axe to grind, their support had been more of a hindrance than a help.

Still, there were bad as well as good effects. Whether or not the Seventeenth Amendment constituted a 'bulwark' against patronage,

Sri Lankan rules, which in one way are no more than a local manifestation of the 'clerk of works' model (see Chapter 1), have no special exemption from normal bureaucratic pathology, as we saw earlier in relation to police and other promotions. Fairness and efficiency were not going hand in hand as they were supposed to.

Ironically, too, patronage was squeezing back in through loopholes in the very rules that were designed to keep it out. Exams may be fair, but *'When exams are delayed, they get people on a casual basis. After a couple of months, or years, all the people on casual basis are made permanent.'* A discretionary choice among staff who had all passed the relevant exam but could not all be promoted might favour the one with the best connections: *'Politically this man is powerful.'* These were the *'5–10% of cases'* to which my interviewee referred.

'The rules' also exacerbated the posture of frightened rigidity at lower levels. Far from oppressive central controls being resented, officials in two separate interviews insisted that ministries passed the buck upwards on decisions they could easily have made themselves. The government auditors, who could already descend on a Ministry Secretary if he or she merely allowed staff to do too much overtime, now had a fresh stick to beat ministries with.

Lastly, putting staffing authority back in bureaucrats' hands while doing nothing to strengthen citizen 'voice' ran the risk of increasing the insensitivity of an all-island administrative service that retained some of the colonial aloofness, with the consequent danger that politicians, as much obliged to deliver benefits to their constituents as ever, would take matters back into their own hands if the bureaucrats cramped their style. After all, even a constitutional amendment could be sidestepped. The government, everyone agreed, had undermined its own Thirteenth Amendment, which created the provincial councils: the head of one of them complained that the government gave powers with one hand and then took them away with the other. Moreover, we have seen that the formal politicization of the PSC in 1972 had merely confirmed what was already the actual practice, despite the PSC's supposed constitutional independence at the time.

The outlook

So the success of the reform would depend on its political support, but this was its most serious weakness. Clearly the majority of parliamentarians had needed to acquiesce for the Amendment to be enacted in the first place. Yet an official closely involved in the reform said that

'I'm afraid that in the year and a half (since the Amendment), it's difficult to get this idea (of independence) seeping in.' Ministers and MPs below the President and the Prime Minister did not support it because *'their influence depends on ladling out of the pork barrel'*, and having made headway with the previous administration, the change of government meant that *'Now we have to start all over again.'*

There was a sense of officials girding their loins for an inevitable trial of strength, the likeliest battleground being the graduate training scheme: might it turn out to be just the latest instance of back-door recruitment of political supporters – of 'push-in'? It would be asking too much to expect the honest officials of the new PSC to prevail in a direct confrontation with the politicians, despite the backing of the Constitution, the staff associations and officials at large; perhaps appointed officials ought not to prevail over elected politicians in a democracy like Sri Lanka's. Two interviewees suggested separately that a confrontation might be avoided if some at least of the graduates were trained to become revenue collectors, posts that could easily pay for themselves, given Sri Lanka's poor record of tax collection. We complete this discussion with the hope that some such imaginative way would be found out of the looming *impasse* in order to preserve the Seventeenth Amendment and extend its scope to the provinces and the education service.

At the time of writing, Sri Lanka was just starting to recover from the tsunami disaster, and civil service management was not uppermost in many minds. Moreover, there was always the risk that political turmoil would derail or sideline the reform, as had happened before, a prospect that the JVP's withdrawal from the coalition government as we completed this chapter in mid-2005 only made likelier. Yet it seemed probable that patronage, which has the resilience of a cockroach, would re-emerge from almost any vicissitude and demand attention once again (and press reports were suggesting that allocation of post-tsunami aid was contaminated by political bias). What form should that attention take? In an ideal world the rising tide of prosperity would raise the public staffing boat, and patronage would take care of itself, as it did in the United States. But that tide will be slow to rise, despite the recent growth that has followed liberalization in South Asia as a whole. Moreover, the experience of Mauritius, a rare structural adjustment success story in the 1980s, shows that growth can leave patronage untouched, while India and Nepal show, conversely, that even in poor countries a central staffing agency can remain an island of integrity in a sea of favouritism (McCourt, 2001c; McCourt and Ramgutty-Wong, 2003; Wade, 1985). Indeed, if Kaufmann et al.'s (2005) finding that governance can cause prosperity means anything at all – that it might be governance that is the tide and the economy that is the boat – it must be possible for governments to act directly on staff management with a real hope of success.

With rule-following bureaucracy one of patronage's 'countervailing forces', and with the importance of institutions so firmly established even among economists (North, 1990), few will doubt that the Seventeenth Amendment was a necessary initiative, seeing that it severed the link between staffing decisions and the political sphere, and reinforced rule-following just as Schick (1998) prescribed. It was also an irrevocable step of the kind which Chapter 6 suggested was the litmus test of political commitment to reform. Managerial devolution and political decentralization are inappropriate institutional remedies in Sri Lanka, for the reasons we have given. But Sri Lanka's initiative was still not sufficient, even in its own terms. There were a number of measures that would strengthen the reform. For example, the Seventeenth Amendment represented an intervention on the demand side of the labour market, but the problem was partly on the supply side too: every year the education system churns out school-leavers and graduates conditioned to look for a job in the public sector. A vocational reorientation of education would do much to alleviate that. There were also technical improvements that could be made to staffing arrangements, such as introducing more predictive selection methods and extending performance appraisal (Armstrong and Baron, 1998; Smith and Robertson, 1993).

However, our analysis suggests that addressing the reform's political weakness should be the first priority. In a country whose President was floating yet another constitutional amendment at the time of writing, this time to abolish her own office (strange to say), public figures too readily believe that deep-seated problems will yield to the stroke of a legislative pen. But patronage is a political problem that requires a political solution. Support for the reform needed to be maximized. The civil service staff associations needed to present a united front, despite the links that some of them have to rival political parties. Donors needed to subordinate their advocacy of pet reforms, whether downsizing, decentralization or even 'pro-poor' measures, to the need to ensure that this fundamental reform actually succeeded.

Most importantly, reform needed the active support of the politicians themselves. In part that meant making efforts to retain the support of the Amendment's original political sponsors and being prepared to sell the Amendment to any new government. But more profoundly, it also meant recognizing that job allocation is not an isolated phenomenon, but part of a patronage system that encompasses all the state's resources. There was a need to find a way to reconcile the independence of civil service management with politicians' not wholly self-serving need to give constituents a reason to (re-)elect them. Patronage expectations built up over 50 years of competitive politics would not disappear overnight, but it would be helpful if the civil service faced up to its image as the people who like to say no, and became more flexible, for example in helping a politician find a way through the maze of laws and regulations in order to get a road widened in his or her constituency. We should remember here that unresponsive bureaucracy is one of the roots of patronage broking. If political supporters of reform could harness 'voice' by selling reform to the public, if the civil servants could show those politicians who are not merely vendors – or, pedantically, brokers – of political pork that they can curb their bureaucratic instincts so that civil service independence need not be at the expense of local responsiveness, then politicians would be more likely to support staffing reform, give up their control of top ministry appointments and extend the reform to the provinces and the teachers.

Despite our reservations, it is worth noting that Sri Lanka's reform has gone as far as it has because it is indigenous: it is 'owned'. We saw in Chapter 6 that ownership is not a sufficient condition for reform success, but Sri Lanka's experience strongly suggests that it is still a necessary one. As with the attempts at downsizing which we reviewed earlier in this book, previous reform attempts based on donor initiatives have not succeeded in Sri Lanka; ironically, despite tough talk from the donors, they have been institutionally unambitious and relatively easy to reverse. There is support here for those who argue that the Holy Grail of policy ownership will take the form of donors respecting, within reason, indigenous priorities, idiosyncratic and unsatisfactory as they may well be, rather than of governments signing up to donor priorities, however rational or even 'pro-poor' those are (McCourt, 2003). A specific example is that further decentralization in Sri Lanka, despite being one of 20 components of what Maxwell (2005) has called the 'meta-narrative', the supposed successor to the 'Washington consensus', would make things worse.[9]

Conclusion: patronage and public staff management

Those of us who study HR and governance lack the luxury of experimental laboratory conditions. In Sri Lanka's case, the electoral hyper-competition prevailing almost since independence, the two insurrections and, most recently and tragically, the *tsunami* in December 2004 have all conspired to deny government a free hand to pursue reform. Yet there may still be lessons that HR specialists and public policy reformers elsewhere can learn from the Sri Lanka case. Believing that patronage broking as a special case of political corruption is a large element in the failure of reform, though by no means the whole story, we have concentrated on how it operates in one South Asian country: its roots, its mode of operation and its effects, both bad and, occasionally, good. We respect Sri Lanka's singularity, but our survey of the patronage literature in the first half of this chapter showed how much it shares with other countries. It is citizens' need for humane access to the resources of government which creates patronage broking in the first place, in Sri Lanka and in many other countries.

Patronage is less a disease that can be cured with a single dose of this or that policy medicine than a stubborn rhododendron bush that needs strenuous spadework to bring it down, exposing its roots and then hacking them off one by one. (Extending the analogy, since job allocation is only one of its branches, tackling the roots may cause other branches like unfairness in land allocation and welfare relief to wither away too.) Institutional reform is a necessary step, but not a sufficient one. The consequent size of the reform task is big enough for an organization to be entitled to put normal management and HR concerns – the micro-level in our governance model (Table 1.2) – on one side and tackle it in a single-minded way. That is what Sri Lanka has been trying to do, rather as the United Kingdom and the United States did in the nineteenth century period of the Northcote-Trevelyan report and the Pendleton Acts. It seems reasonable to suggest that the method outlined here is applicable to other countries: institutional or macro-reform to recover the independence of the civil service combined with measures to build political support and increase the responsiveness of those 'official channels' that most of us would be only too happy to use if we thought we could rely on them.[10] That may also be true of our analysis of the fragility of Sri Lanka's reform, which was pressing too heavily on a slender institutional base supported mainly by the civil service lobby, and equally true of the imagination and persistence needed to make it stick.

'The bloody horse' of the 'third phase' of reform never really did materialize in Sri Lanka, but instead a 'horse of a different colour', to adapt the French phrase, entered the ring. The challenge at the time of writing was to nurture it and create a benign environment so that it would not take fright and bolt off after its forerunners. With that task done, and the integrity of government established, there will be an opportunity to switch attention to using strategic management and strategic HRM to improve the performance of government, professional concerns that will allow HR scholars and practitioners to bring their normal expertise to bear in order to improve government's efficiency and its responsiveness to citizens' needs.

8
Malaysia: History and Path Dependence

Path dependence in development studies and governance

So far in this book we have explored the influence of management models, institutions and politics on staff management, and we have explored commitment and patronage as aspects of the latter. We now descend to our deepest level of analysis, exploring the way in which staff management, and governance in general, are conditioned by the historical development of the civil service in one developing country.

Previous chapters, and particularly Chapter 6, have touched on the history of staff management in developing country governments. This reflects the way in which the history of development has been elevated from an antiquarian pursuit to a live explanation of the progress of development in recent years. That in turn is the result of the emergence of 'path dependence' as an account of the history of technology and political institutions. Our application of the concept to Malaysia's experience necessarily entails a critique of the concept itself.

Coined by David (1985), 'path dependence' has come to be seen as a key to understanding the way economies, organizations and polities behave. It began as an economic heresy.[1] Neo-classical economics had assumed that rational economic actors would make optimal and unconstrained choices. David, Arthur (1989) and others, dwelling on episodes in the history of technology like the triumph of the manifestly sub-optimal QWERTY typewriter keyboard in the English-speaking countries. An intrinsically inferior technology might prevail because of a 'founder effect' whereby learning processes and further investment would generate increasing rather than diminishing returns.

Thus path dependence in technology boils down to a three-stage process: an initial 'critical juncture' when the path is embarked on

159

(such as the adoption of QWERTY); increasing returns after adoption of the path; and 'lock-in', as each step down the path increases commitment to the initial choice and reluctance to change direction. Since actions in the present are conditioned by decisions in the past, this is a view in which 'History becomes important', as Arthur says (1989, p.128).

Following Arthur, analysis based on path dependence has fanned out to studies of industrial and business development, both in industrialized and developing countries (Eriksson *et al.*, 2000; Hall, 1999; Krugman, 1994; Meyer-Stamer, 1998; Noda and Collis, 2001; Redding, 2002; Schilling, 2002); and also, crucially for us, to the development of political institutions, in Latin America (Collier and Collier, 1991; Mahoney, 2001, 2003) and – in a manifestation that many readers will know – the development of Italian regional government in Robert Putnam's *Making democracy work* (1993), the source of our ubiquitous interest in 'social capital' (see also North, 1990[2]). Political path dependence writers were enormously ambitious. Where the technological paths had ranged modestly from 20 to a hundred years, the political paths could stretch out over half a millennium or even more. Putnam believed that the door leading to the path of civic development from the south of Italy clicked fortuitously shut in the twelfth century. Mahoney (2003) identified the almost equally distant founding of Spain's colonial empire (Mahoney, 2003) as a critical juncture in Latin America's political history, when political and social institutions were created which ironically favoured the subsequent economic development of the imperial periphery over the core; for example, of Argentina over Bolivia.

In short, path dependence's sudden ubiquity and the flexibility that allows scholars to use it to make sense of short- and long-run change in organizations, technology and polities, and at national, sectoral and organizational levels of analysis to boot, are the reasons why the political economist Robert Bates has said that 'History, discourse, institutions, structures, symbols, path dependency ... mark the agenda ahead' for development studies (1993, p.1080), and why it is increasingly assumed to be an intrinsic feature of the whole development process, with Maxwell roundly declaring that 'The first rule ... should probably be that development is particular and path-dependent' (2005, p.1).

'Critical junctures' versus incrementalism in historical development

There are, we suggest, three largely unexamined problems with the path dependence analysis. The first is the rejection of an incremental view of historical progress. Path dependence views history as a gigantic railway network, where travel is in a straight line until a point switch abruptly sends the train down another line. This contrasts with the mainstream historical view in which, in the words of the German philosopher Leibniz, 'nature does not make leaps' (quoted in Gerschenkron, 1968, p.19).[3] The French historian Fernand Braudel is representative here. Speaking in his greatest work of the development of the Mediterranean world in the reign of Philip II of Spain, he says: 'There is no single conjuncture: we must visualize a series of overlapping histories, developing simultaneously' (1973, p.893). Similarly, while isolating the decline of the peasant economy as the crucial trend in modern France, he emphasizes that 'I shall make no attempt to identify some irrevocable turning-point' (1990, p.401). Rather than a railway, history here is like a language, developing incrementally and imperceptibly.

Path dependence and historical causation

The second problem concerns the nature of historical causation. While a 'critical juncture' represents a confluence of heterogeneous social and economic factors, *they coalesce into a single cause*. Thus the consolidation of the political dispensations in northern and southern Italy, and in Latin America's imperial core and periphery, becomes *the* single explanation for their subsequent respective political development. Again, this contrasts with mainstream historiography: 'History seeks for causal wave-trains and is not afraid, since life shows them to be so, to find them multiple' (Bloch, 1954, p.194). Similarly, 'The examination candidate who, in answering the question "Why did revolution break out in Russia in 1917?", offered only one cause, would be lucky to get a third class. The historian deals in a multiplicity of causes' (Carr, 1987, p.88). That is why Braudel aspired to write 'total history': to provide a complete explanation unrestricted by academic disciplinary boundaries.

Political agency in path dependence

The third problem concerns the path development view of the role of political agency – of human individuals and groups, in other words. Politicians only have real freedom to act at a critical juncture, and not necessarily even then. In the centuries-long gaps between junctures, they have no choice but to eke out 'normal governance'[4] as machine-minders on a political assembly line.[5] Path dependence 'locks in', but cannot unlock.

Thus path dependence in its strict form has a radical and perhaps even fatal implication for governance interventions, and indeed development policy interventions as a whole. If political actors, including governments, have no choice but to soldier on down the path that choice or contingency decreed for them long ago, purposeful action in the short or even medium term becomes futile. For example, nothing short of a once-in-every-500-years critical juncture, one fears, will make a government move towards the Millennium Development Goals (MDGs) unless its path decrees it already. Indigenous development activists, international policy mongers in the development agencies and the consultant and academic communities, with our ever-ready blueprint models – we are all wasting our time. In normal circumstances there is no such thing as policy transfer or policy learning.

The Malaysian Civil Service

The development of staff management in the Malaysian civil service is the vehicle for our exploration of the influence of history. When set against the lamentable performance of the civil service in so many developing countries, Malaysia seems to represent a beacon of efficiency, having 'distinguished itself in the developing world as a country which ... has demonstrated ... a significant improvement in the strength of its administration ... The public service ... has ... undergone major changes within a short time frame, representing a fundamental shift in paradigm' (Sharma, 1998, pp.431–2). As we saw in Chapter 1 (Table 1.5), the World Bank's governance index places it on the 81st percentile of countries worldwide. This is against an average placing on the 50th percentile for countries in the East Asia region; even the middle-income countries among which Malaysia is numbered appear only on the 63rd percentile (Kaufmann *et al.*, 2003).[6] The Malaysian economy has done well, but its bureaucracy, apparently, even better. Thus the former Chief Secretary to the government states with a minimum of undue modesty that 'The rapid economic growth experienced by the country during the past few years can be attributed to the continuing efforts of the Civil Service in implementing the Malaysia Incorporated policy' (Sarji, 1995, p.135).

And so for officials from other developing countries setting out on study tours, all roads have led to Kuala Lumpur (Sarji, 1995, p.xiv). Quite rightly so, according to bureaucracy's most persuasive current advocate, slashing the Gordian knot of path dependence:

The challenge of emulating East Asia's bureaucratic effectiveness may be less daunting than the stereotypical 'Confucian super-bureaucrat' image might suggest. Meritocracy and organizational coherence can be secured ... in a variety of institutional forms. Most countries should be able to find one suited to local history and politics. (Evans, 1998, p.73[7])

In short, 'If Malaysia can do it, why can't you?' The status of Malaysia as an exemplar of governance is based on the assumption that its experience is transferable, rather than the culmination of an idiosyncratic 'path'. What, then, has been the nature of Malaysia's civil service management success? How path-dependent has success been, and how much of it depends on critical junctures in Malaysia's history? Finally, how realistic is it to expect other countries to emulate Malaysia's performance in the way that Evans says?

Society, economy, politics and the civil service

Society

The deepest social root of civil service management, we suggest, is the premium placed on authority. Citizens 'will not readily challenge any ... government official, even one whom they believe to be corrupt. Even to hear criticisms of their leaders will sometimes cause them to feel uncomfortable or irritated ... obedience and respect for authority are a key factor in Malay social attitudes' (Taib and Ismail, 1982, pp.112–13). It is a longstanding feature – Andaya and Andaya in their history of Malaysia talk of 'an earlier age when Malays sought guarantees of just rule from their kings in return for promises of unswerving loyalty' (2001, p.339) – but it was reinforced by British administrative culture, including the fact that as in other colonies, the British chose to rule indirectly through the native rulers (Mansor and Ali, 1998). Consequently, 'popular ... deference to the Westernized elite – particularly civil servants – was the rule rather than the exception' in the post-independence period (Embong, 2002, p.22). Echoing this analysis, Scott (1968, p.252) observes that 'the traditional reliance on high-status leadership has created a situation tailor-made for domination by the administrative elite. Both the bureaucrats and those they guide find this relationship quite natural and appropriate.' All of this is reflected in Hofstede's (1980) well-known research, in which Malaysia is actually the country with the highest score for 'power distance', defined as the extent to which cultures accept the right of superiors to exercise power over subordinates. The onus is on those allergic to 'culturist' explanations to account for the range of sources that emphasize this factor in Malaysia.

The second major social influence is Malaysia's ethnic composition, and the attitudes that flow from it: 'identity has hinged on ethnicity', says Case (1995, p.102), echoing what Eriksen said about Mauritius (Chapter 3). Despite differences within the indigenous community or 'bumiputeras' (a Sanskrit word meaning 'sons of the soil'), the politically vital cleavage is between the mostly Malay bumiputeras as a whole and the descendants of the Chinese and (mostly South) Indian immigrants originally imported by the British colonial rulers to work in new economic activities, notably rubber plantations and tin mines. As in other former colonies with a wealthy settler minority – Ireland and Zimbabwe spring to mind – there is a sense that the minorities whose parents or ancestors were settlers are there on sufferance, and that independence in 1957 was the proper opportunity for the poor majority to assert its culture and interests at the settlers' expense (Scott, 1968; Taib and Ismail, 1982, pp.122–3). Hence the comment in a recent book that 'There are still significant numbers of non-Malays ... (who) insist in challenging Malay alpha status ... Fortunately, their numbers are small and declining' (Musa, 1999, p.225). A retired very senior official believed that *'You go back to ancient thinking: this is their country and they want to dominate.'*

Some observers have suggested that ethnic identity has begun to weaken or fragment (Choi, 2003; Thompson, 2001; Weiss, 1999), leading Case (1995, p.107) to make the intriguing suggestion that there is now room for 'Farsighted leaders (to) innovate within the parameters of cultural familiarity, couching initiatives in enough palliatives that they can nudge cultural change along a desired, or at least less determinist, trajectory.' This is reflected in political moves to sponsor a single Malaysian identity, or *'Bangsa Malaysia'* (Collins, 1998). There does seem to have been some movement from an ascriptive to an achievement orientation, to use the anthropological terms that we introduced in Chapter 3.

Economy

It is well known that over the last quarter century, Malaysia's economic performance, as one of the 'Asian tigers', has been good, with steady growth through most of the 1980s and 90s until the 'East Asian crisis' at the turn of the century, when the economy contracted by 7.4 per cent in 1998. At the time of writing, the upward trajectory of growth seemed to have been re-established, albeit at a less precipitous rate than before, with GDP growth projected at 5.3 per cent for 2004.

The strength of the economy over the period, allied to a certain self-confidence among the policymaking elite, allowed the government, controversially, to reject the IMF's money and advice in 1998 (Hilley, 2001), and it no doubt took some satisfaction when the IMF subsequently ate its words and 'congratulated the authorities for Malaysia's strong economic performance and their skilful and prudent macroeconomic management' (IMF, 2004b, p.4).

It is important to note that growth has been, in the current jargon, 'pro-poor': strong performance went hand in hand with the pro-Malay NEP measures, allowing the Gini coefficient (the accepted measure of income inequality) to decline from 0.513 in 1970 to 0.445 in 1990 (Gomez and Jomo, 1997, p.170). The orthodox view is that NEP-style meddling in the free market must act as a brake, but the statistics of growth cannot be gainsaid, and the government analysis in its Second Outline Perspective Plan of 1988 that the NEP was pro-growth because it delivered the essential 'atmosphere of peace and stability' is very plausible (Chowdhury and Islam, 1996).

Politics

Having created Malaysia's principal ethnic cleavage through importing Chinese and Indian labourers, the British could not, or at any rate did not, do enough to prevent the democracy they created in the years leading up to independence from being 'tethered to the underlying socioeconomic structures' (Case, 2002, p.103). Political parties correspond to the main ethnic groups: UMNO (United Malays National Organization), MCA (Malaysian Chinese Association) and MIC (Malayan Indian Congress). Yet it is fascinating to observe that these ethnic-based parties have opted to cooperate rather than confront, so that all post-independence governments have been cross-communal coalitions with UMNO as the dominant partner, the current manifestation being the *Barisan Nasional* (National Front; BN for short). Political scientists have called this style of government 'consociationalism' (Crouch, 1996, chapter 9); in Malaysia it became known as 'the bargain'. As Malaysia's first prime minister, Tunku Abdul Rahman, put it: 'The Malays have gained for themselves political power. The Chinese and Indians have won for themselves economic power. The blending of the two ... has brought about peace and harmony.' (Case, 2002, p.105). Since 'political power' included the power to shape the bureaucracy, 'the bargain' ratified what Crouch (1996, p.237) calls

'The old stereotypes – Malay bureaucrats and peasants, Chinese business and tradespeople, Indian professionals and estate labourers.'

Consociationalism only works when the consociating groups think they are getting enough out of it. The fragile 'bargain' fell apart on May 13 1969, when ethnic rioting followed a general election perceived to have tipped the scales towards the Chinese. The government, Malay-dominated as ever, responded by strengthening the Malay side of the deal. The point of the celebrated 'New Economic Policy' (NEP) introduced in 1971 was to give Malays a foothold in the economy through government measures such as putting pressure on businesses to accept Malay partners. In the civil service, the NEP accentuated the pre-existing bias towards civil servants of Malay origin. The stereotype of the Malay bureaucrat persisted, but a competing stereotype of the Malay entrepreneur or *rentier* (Gomez and Jomo, 1997) began to emerge.

Consociationalism also only works for 'as long as the masses are docile and deferential and are prepared to entrust their leaders with the responsibility to safeguard the community's interests' (Crouch, 1996, p.153), something that the deferential character of Malaysian society has permitted. What has variously been called Malaysia's 'soft authoritarianism' (Means, 1996), 'quasi-democracy' (Zakaria, 1989), 'semi-democracy' (Case, 2002) and – most expressively – its 'repressive-responsive regime' (Crouch, 1996) is at once an obstacle to full democracy and the indispensable condition that allows democracy to operate at all.

When consociationalism does work, it is by co-opting potential opposition. We have seen already how parties representing the three main ethnic groups are part of the governing coalition. The urge to co-opt has even embraced the main public sector trade union, CUEPACS, whose successive presidents have tried 'to outdo their predecessors in obtaining government approval' (Jomo and Todd, 1994, p.160), and whose current leaders boasted of their *'smart partnership'* with the government in our research interview. There may have been an energetic policy debate within what Khoo (2003) calls the 'party-bureaucracy-class axis', but it has been conducted over the heads of the rank and file. The result is that much political activity is micro-politics: jockeying for position within the government, so that 'UMNO general assembly elections have often been conceptualized as Malaysia's "real" elections', in which party officials are alleged to have bartered their votes for some kind of reward (Case, 2002, pp.111–12).

The British may have failed to prevent politics from becoming ethnic-based, but they succeeded in defeating the Communist insurgency in the so-called 'emergency' of the 1950s. Through a combination of military repression and 'hearts and minds' tactics that the United States was to imitate disastrously, 'strategic hamlets' and all, a decade later in Vietnam, they effectively destroyed the extreme left, so that following independence there was no significant pressure to adopt anti-capitalist economic policies. As a result we do not see the disruptive cleavage between pre- and post-liberalization policies evident recently in countries like Tanzania and India, not to mention China.

Employee relations

Scholars depict a strongly top-down style of employee relations with roots in the 'emergency' period to suppress communism in the labour movement, and bolstered by the current imperative to provide a favourable environment for foreign manufacturers with their typical hostility to unions (Bhopal and Rowley, 2002; Jomo and Todd, 1994; Kuruvilla and Erickson, 2002; Mansor and Ali, 1998; Mellahi and Wood, 2004; Todd and Peetz, 2001). This is reinforced by the deep-seated social or cultural tendencies that we reviewed earlier. Management style tends to be paternalist; on the other side of the coin, worker style is compliant. There is little diminution of managerial control and little involvement by workers or their union representatives in management decisions. Jomo and Todd go so far as to conclude that unions are 'a sad and pathetic caricature of contemporary British unionism even after ... Thatcherism' (1994, p.170; see also Parasuraman, 2003, p.63).

The civil service itself

There is a second sense in which Malaysia is an 'intermediate' state (see endnote): in terms of the classic politics/administration split. Malaysia's bureaucracy is neither wholly insulated from political influences in the way that Minns (2001) found South Korea to be, nor wholly politicized in the manner of South Asia.

Politicians and bureaucrats shared an identity of outlook in the period just after independence. They had, after all, sprung from the same root. UMNO's first leader, Datuk Onn Jaafar, was a civil servant, and the political elite was drawn largely from the civil service (Puthucheary, 1987, p.95). For the civil service, the decade of the 1970s was the golden age, when the so-called 'administrocrats' enjoyed 'a position of power perhaps unequalled by any other civil service in a democratic country' (Puthucheary, 1987, p.107) and when the key policy that they had to implement was the ambitious NEP, making inroads even into the previously inviolate private sector. Malaysia was 'an administrative state' (Esman, 1972) or a 'bureaucratic polity' (Crouch, 1996, p.199). It was equally the golden age of development administration internationally, a time when a study of neighbouring Thailand declared that 'The subject of bureaucracy has acquired a new lustre, a result of current concerns with the emergence of a host of new nations' (Siffin, 1966).

By the mid-1980s the bureaucratic party was over, even if Malaysia ended up with less of a hangover than many developing countries (appropriately enough for a country with an abstemious Muslim majority). Prime Minister Mahathir Mohamad may have espoused a policy of 'Look East', including for the civil service (Taib and Mat, 1992, p.432), but in the period of the National Development Policy (NDP) from 1990 onwards he took his cue from the West and specifically from the former colonial power, imitating Margaret Thatcher's privatization programme and her anti-civil service rhetoric (Gomez and Jomo, 1997). Criticism of inefficient public enterprises and of the public sector's hostility to free enterprise became the order of the day (Khoo, 2003, p.46), 'deification of private enterprise coupled with denigration of the Civil Service', as an observer of the British scene commented at the same time (Sampson, 2004, p.112). Meanwhile, some 'lustre' – and some influence – had rubbed off the civil service and on to the new bumiputera entrepreneurs whom the NEP had conjured into existence. The rate of increase in the civil service, which had employed a 'staggering' quarter of the entire workforce in 1983 (Milne and Mauzy, 1999, p.7), now slowed down.[8] 'To this day,' Khoo concludes (2003, p.177), 'The bureaucracy has not recovered its early NEP pre-eminence. It is a junior partner of "Malaysia Incorporated" and remains burdened with criticisms of inefficiency.' Where six of the seven members of the first post-independence Cabinet had been civil servants (including the prime minister), by 1987 that was true of only three out of the 14 UMNO ministers (Crouch, 1996). Perhaps the consociational sympathy towards CUEPACS is a legacy of the 'lustre' era: *'When we present anything to the PM, he always says: Have you talked to the unions?'*

One way of reacting to criticisms of inefficiency is to acquire the trappings of efficiency in the hope that the substance will follow. The energetic Chief Secretary to the government, Ahmad Sarji, recounts how the civil service introduced Client's Charters and TQM in its ISO 9000 version (both acquired off the peg from Britain once again), together with home-grown initiatives such as the 'policy on the assimilation of Islamic values in the civil service' (see Sarji, 1995, p.207). Even if these measures often had a foreign provenance that was part of their prestige value, they were still genuine indigenous initiatives for which the World Bank or other external agency could claim no credit. Moreover, their emphasis on accountability, managing public complaints and evaluation was characteristic of a government that could be 'responsive' as well as 'repressive'.

We should note the strongly centralized nature of public administration. The political backdrop is 'the ongoing struggle by the centre to restrain centrifugal tendencies', which Andaya and Andaya (2001, p.339) attribute to basic geography: think of the tract of ocean that separates West from East Malaysia. In an ostensibly federal system, 'State departments are in fact operating agencies of the federal government' (Puthucheary, 1987, p.103). When we asked a state official in an interview about the state government's approach to staff appointments, and then about its approach to pay, his reply was the same in both cases: *'We adopt 100% federal policies.'* Yet Andaya and Andaya also note that there is little sign of separatism. Sabah and Sarawak are not incipient Bangladeshes.

Affirmative action in the civil service

However good Malaysia's civil service performance may have been, would it have been better still without the government's affirmative action policy, the political reflection of Malaysia's precarious ethnic mix? We need to note this crucial and distinctive aspect of civil service management, blamed for bureaucratic inefficiency by Emsley (1996, p.72), Gomez and Jomo (1997) and Milne and Mauzy (1999, p.57), but a major element of 'the bargain'. While its political benefit is clear, one can still ask if the efficiency cost has been excessive, especially given the changes that have made Malays less dependent on the public sector for a stake in the economy.

Affirmative action in employment was certainly an important element in the NEP, which in this sense extended Malay privileges from the public to the private sector. The Industrial Co-ordination Act of 1975 required firms to employ 30 per cent Bumiputeras on pain of having their licences revoked (Andaya and Andaya, 2001, p.314). Admittedly, a glance across the causeway that separates Malaysia from Singapore to the complaints of discrimination against Malays there would entitle the government to point out what the Chinese-dominated private sector might do if left to its own devices (Ganguly, 1997). But affirmative action in civil service staffing actually predates the NEP, having its origin in the colonial period, as we have pointed out already. Recruitment quotas for the administrative elite were introduced in 1952, and continued unaltered after independence, which in this sense was no kind of 'critical juncture'. Gradually, Bumiputeras increased their predominance in the civil service as a whole, with Means (1991, p.297) asserting that 'Through giving recruitment and promotion preferences to Malays, the whole structure of government has become a bastion of Malay power and the major avenue for Malay professional and economic advancement' (see also Gomez and Jomo, 1997). Crouch (1996) reports that in 1989, 19 department secretaries were Malay, two Chinese and one Indian, and that 88 per cent of deputy secretary-generals were Malay. There has never been a non-Malay Chief Secretary, let alone Prime Minister. By contrast, multi-ethnic and middle-income Mauritius had had both a prime minister and a Chief Secretary from minority ethnic groups by early in the new century, as we saw in Chapter 3.

Turning from race to gender, the number of women working in the civil service has dramatically increased from a low base. By 1999, the civil service was 40 per cent female, with 40,000 more women than in 1990 (Andaya and Andaya, 2001).

Interview findings

Interview details

Eight interviews were held with serving and retired officials in central ministries and agencies. Three interviews were held with officials in line ministries. We also interviewed two members of the national executive of CUEPACS, the trade union that represents middle- and lower-grade civil servants, and we ran a focus group (Morgan, 1997) of serving and retired civil servants from different Ministries to give the point of view of a lower level in the hierarchy. We also drew on similar interview data obtained in 1998. Interviews covered the same topics as the other studies in this volume, with the addition of affirmative action, which as we have seen is a distinctive feature of HRM in Malaysia.

Strategic integration

More of the strategic elements were present in Malaysia than in any of the countries discussed in this book except Namibia (Chapter 9). Political stability has allowed the government to develop a good overall strategic capacity, manifested in the well known and much imitated national 'Vision 2020' which provides clear long-term targets, and there is an Economic Planning Unit within the Prime Minister's Department responsible for implementing it. The government has set up several central strategic bodies. There is a strategic apparatus at the level of ministries in the form of mission statements and key performance indicators, and it seems to be developing: KPIs, for example, are a personal emphasis of the new Prime Minister.

What the government tends to do, however, is to make specific HRM responses to specific policy issues. For example, at the time of our interviews the government believed that it had been outsmarted by the government of Singapore in recent negotiations over access to water supplies. It therefore asked INTAN, the National Institute of Public Administration, to provide training for senior officials in negotiation skills. Similarly, when Mahathir decided that the civil service would benefit from TQM, he handed implementation to MAMPU. When he decided that there needed to be a response to complaints from the civil servants' trade union about unfairness in performance management (see below), the Public Service Department got the job of sorting it out. There is a sense of government knowing where the HRM levers are and using them when it needs to – and of the machine responding when the levers are pulled. One can make a good case for saying that there is a 'big picture' in the form of a sustained emphasis on improving civil service performance to which individual measures like TQM contribute. But it would be false to say that there is any overall HRM strategy in the classic manner of Fombrun *et al.* (1984) and many others. Specific responses to specific issues is not the same as a single integrated strategic response to which all HRM activities contribute.

'Strategic' has an interesting alternative meaning in the civil service vernacular, as a term for someone who *'knows what side his bread is buttered on'*. A 'strategic' officer is a networker, schemer and intriguer. He or she may *'get things done'*, but always *'to their own personal advantage'*. In this high-power distance society, their focus is on the boss, on *'being at the airport when the boss is going and coming back, carrying his bags'*; *'If the minister has a family day, you should be there.'* It will be *'tough'* for someone who is not 'strategic' to get ahead.

Line manager ownership

One reason for the lack of strategic integration is that responsibility for HRM was every bit as centralized in Malaysia as it is in most New Commonwealth countries (McCourt, 2003), and pressure to devolve was limited. True, it was a former senior Finance official who complained that *'If you want to "vire",[9] you have to go to Treasury. Can you imagine the bureaucracy? The fellow in Treasury, a junior fellow with five years' service, is saying no.'* But where the head of a major service department in Mauritius was enormously frustrated by his lack of power (*'You want people to behave as managers, but you're not giving them the opportunity'*), his equally dynamic exact counterpart in Malaysia was quite satisfied. Despite some frustration, he believed that *'We still need regimentation, directives from the centre.'* One level down, the departmental HRM staff whom we interviewed agreed: *'I think the current arrangement is good'*, said one; *'Level of delegation is appropriate,'* said another. Thus when PSD did delegate some junior appointments, it was merely *'because they just couldn't cope'* with the volume of applications. At the centre, there was the same 'balkanization' that we have seen already in this book: PSC responsible for appointments, the Ministry of Finance for pay, PSD for promotion and employee relations, and INTAN for training. There was no sign of any of that changing.

Employee selection

The Public Service Commission is the body responsible for employee selection, given that only junior appointments are delegated. As in the other Commonwealth countries discussed in this book, its remit is specified in the national Constitution. Unlike its Tanzanian counterpart (Chapter 4), it enjoys both *de jure* and *de facto* independence. The government seems not to lean on it even at election time, and, crucially, the cycle of appointment for its Commissioners is separate from the electoral cycle. A relevant official talked of meetings with the Prime Minister and the Chief Secretary giving him no sense of any direction that the government would like the PSC to take. The Mauritian complaint that *'You must dance to the music of the one who appoints you'* (see Chapter 3) is not voiced in Malaysia. Politicians' occasional attempts to act as patronage brokers for their constituents bear little fruit. The negative aspect of this, mentioned already, is balkanization: an independent, freestanding PSC cannot be an effective strategic lever.

Dealing with no fewer than 350,000 applications in 2003, the PSC has partly computerized, and candidates can now apply online. There has also been some professional improvement: assessment centres are used for certain senior appointments, and there is limited use of psychometric measures like the 16PF personality questionnaire. But otherwise the staple diet is little different from Sri Lanka's: academic-style examinations and structured interviews conducted by untrained interviewers and not based on competence data, although decisions are at least based on scores.

Overall, therefore, appointments appear to be fair (though see 'affirmative action' below) and somewhat efficient, but as in Sri Lanka still fall short of what recent research and textbooks, such as Conway *et al.* (1995) and Cook (1998), regard as good practice.

Performance management

The government's approach to performance management is the area of greatest recent activity, and the one that most exercised civil servants at the time of our research. We therefore discuss it at some length.

In 1992 Malaysia replaced the 'annual confidential report' system inherited from the British with a standard performance appraisal system, called the 'New Remuneration System' (NRS). It included a PRP element that emulated governments like New Zealand and the UK (not to mention many private companies), but which went further, as far as we are aware than any other African or Asian government. It meant that managers who had little say in who joined or left their departments would at least have some control over the staff who were with them at any given moment. Accordingly, official sources cited it as one reason for a dramatic improvement in civil service performance. But it is clear from Shafie (1996) and from our interviews in 1998 that there were serious problems from the start. Some of them were generic ones that we should not underrate simply because we have seen them all too often elsewhere: that it wasn't properly strategic; that managers lacked the skill, the training and even the basic belief to do it properly; and a yawning gap between the number of staff who qualified for a PRP bonus and the number who actually got one.

We should enlarge on the last of those problems. PSD had to bow to the Ministry of Finance, which decided that only 5 per cent of staff in each department would qualify for an NRS bonus. There is nothing specifically Malaysian about this – finance departments everywhere tend to dominate, and to agonize about losing control of pay decisions – but it is a textbook illustration of how in the absence of 'horizontal integration', HRM activities can pull in different directions and almost cancel each other out, especially when Finance has delegated very little to line departments. Staff were quick to complain that motivating the select 5 per cent was at the expense of demotivating the other 95 per cent.

But there were also three distinctive problems. The first was dependence by line ministries on the central department. We should explain to readers whose experience of organizations is of 'line' functions like Production having priority over 'staff' functions that PSD dictates to line ministries: *'whatever comes from ... PSD, that's it, without any thought for the objectives (or) the impact.'* Yet on the other side of the power distance coin, line ministries take this lying down. Indeed 'most departments are overly dependent on the PSD to solve issues that they could solve themselves', according to Shafie (1996, p.347).

The second problem, manager bias, is of course universal, but has a specific Malaysian twist. The national 'atmosphere of peace and stability' on which the government has rightly congratulated itself has not dissolved ethnic suspicions. CUEPACS leaders with their closeness to government were not willing to say that this might be a problem, but staff were a little less reticent. An officer who asked her boss why she had not got a bonus which she thought she had earned was told that *'other considerations have been taken into account.'* When we asked her what those 'considerations' were, she replied guardedly, *'I think in Malaysia we are quite a racially mixed sort of community so there are always "considerations"'.* It appears to be partly for this reason that the government acted to reduce the power of the individual line manager in making pay decisions by introducing the MRS system.

Lack of support from CUEPACS was the last of the distinctive problems. When CUEPACS raised the 'yawning gap' and bias issues, the government, in 'responsive' mode, agreed to act. In fact, for 'government' we should read 'Mahathir': *'The Prime Minister was now asking CUEPACS to put up another memorandum to overcome the problem'*, said CUEPACS. Having personally, and characteristically, chaired all ten meetings of the committee that designed the original scheme, it was not surprising that he was instrumental in designing the new one, according to senior staff. He thought the best way of avoiding bias would be to go back to the old civil service examination. But the 'Malaysian Remuneration System' which duly emerged in 2002 turned into an instance of the law of unintended consequences. The examinations took on a life of their own. For example, only 0.87 per cent of the 130,000 teachers actually 'passed' the relevant exam, to the fury of CUEPACS, who returned to it again and again in our interview: *'Even in the last system we can get 5% yearly, so now we are getting less than what we got in the last system.'*

With other services apart from Education following a slightly different but not necessarily better approach, CUEPACS lobbied the new Prime Minister, Mahathir having retired in the meantime. It was futile for a department head to dismiss complaints from staff who had 'failed' the exam with the Malay proverb *'If you can't dance, don't say the floor is uneven'*. The PM heeded the unions, PSD was ordered to sort out the mess, and at the time of our interviews, a specially convened task force was holding daily crisis meetings. It was clear that exam scores were being moderated to ensure that the number of staff qualifying for the bonus would not fall below the magic 5 per cent figure which was half the reason for CUEPACS' hostility to the original scheme. The original objective of using performance management as a vehicle for instilling a culture of performance had been buried under the avalanche of politicking which the scheme's design flaws had triggered.

Affirmative action

Given the constitutional disapproval of discussion of this issue, it was predictably difficult to gather data. Despite its centrality, we were told that statistics were not available about percentages of men and women and so on at different levels of the kind that employers are legally obliged to furnish in Northern Ireland and South Africa, two countries where affirmative action is equally salient. We managed, however, to obtain the following statistics for entry to the elite Administrative and Diplomatic Service, see Table 8.1:

Table 8.1 Ethnic and gender composition of recruits to the Administrative and Diplomatic Service

Year	Male	Female	Female as % of total	Bumi: Malay, Sabah, Sarawak	Non-Bumi: Chinese, Indian	Non-Bumi as % of total
1998	64	16	20.0	72	8	10.0
2001	133	111	45.5	229	15	6.1
2002	191	130	40.5	286	35	10.9
2003	163	112	40.7	241	34	12.4

The figures for 1998 tally exactly with what the PSC told us in an interview in 1998: *'There are quotas for male and female – a department might request 15 men and 5 females'*, and with Ahmad *et al.*'s (2003, p.96) account. They report that in 1995, 'The selection ... gender ratio was ... 4.1 in favour of males ... at the administrative request of the Public Service Department,' even though women 'were generally the better performers during the exercise'. Despite 'a furious (internal) debate', PSC ultimately knuckled under.

The judgement that women were 'generally the better performers' must be taken seriously, as one of the authors was actually a Public

Service Commissioner in 1995. No doubt there are exceptional jobs, such as those involving certain religious duties, where being a man is what British employment law calls a 'genuine occupational qualification'. But those aside, we suggest that the above data constitute evidence of discrimination contrary to Article 8 of the Malaysian Constitution. The government as employer had deliberately preferred to take less able men, by definition likely to provide a lower quality of service to the citizens of Malaysia. Moreover, the PSC had shown itself unable or unwilling to resist pressure from department heads in the way that the constitution was framed to forestall.

It is clear that at the turn of the century the situation changed dramatically in women's favour, though still not as much as one might expect, given that already by the mid-1990s the ratio of female to male graduates was 60:40 (Ahmad *et al.*, 2003), and that women were 'generally better performers' in the 1995 PSC recruitment. It may be more accurate to say that the informal female quota has been relaxed rather than that the PSC has become gender-blind overnight.

Turning from gender to race, the PSC did not come near its 20 per cent quota in any of the four years for which we have figures, despite a relevant official's claim that '*Now we are taking between 17 and 19%.*' This was hardly surprising, since only 1.9 per cent and 2.2 per cent of the 350,000 civil service applicants in 2003 were Chinese and Indian respectively (PSC data). A relevant official put that down to '*social belief, economic – most Chinese are not interested to work in government because of pay.*' But Navaratnam, himself an (Indian) ex-Deputy Secretary of the Ministry of Finance, says it is rather because 'most non-Malays are discouraged to apply ... believing it will be a waste of time' (2003, p.633). Be that as it may, one can see why one relevant source declared an objective '*to increase the non-Malay intake,*' including through advertisements in non-Malay newspapers, (although another said there was '*no specific programme to encourage (them) to apply*'). One can also see why, contrary to our expectation, non-Bumiputera informants in two separate interviews supported the constitutional quota, seeing it as a buoyancy aid that would stop non-Bumiputera representation from sinking without trace rather than a weight belt that would stop them from rising too far. In fact those few non-Bumiputeras who did apply were disproportionately likely to be appointed, forming 12 per cent of appointees from a pool of only 2 per cent of overall applicants.

At the higher promotion levels, interviewees confirmed that the allocation of top positions reported by Crouch for 1989 has not changed.

There is still an *'unspoken rule about who will be secretary-generals'*. Moreover, there are *'sensitive'* ministries such as Education, Home Affairs and Rural Development, central to Bumiputera interests, which may be even less favourable to non-Malays. PSD is one of them, as it is in charge of civil service promotions, which are a central plank in the edifice of affirmative action.

So the government continues to promote the Bumiputera interest in public employment through social engineering, with PSC and PSD doing their bit in 'balancing the races (and also the sexes) ... a crucial role in the development of contemporary Malaysia' (Wu, 1990, p.84). But apart from the impact on efficiency, it has been too successful for its own good, and now finds itself in the slightly embarrassing position of beckoning the same non-Malay applicants with one hand that it had previously waved away with the other.

Improving HRM in the Malaysian Civil Service

Based on the evidence reported here, we suggest that relative to the other countries studied in this book, we can characterize HRM in the Malaysian civil service as genuinely performance-orientated, though that is in tension with the government's affirmative action programme, which means that the best person is not always preferred; quite strategic, given strong central strategic agencies and the apparatus of strategic management, even though that does not extend fully to HRM; highly centralized; and with partial evidence of normative models in activities like employee selection.

In the light of that characterization, what might be the priorities for improvement? One very senior interviewee, referring to a wide-ranging report written by two American academics in the mid-1960s (Montgomery and Esman, 1966), pointed out that *'Every respectable conglomerate has a review every 10 years something, our last was the Montgomery report. We never had one since.'* Something equally broad would be desirable in Malaysia, consolidating the piecemeal reforms of the last 20 years. Perhaps South Africa's Presidential Review Commission (Government of South Africa, 1998) offers a recent model. Pending such a review, our priorities are as follows.

Strategic integration. Government should extend its strategic approach to the way it manages its staff. Like many organizations, the government is not aware of the way in which HR can be a strategic lever, facilitating the achievement of its objectives. The central agencies – Finance, MAMPU, PSD, PSC and INTAN – should join forces to ensure that there is a consistent strategic approach across the key HR activities of employee selection, pay, performance management and training.

Line manager ownership. We have noted that centralized management of HR is a constraint on strategic integration. We have also noted that there is little pressure from departments in this top-down managed system for further delegation, and that there is some fear of favouritism increasing if departments make their own decisions. But we judge that there is scope for further delegation. It could be done on a pilot basis initially. Doing even this much would probably require the personal authority of the prime minister, vital in this power-distant society. The example of staffing devolution in the British civil service, whose influence remains strong, might also count for something. However, it must be admitted that it is over 20 years since the UK delegated staffing authority. Malaysia has adopted other British initiatives, such as citizen's charters, but not this one.

Employee selection. It is likely that the PSC's current predominantly examination-based approach has a weak predictive validity: good candidates are probably rejected and poor ones selected. Subject to recommendations we make under other headings, the PSC should dramatically extend its use of psychometric selection methods such as verbal critical reasoning tests.

Performance management. An outsider cannot help but feel that the government could have avoided getting into its well-intentioned muddle if it had used a consultant or other expert from outside the civil service to advise on scheme design and implementation. At the time of writing, the government had already taken some remedial action. But starting from where the government was, the priorities would seem to be: liaison between Finance and PSD to ensure that the quota for merit awards is both affordable and in line with the staff expectation that the government has helped to create; simplifying the assessment process as far as possible; and improving managers' conduct of performance assessment by providing training and briefing.

Affirmative action. This is a sensitive topic where suggestions can easily be misconstrued. However, we agree with Case that there is 'scope to innovate within the parameters of cultural familiarity'. Malaysia is now a very stable society in which Bumiputeras are the clear majority and have a strong grip on political power. Some of what was intolerable in the fearful atmosphere of May 1969 may be tolerable today, and the accession of Prime Minister Badawi may provide the opportunity for an initiative. On one hand, the 30 years since the NEP have not been enough to end the relative disadvantage of Bumiputeras.

On the other, advantaged communities still have disadvantaged members, including those Indians who still live in what one interviewee called the *'green ghettos'* of plantations; and there is the view held by many that affirmative action has been a brake on public sector efficiency.

In the long term, the government should consider moving from a strategy of affirmative action to a more nuanced strategy of social inclusion, targeting disadvantage in terms of income rather than ethnic group membership. It should switch from its quota model, originally modelled on the system designed at independence in India to advance disadvantaged castes, to an anti-discrimination, equal opportunities model. Crucially, this would outlaw discrimination *at the point of selection*. It would no longer be possible to set quotas, formal or otherwise, for recruitment of men, women or ethnic groups. This is important because it is discrimination at the point of selection that lowers the quality of entrants to the public service, and in consequence the quality of service to the public. Such a law would still allow special training of other measures stopping short of the point of selection.

We do not underestimate the challenge this will pose to the government, both politically and constitutionally: an amendment to the Constitution will be needed, and it will require the assent of the Conference of Rulers (Article 38, 5). A period of public education and consultation, and a phased implementation, would be necessary.

Discussion: path dependence and history in the Malaysian Civil Service

How much mileage is there in a path dependence explanation of HRM in the Malaysian government? The plausible candidate for 'critical juncture' is the formation of the civil service under the British. It cemented a British administrative structure for the civil service; a British orientation that was still evident in the 1990s with the adoption of 'citizen's charters' and Total Quality Management; and the central role that the civil service was going to play in 'the bargain', of which the recruitment quota is the visible expression. A factitious precision could even pinpoint the establishment in 1954 of the Federal Establishment Office, PSD's precursor, as a key date. It is in keeping with the path dependence view that we cannot regard either independence or the NEP period which followed the May 13 riots as a critical juncture, dramatic though they undoubtedly were. The civil service structure was already solid enough – sufficiently 'locked in' – to ride out those two episodes, which we can therefore discount in the same way that Putnam discounted the *Risorgimento* and Mahoney discounted Bolivar; we must be a little Olympian too. For the foreseeable future, we are likely to see only 'normal governance' in the basic structure of government. That matters because the structure militates against devolution and line manager ownership. The affirmative action measures are less stable – they have their critics, especially and naturally among the non-Malays – but not very much less. Granted, the path that followed this 'critical juncture' has been much shorter than the corresponding one in Latin America, but then Malaysia's colonial experience and independence alike are hugely more recent than Latin America's, let alone Italy's continuous political development over a millennium and more.

In other ways, though, path dependence as applied to Malaysia entails a reductive emphasis on a single cause that requires us to ignore five contributory factors that we have identified: the pervasive respect for authority, rooted in royal history but reinforced by British administrative culture; Malaysia's ethnic make-up, the consequence of British importation of Chinese and Indian labourers; the stable and buoyant economy; the National Development Policy of 1990; and the personal role of former Prime Minister Mahathir Mohamad.

Justifying their importance is necessarily an exercise in counterfactual history (Ferguson, 1997): how would things have been different without them? Without the respect for authority, Malaysia would have been a less stable country, and harder to govern. Mahathir would have had less room to manoeuvre, Malaysia resembling Britain in its willingness to vest considerable authority in its prime ministers.[10] Without the ethnic mix, with the Malays becoming a disadvantaged majority in what they tended to see as *their* country, Malaysia would have had no more need for the paraphernalia of quotas and the whole NEP than monoethnic Swaziland. Without the healthy economy, civil servants would have earned less and probably been less efficient and honest: we know from World Bank research and from common sense that there is a correlation between wage levels and 'moonlighting' (Van der Gaag *et al.*, 1989); the government would have had less money for initiatives like Citizen's Charters; and it might have found itself carrying out civil service reform Washington-style, attempting to reduce civil service numbers just as ineffectually as most countries that followed the World Bank model in the 1980s and 90s (see Chapter 2). Without the National Development Policy, the civil service would have retained its predominance in national life. Finally, and whether or not he was 'more acted upon than acting', like Braudel's Philip II of Spain (1973, p.19), it seems reasonable to accept that Malaysia without Mahathir would have been a very different place.

As we have seen, the path dependence view entails indifference to the 'normal governance' that occurs between 'junctures'. Yet even if we take the formation of the civil service as the operative juncture, who will maintain that nothing significant has happened in the following half-century? Our judgement is that the five factors above, taken together, count for a great deal. Thanks to them, the civil service has expanded out of recognition, swollen and then shrunk in prestige, become feminized, remained relatively honest and, in Evans, Jomo and Sarji's analysis at least, contributed crucially to Malaysia's economic success – to mention only factors that we have discussed in this chapter. All this has happened while the civil service in so many developing countries has gone backwards. Study groups would not be beating a path to Kuala Lumpur to visit the civil service as it was in 1960. Moreover, agency has mattered a great deal, and not only at the putative 'critical juncture', even if Mahathir's personal authority was affected by long run factors of which he himself was the product, such as the need to appease the Malay majority.

There is indeed a sense in which the consolidation of the civil service in the early 1950s placed Malaysia on a path from which it has not deviated. Counter-intuitively, but echoing Putnam and Mahoney, the difference that independence made was more apparent than real. But that is not the whole story. First, the 'critical juncture' has its own roots in Malaysia's social history. Second, there have been cumulative 'Darwinian' developments in the *content* of civil service management in which the agency of Prime Minister Mahathir was significant, and they have changed the civil service out of recognition. Third, if the *structure* has stayed the same, that is not only because government has invested in it and gained increasing returns, but because many would think it appropriate if it was introduced today for the first time. In this 'power distant' and highly centralized country, there was no appetite even in line departments for structural reform: *'Level of delegation is appropriate, despite the problems'* was a typical interviewee response. In short, path dependence as applied to Malaysia requires a reductive and doctrinaire insistence on structure stability at the expense of content innovation, and in the end the mainstream historical view of Braudel and others carries greater explanatory force than the path dependence view.

Thus when we apply it to Malaysia, path dependence as a *political* explanation[11] is most convincing where it is (unconsciously) most derivative and least convincing where it is (self-consciously) most original. Its stress on using the often very remote past to explain the present has been helpful to development scholars, and development actors even more, living as we all tend to do in a perpetual and voluntarist present; but in its essentials it mostly recapitulates Braudel and others, and its emphasis on decisive critical junctures makes it simply the latest in a long line, however distinguished its members, of reductive single-cause explanations. In short, past dependence, yes; path dependence, no.

Conclusion: history and governance

The new emphasis on history which we owe to path dependence has the positive value of according developing countries the dignity of a history. It was as recently as 1965 that the Regius Professor of Modern History at Oxford felt able to remark that Africa has no history, merely 'the unrewarding gyrations of barbarous tribes in picturesque but irrelevant corners of the globe' (Trevor-Roper, quoted in Evans, 1997, p.178). It is, moreover, a history that we must reckon with, since 'History cannot be swept clean like a blackboard' (Said, 2003, p.xiii). For vulnerable countries, possibly including Iraq at the time of writing, history is a bulwark against the grandiose schemes of self-styled builders of democracy and other false friends.[12]

But there is also a negative implication. Template models of 'good practice', including the SHRM model on which we have focused in this book, will only prevail if they go with the grain of a country's history. This increases the difficulty of reform initiatives that were difficult enough to begin with. Yet 'things and actions are what they are, and their consequences will be what they will be; why then should we seek to be deceived?' (Bishop Butler, quoted in Berlin, 1978, p.1). It is the job of scholars to find a way of showing policymakers how an understanding of history can be an asset. We can do that through helping them to recognize when it is time to cut their losses, but also through increasing the likelihood that policy initiatives such as the Millennium Development Goals – on which we focus in our next chapter – will bear fruit.

As usual, we caution against reading too much into a single case. But the lasting value of path dependence may well lie in directing our attention to the way in which history shapes and constrains the options of policymakers. Clark and Rowlinson (2004) have argued the need for a 'historical turn' in business studies, and it is now time for history to join the other social sciences in order to enhance the study and practice of governance and of development policy at large. We should show our gratitude to the pioneers – David, Arthur, North, Putnam, Collier and Collier, and Mahoney – by capitalizing on their discoveries in order to enhance design of development programmes, and not least of programmes for the reform of public staff management.

9
Namibia: The Human Resource Crisis in Health in Africa

Institutional and HR capacity in health

Readers for whom the last few chapters have wafted away into strato-spheric clouds of political and historical speculation will be relieved that our final case study brings us down with a bump to an intensely practical issue in the governance of developing countries: promoting the health of their citizens. In earlier chapters we explored the extent to which governments are practising 'strategic' HRM, which we defined in Chapter 1 as the integration of the activities of staff management with government's overall strategic objectives (and also with each other). What could be more strategic than a national target for reduc-ing maternal mortality by three-quarters? For that, along with ambi-tious targets for child mortality and disease reduction, is what Namibia and all the other governments of the world committed themselves to when they signed the United Nations' Millennium Declaration in September 2000. Reducing child and maternal mortality by 2015, and also the deadly diseases of HIV/AIDS, malaria and TB, is the thrust of three of the eight 'Millennium Development Goals' (MDGs). The Millennium Declaration represents a new direction for development thinking, departing from the 'big private sector and small state' model that was dominant in the 1980s and for most of the 1990s, and whose staffing expression was the 'downsizing' model of reform which we dis-cussed in Chapter 2.

Nevertheless, five years on from the Declaration, the UN's own status report showed that little progress on the health Goals had been made in sub-Saharan Africa. Rates of child and maternal mortality, and like-wise malaria and TB infection, all remained stubbornly high – the TB rate was actually increasing. With measles immunization rates staying low and a HIV/AIDS infection rate that was stabilizing but not falling (which in practice meant a growing number of people succumbing to full-blown AIDS), sub-Saharan Africa was worse off than anywhere else in the world.

The causes are beyond the scope of this chapter. But it is clear that national governments will have to play the leading role in any solution. The 'small state' which has divested or privatized many of its functions is unequal to the task. In fact the need for governments to take a lead, particularly in the fight against HIV/AIDS, is the very first argument that Francis Fukuyama (2004) advances in his recent book *State Building* to persuade his readers that the state is fundamentally a good rather than a bad thing, and that our priority should be to strengthen the capacity of weak states rather than cut strong but predatory ones down to size. Treating AIDS, Fukuyama points out, requires a robust public health infrastructure and comprehensive public education. Even if poor countries need help to tackle the problem, they also need institutional capacity of their own, if for no other reason than to channel the resources that might come from outside.

It is also clear – to come now to the point of this chapter – that the way governments manage their health workers is an important part of their institutional capacity. While the budgetary imperative to rein back spending on staff hasn't gone away, we have started to hear a different story in the health sphere from the downsizing narrative that was the subject of Chapter 2, a story about the positive contribution of health workers to public health, rather than their negative drain on public expenditure. For example, we have realized that the more doctors, nurses and midwives there are, the lower maternal, infant and child mortality rates will be (Anand and Baernighausen, 2003; Khaleghian and Gupta, 2005).

Yet despite what we know about the potential contribution of health workers, their actual contribution is woeful. One reason why sub-Saharan Africa is so far from meeting the health MDGs[1] is that while Africa is estimated to have 25 per cent of the world's diseases, it has only 1.3 per cent of its health staff. Despite dramatic scaling-up of plans – Malawi, to take one example, was planning as we wrote for a twenty-fold increase in Anti-Retroviral Therapy (ART), a crucial component of AIDS treatment – the World Health Organization (WHO) was obliged to admit that it would not reach its own '3 by 5' target of giving AIDS drugs to three million people in developing countries by the end of 2005, and staff shortage was again one of the reasons it gave (Allen, 2005). Botswana's estimate that introducing

ART would require 29 and 8 per cent more doctors and nurses than it already had – and no fewer than 179 per cent more pharmacists – gives an idea of the size of the HR task (De Korte *et al.*, 2004).

It was against this background that Dovlo (2004) proposed equipping 'mid-level cadres' to do the work of high-level staff who are at a premium, and Wyss (2004) proposed the following in his review of the HR implications of the MDGs:

- Recruit more staff from underrepresented groups and regions
- Distribute staff better across rural and urban areas
- Improve performance management
- Improve training
- Improve the policy framework

However, the reality is that while demand for health staff is increasing, the supply is decreasing, and will decrease further if current trends continue. One reason is the 'brain drain' of skilled staff going abroad or moving from the public to the private sector (High-level Forum on the Health MDGs, 2005). The OECD estimated in 2002 that no fewer than six out of every hundred health workers in the UK were South Africans (OECD, 2002). What point was there, for example, in South Africa planning to create 12,000 new health posts when it already had 29,000 that it couldn't fill? Moreover, health worker numbers in Africa have often not kept up with population growth, not least because of the cutbacks on staffing of the type discussed in Chapter 2, which often do not distinguish between health staff and staff in other government activities which are less of a priority and where there might still be scope for reducing numbers.

The Namibian health service

We chose Namibia for our case study of HR in health because its health service is seen as having done well in providing basic public health facilities and managing its staff, reflected in health indicators that are relatively good in regional terms. In some ways it is not a typical sub-Saharan country. The World Bank classifies it as upper-middle income, largely because of its mineral wealth, and it has a small population of just under two million despite its large area, much of which is desert. Roads and other parts of the infrastructure are very good. But in other ways it is typical. As we saw in Chapter 1,

Namibia's human development rating is low, partly because the health of a large section of the population is closer to poorer countries in Africa than national averages suggest. That in turn reflects the apartheid legacy of income inequality and a skewed provision of services. There are also serious gaps in the health infrastructure. Namibia is one of six African countries which have no graduate medical school, so doctors have to be trained or imported (JLI, 2004). At ministry level there are vestiges of top-down management and bureaucratic habits, partly again a result of *'Inheritance from the apartheid days ... After independence the old bureaucrats indoctrinated the new people'*, but also of sheer *'inertia'*.

But the most alarming thing that Namibia has in common with its neighbours is the level of HIV/AIDS and TB infection. In 2003 it was estimated that 210,000 people were living with HIV/AIDS, more than one in ten of the population; only Namibia's southern African neighbours – Botswana, Lesotho, South Africa and Swaziland – had higher rates (UNAIDS, 2004). Knock-on effects included HIV infection of health workers, with prevalence among ante-natal attendants of 8.4 per cent as early as the mid-1990s. The TB infection rate, at 676 for every 100,000 people, was the highest in the world. Moreover, over 45 per cent of TB sufferers were also HIV positive, as TB is the most serious of the opportunistic infections to which HIV carriers are liable to fall victim. As a result, life expectancy, which had been 60 years in 1991, had dropped to 42 by 2002.

Even the relatively sound health infrastructure creaks under the weight of these problems. Focus groups which we conducted with hospital and clinic staff in both the capital and a district headquarters showed that as well as heroic dedication, staff are often exhausted and demoralized:

> *You get so demotivated because you're doing the same thing all the time, but have no time to ask patients if they are really OK. In the old days – five years ago – TB patients were healthy, just needing medication once a day. Now they need to be bathed, turned ...*[2]

The precipitous rise in HIV/AIDS and TB has created a dilemma in health strategy and staffing. Unlike some other countries in the region, Namibia has made steady progress in realizing a long-term strategic vision for health care, as we shall see. But its relatively settled structure, an achievement that should not be taken for granted, is now in tension with the need for an urgent response which matches the scale of the HIV and TB crisis. That tension is one of the principal themes of this chapter.

Interview findings

Interview details

In this chapter we descend not only from the theoretical to the practical, but also from the level of government as a whole to the level of a single government ministry, the Ministry of Health. We take, as it were, a vertical rather than a horizontal slice out of the structure of government, gathering data from the Ministry's headquarters, but also from the central ministries that are 'above' them and from hospitals, clinics and a regional headquarters that are 'below'. Twenty-two interviews were held in May and June 2005. The people we interviewed, identified by current and former HR staff in the Ministry of Health and Social Services as carrying a key responsibility for the design of operation of HRM systems, were as follows:

- Two officials in the Department of Public Service Management in the Office of the Prime Minister
- Three officials in the Department of State Accounts in the Ministry of Finance
- Deputy Minister and the Permanent Secretary of the Ministry of Health and Social Services
- The Under Secretary of the Department of Policy Development and Resource Management, the Department responsible for HR in the Ministry of Health)
- Three current and former officials in the above Department
- Staff involved in health training programmes in the University of Namibia
- Staff in the National Health Training Centre, both central and regional
- Managers in a regional health administration
- Managers at Katatura hospital, Windhoek
- Staff in the (USAID-funded) Centers for Disease Control (CDC)
- Staff in two other international agencies active in the health field

We also ran three focus groups of more junior staff at a central hospital and two clinics, one in the capital and one in a regional headquarters.

Strategic human resource management

One of the most successful features of the Namibian health service is that it is a relatively well integrated system, not only within the Ministry of Health but across government as a whole, as Figure 9.1 shows.

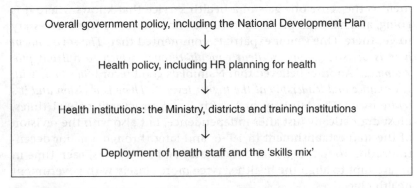

Figure 9.1 The integrated system of health provision

The foundation document is Namibia's 'Vision 2030' (Government of Namibia, 1998). It is not unique to Namibia: it derives ultimately from Malaysia's well-known 'Vision 2020', referred to in Chapter 8, and both Botswana and Lesotho in the region have versions of their own. One level below it is the National Development Plan process; Namibia is now in the period of its second Plan (2001-06). One level below that again is health policy. The basic framework was laid down at the time of independence in *Towards achieving health for all Namibians: A policy statement* (1990), which the government reviewed in 1997. The thrust of health policy is reflected in the five-year *Human resource strategic plan 2000/1–2004/5*. There is also a 'Public Service Charter' for government as a whole, modelled on the 'Charter for the Public Service in Africa' (in which Namibia played a leading role) and ultimately on the UK's 'Citizen's Charters'. It sets out standards of behaviour, including courtesy to clients, to which public servants should cleave. One can find written evidence of what we called 'strategic integration' in Chapter 1: HR issues do get addressed in the context of strategic programmes. There are, for example, sections on HR in both the *National strategic plan on HIV/AIDS 2004–2009* and the *Guidelines for the prevention of mother-to-child transmission of HIV (PMTC)*.

Such documents have their limitations. We noted in Chapter 1 that experts on strategic management and project planning like Mintzberg and Korten have long emphasized that it is the quality of strategic thinking, rather than the content of strategic documents, which have a short shelf-life, that is crucial. The full 30-year HR Plan, for example, was never finalized because of a ministry restructuring which overtook it. However, what is more important than any particular policy document is the sense one gets of a health service that knows where it is going, and has been prepared to revise and restructure when necessary to get there. One senior expatriate commented that *'The environment here is decisive ... an excellent conduit through which to roll out programmes.'* Another believed that Namibia's good record *'has to do with governance and leadership at the higher level ... There is a vision and it's really used.'* The Ministry of Health has restructured several times, most dramatically just after independence, but also with the revision of the staff establishment in 1996, and later through a major decentralization to four regional directorates and 13 regions, each time in an attempt to align the health service more closely with government health objectives.

However, Namibia's relatively strong strategic framework still had one fundamental deficiency. The *National Strategic Plan on HIV/AIDS*, contained no estimate of the current level of HIV infection, despite being two hundred pages long and covering every relevant area of government activity; and, crucially, it stopped short of setting a target for reducing infection rates, or of showing how its literally hundreds of proposed activities would reduce the number of people who were infected or who would die. In the public management jargon, those activities were 'outputs' rather than 'outcomes', means rather than ends (McCourt, 2001d).[3] When only eight months later the government did set the target which the standard format for applications to the Global Fund to Fight AIDS, Tuberculosis and Malaria required (Global Fund, 2004), it was the modest one of reducing HIV prevalence among 'younger age groups' by 5 per cent over the five years of the project – which at best would reduce overall prevalence from 10 per cent to 9.5 per cent of the population.

The government's reluctance to offer up an ambitious target as a hostage to fortune is understandable, especially when it needed to keep a lid on public spending at the same time. After all, even the much admired New Zealand government of the late 1990s fought shy of setting outcome targets. The Labour government elected in 1997 in the UK did set itself no fewer than 600 such targets in a mood of post-election euphoria; the responsible minister was prescient enough to describe them as '600 rods for our own back' at the press launch in 1999 (McCourt, 2001d).

But the Namibian government's reluctance meant that its actions would almost certainly not rise to the scale of the problem. It also meant that the donors, and particularly American donors in whose aid strategies the HIV/AIDS campaign is a central plank, were in the strange position of displaying a greater sense of urgency towards Namibia's health problems than Namibia's own government, and of trying to persuade the government to speed up its response, even if that meant cutting across the well established health strategy. Thus arose the tension between long- and short-term priorities to which we have already alluded, and to which we will return.

HR at government and ministry level

The requirement to advertise almost all vacancies externally which comes from the government's commitment to affirmative action (see below), and the deliberate delay in filling vacancies which results from the overall budget deficit (7.5 per cent of GDP in 2003/4) are just two examples of the impact of central government on health staffing. For as long as governments manage their public servants centrally – and we saw in Chapter 3 that they have good as well as bad reasons for doing that – tedious restrictions like these will persist.

At ministry level there was an anachronistic split which no one in the ministry defended between its departments of Human Resource Management and Human Resource Development, with HRM playing the 'clerk of works' role of handling leave forms and other HR housekeeping, and HRD dealing with training, but also taking initiatives such as marketing careers in health to school and college leavers. To some extent strategic tasks fell between the two stools, so that a strategic HR response to health policy objectives tended to come from the policy side rather than the HR side. One informant with experience of both sides said that *'You will find a HR response to HIV/AIDS in the HIV/AIDS division, but not in the HR division. It's usually driven by the programmes.'*

Line manager ownership

Despite central controls, staff management is still more decentralized in Namibia than in any of our other countries. Ministries appoint their own staff up to and including the permanent secretaries who are the official heads of ministries, and it is local staff who make the appointments, with HR staff merely acting as secretaries. Politicians seem to keep out of staff appointments except, of course, the very senior ones that only they can make. Even then, their influence is marked only in *'sensitive'* ministries like Defence. Politicians seem to disagree with their

Sri Lankan counterparts that the only way to get senior officials to implement your policies is to appoint them yourself. On the other hand, there is no sense either of Sri Lanka's ideological divide between politicians and officials.

The central controls that persist were resented most fiercely at the sharp end. If a matron resigns in a district, a senior district officer complained, the request to replace her has to go first to headquarters, then to Finance and OPM (despite OPM's claim that these appointments have been decentralized). Up to three months are lost before the post can even be advertised. At the lowest level, a local health centre manager was beyond resentment: *'We just take what we're given.'*

However, at the other end of the system Finance officials were surprisingly relaxed about giving more power to ministries: *'I'm neutral on corruption as between a centralized and a decentralized system,'* said one of them, who believed that the only way that ministries would ever learn to manage budgets was by being made to. With a move to 'programme budgeting' trailed in the finance minister's 2005 budget speech, it looked likely that ministries would soon have greater freedom – with the notable exception of pay: experience with performance-related pay suggested that devolving pay decisions would create a temptation to indulge or victimize their staff that some managers might not be able to resist.

Employee selection

The driving force behind Namibia's employee selection procedures is affirmative action. As in Malaysia, Namibia's newly independent government inherited a society with a (white) settler community that was richer and better educated than the indigenous majority. However, whereas UMNO in Malaysia was the unapologetic organ of the Malay community, the South West African People's Organization (SWAPO) in Namibia espoused non-racialism and had a small but significant white membership, just like the African National Congress (ANC) in South Africa. It wanted to 'redress the racial balance', but it also wanted to abolish the race discrimination that was apartheid's hateful essence.

Clearly these two desires were contradictory. The Ministry of Health's Personnel Procedures Manual defined affirmative action as

> a process whereby action is taken to end unfair discrimination … without evoking perceptions of reverse discrimination among certain groups.

But the Manual also stated that

Government expects managers to ... consider primarily disadvantaged persons when they recruit new staff members (Ministry of Health and Social Services, 2004, p.89 and p.6 respectively).

It is not clear how 'advantaged persons' could be ruled out without evoking the perception of reverse discrimination. To be sure, the government could only change the composition of the workforce over any politically realistic timescale by preferring relatively unqualified black candidates over white candidates, in a context where whites historically have been better educated than blacks. But doing so drove a coach and horses through the ideology of non-discrimination. Hence the contradiction.

However, Namibian practice was still considerably more transparent than Malaysia's. Remarkably and almost uniquely, the affirmative action imperative meant that posts at every level were open to competition from outside, which led managers to complain that they could not use discretionary promotion as a way of retaining staff. Affirmative action has also produced procedures that are more explicit than in any of the other countries that we discuss in this book. There was written guidance for managers on how to draw up job descriptions, and managers were expected to keep records of their reasons for shortlisting and appointing candidates. Rejected candidates could appeal, and the appeals procedure had sharp teeth: appellants were successful in no fewer than 20 of the 25 appeals brought in 2003/4 across government as a whole (Public Service Commission, 2004). This is in sharp contrast to Swaziland on the opposite side of southern Africa, where we saw in Chapter 6 that internal procedures are so unsatisfactory that the government loses case after case in the courts on issues which could have been resolved internally.

Namibia's procedures do not go beyond what Cook (1998) has called the 'classic trio' of application, shortlisting and interview: there is little if any use of tests or assessment centres. Strictly speaking, what organizational psychologists call a 'validation study' would be needed to demonstrate that these elaborate procedures have made a difference to the quality of staff appointed and the work they do. But we saw in Chapter 1 that experience elsewhere gives us good reasons to believe that they will. Apart from that, transparent procedures like these will tend to increase citizens' confidence in the way government manages its staff on their behalf (World Bank, 1997).

Performance management

Following independence, a performance management scheme which included a performance management pay element was introduced across government as a whole. Assessment by managers was intensive, taking place once a quarter. It was possible for good performers to get two salary increments ('notches') or even three in a single year. However, the scheme foundered in 1998 in a welter of accusations of nepotism: *'The old scheme failed because it was too subjective,'* said one informant; *'friends of bosses got notches'* said another. There were also suggestions of what in Chapter 8 we called 'leniency bias': *'Managers were giving everyone the notch'* because they were *'just afraid to say no'*. The scheme as a whole was seen as *'arbitrary'*, leading to complaints from the powerful trade unions. At the time of our interviews a new 'Performance Management System' was being piloted in the Ministries of Labour and Agriculture after a lapse of seven years. Significantly, the emphasis in the new scheme was on competencies; managers would have no power over pay.

Overall, Namibia's performance management experiments have followed a similar trajectory to those in Mauritius and Malaysia (Chapters 3 and 8): the belated introduction of a scheme with a pay element, intended to introduce the culture of performance, quickly falling foul of particularistic tendencies in the broader society, but also of the sheer inability of managers to deal fairly with staff; and the tentative re-introduction after a cooling-off period of a watered-down scheme which emphasized employee development rather than pay, and which still had to prove its worth.

Training and the health 'skills mix'

Chapter 1 explained our exclusive focus in this book on employee selection and performance management among the various HR activities. In this chapter we abandon that self-denying ordinance in order to discuss staff training, for the simple reason that it is the activity where the most interesting actions have been taken. Like affirmative action in Malaysia (Chapter 8), it is too important to ignore.

The context for our discussion is the mixed fortunes of training in development thinking since the 1960s. In the period between independence and 1990, improving public staff management, 'capacity building' (Hilderbrand, 2002) and even developing public administration became all but synonymous with training public employees once the basic state structures were in place. There were two principal vehicles for this. The first was the national administrative staff colleges like INTAN in Malaysia and MIPAM in Mauritius which newly independent countries set up to provide pre- and in-service training for their civil servants. The second was the overseas scholarship programmes which took up a hefty share of aid agency and government training budgets. All this activity was based on a simple 'skills deficit' premise: developing country governments were seen as underperforming at least in part because their staff lacked skills, and training was seen as *the* way of making up the deficit.

But training has fallen from grace. The training-led model of public staff management began to decay in the late 1980s, for four reasons. The first was the pressure to reduce public spending which resulted from the two oil price shocks of the 1970s; training is notoriously one of the first spending items which organizations everywhere cut when they get in trouble. The second, consequent reason was the absurdity of training new staff at the same time as trying to save money by 'downsizing' the staff that governments already had. The third, insidious reason was the loss of belief in training as a form of development assistance. It had become equated with 'trainingism', just as we saw in Chapter 1 that management became equated with 'managerialism': training as an end in itself, serving the vested interest of training providers and of the trainees who pocketed what they saved from their training allowances (Turner, 1989). When the critique was applied to official UK aid spending on training, it was a convenient pretext for a Conservative government that was happy to see aid spending decline to withdraw almost completely from standalone training (Hulme, 1990).[4] Finally, spending less on training was the opportunity cost of the recognition that training was not the be-all and end-all of public management: to some extent spending migrated to support for programme budgeting, 'results oriented management', performance management and so on. Those who suggested that training could still be effective if it was better targeted and more 'strategic' (such as McCourt and Sola, 1999) were swimming against a powerful tide.

The health service in Namibia has bucked this trend. To understand why, we need first to grasp the concept of what Buchan and Dal Poz have called the 'skills mix': the appropriate mixture of skills and jobs that health services need. For example, they suggest that 'there is unrealized scope ... for extending the use of nursing staff and for further development of care delivery led by nurses/midwives' at the expense of tasks currently done by doctors (2002, p.579).

Namibia's health staffing hierarchy at independence is shown in Figure 9.2.

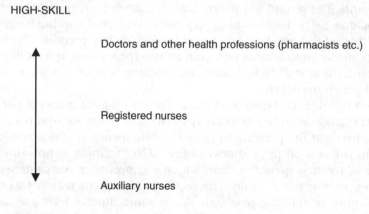

HIGH-SKILL

Doctors and other health professions (pharmacists etc.)

Registered nurses

Auxiliary nurses

LOW-SKILL

Figure 9.2   The pre-independence staffing care structure

This structure created two problems. The first was the skill deficiencies caused by the gaps in the structure. At the top, there was no provision for clinical specialization, and at the bottom, auxiliary nurses were mostly untrained and could not provide specialized care. Throughout the structure there were staff shortages, caused by the delay in providing high-skills training, and also by loss of high-skill staff who were attractive to the private sector, and likewise by movement from rural to urban areas.

The staffing structure at the time of our study after 15 years of independence is shown in Figure 9.3. This structure was the outcome of a large number of separate initiatives. The most impressive was the scheme to upgrade auxiliary nurses to enrolled nurses. Described as a *'milestone'* in Namibian health care, it had its origin in the move to primary health care following independence, and a 1992 report called *Integrated health care delivery: The challenge of implementation*, prepared with support from WHO. The next step was to recognize that a system of 'sub-professional' training was the most relevant and affordable way of supporting national primary health care priorities. Donor support was important, but once again it supported indigenous plans rather than substituting for them. An example of this is that the enrolled nurse training structure was inaugurated with skeleton staff

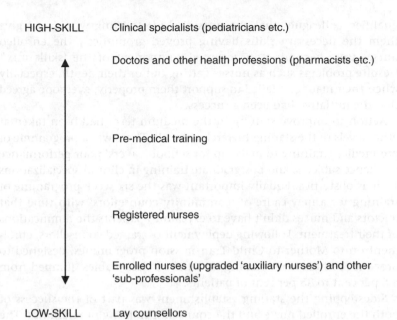

HIGH-SKILL   Clinical specialists (pediatricians etc.)

Doctors and other health professions (pharmacists etc.)

Pre-medical training

Registered nurses

Enrolled nurses (upgraded 'auxiliary nurses') and other 'sub-professionals'

LOW-SKILL   Lay counsellors

Figure 9.3   The current staffing care structure

before donor resources began to flow. Consequently, donor resources were effective through simply adding to a structure that already existed, for example by providing funds for supplementary tutors to be appointed.

A National Health Training Centre was established in Windhoek, with four regional centres around the country, a network described by a donor-funded expatriate as a *'phenomenal resource'*. Its courses had been running long enough at the time of writing for positive results to be evident. There was a very high training completion rate: 97 per cent in one regional centre. In at least one northern district, patient mortality rates improved following enrolled nurse deployment. Staff themselves were entirely positive about the scheme, especially the former auxiliary nurses who were its main beneficiaries: *'It was an eye-opener – we thought we were doing the correct things.' 'Now we can manage the clinic alone, there is more responsibility. Salary-wise, it is better too.'* One worker put the advantages in a homely way: *'You dusted off for the sake of dusting off, now we know why.'* Finally, it was perhaps as positive a sign as any that private clinics and hospitals were willing to employ some of the enrolled nurses themselves. With the fears of better qualified colleagues that the nurses' short training would not give them the necessary skills having proved groundless, the enrolled nurses were becoming an accepted component of the 'skills mix'. Despite problems such as nurses getting out of their depth, especially when their managers failed to support them properly, everyone agreed that the initiative had been a success.

Action to improve staffing in the medium term had been taken at other levels of the staffing hierarchy as well. There was a programme of pre-medical training to make up for school-leavers' poor performance in science subjects, and postgraduate training in clinical specializations such as obstetrics. Equally important was the six-week programme of training for a new cadre of 'community counsellors' with time that doctors and nurses didn't have to explain to patients the ramifications of their treatment. Following deployment of trained counsellors, enrolment on to Mother to Child Transmission programmes, designed to prevent mothers from passing on AIDS to their babies, jumped from 8.5 per cent to 85 per cent of patients.

Sidestepping the staffing establishment was part of the success of both the enrolled nurse and the counsellor training programmes. The point of a staffing establishment is to keep a lid on spending by making it hard for ministries to create posts, but it also makes it hard to respond quickly to a new need. This was avoided by giving trainees the status of students rather than employees so that they would not be part of the establishment. Similarly, the counselling scheme was managed by the Red Cross, and counsellors were formally Red Cross, not government employees.

Altering the 'skills mix' by lowering the fences between the traditional health professions is an example of what has been called 'functional flexibility' in the context of the new SHRM model, as we saw in Chapter 1. It is supported by international evidence that using nurses and care assistants to do what has traditionally been doctors' and nurses' work, is not at the expense of quality of care (Buchan and Dal Poz, 2002; Dovlo, 2004).

These changes aligned staffing much more closely with the health priorities of the new government. This, we suggest, is an example of the Mintzbergian 'strategic thinking' model of strategy rather than the blueprint model. What was crucial was the shared understanding about the need to shift the health system from apartheid provision to provision for all Namibia's citizens, and from curative-based to preventative medicine, a result of the focusing of minds that came with the liberation struggle. Without it, the health service would have been like an anthill when the Queen has been removed, and no strategy document, however elaborate, would have been a substitute.

Discussion: HR and the health crisis

Strategy, urgency and commitment

At the start of this chapter we noted how the MDGs represent a new departure in development thinking, and how public staff management has come to be seen as central to realizing them, especially in health. This chapter has explored what that means in practice for one sub-Saharan country. Namibia has patiently built up a strategic framework for health policy in the context of government policy as a whole, including strong training arrangements at every level of health staffing, and it has brought HIV/AIDS under the strategic umbrella through its National Strategic Plan for HIV/AIDS. The framework is imperfect, but expatriates who know other African countries felt that it works relatively well. Its major weakness is that it has not kept pace with the rise in HIV/AIDS and TB infection: the community counselling service, still at the pilot stage when we did our study, was the only specific response. That is the source of the tension between building long-term capacity in a strategic context and responding to the relatively short-term demands of the AIDS and TB crisis, which we now address.

In a way the tension ought to be a false one, for the crisis has not come out of a clear blue sky: it was as long ago as 1986 that Namibia's first four cases of AIDS were identified. Strategic management is by definition a long-term activity, but the period over which AIDS and the associated rise in TB infection have developed comfortably crosses the strategic time threshold. AIDS and TB have become an urgent issue because it is only very recently that governments in southern Africa, including Namibia's, have begun to follow Uganda's example in being candid with their citizens and then acting decisively (Uganda, as it happens, was the ultimate model for Namibia's counselling programme). As a result, infection rates have been allowed to creep upwards. In Uganda, the percentage of pregnant women attending antenatal clinics who were HIV positive went down from 31 to 14 per cent between 1992 and 1998. In Namibia, it went up from 4.2 to 17.4 per cent over the same period, and by 2002 it had risen further to 22 per cent – and this in a country that is much richer than Uganda, showing that money is only part of the story.

The dilemma that Namibia was facing at the time of writing was to find an adequate response to the particular problems of HIV/AIDS and TB without damaging the strategic framework. On the one hand, policies have succeeded in Namibia as much because of the framework in which they are set as because of the policies themselves. On the other hand, the very solidity of that framework has militated against responding to a pandemic which has no respect for strategic timetables. The picture is complicated by the government's emphasis on the framework being in conflict with donors' emphasis on the problems.

Fundamentally, we suggest, this is a problem of political commitment. It is significant that WHO (2005) believes that the crucial factor in Uganda's success was political commitment. UNAIDS' (2004) global report calls for 'strong leadership and concrete commitment from all sectors of government and society', and it may be equally significant that a whole section is devoted to the same topic in Namibia's AIDS Strategy document. If we apply the model of political commitment that we outlined in Chapter 6 to Namibia, we can see that the 'antecedents' of commitment in the form of political and administrative capacity are present, but that the 'elements' are defective in one important way. While Namibia's commitment to tackling the pandemics is voluntary, explicit and public, it is not challenging: as we saw, no target has been set for reducing the scale of infection.

We do not wish to go over the political ground that we covered in previous chapters. However, we noted in Chapters 2 and 6 that commitment is partly a function of the quality of advice that officials give to politicians. Officials need to propose a realistic target for reducing infection rates, one that takes account of the resources needed, including the human resource.

Relationship with donors

The relationship with donors, touched on in the last section, is a relevant factor. As a relatively wealthy country, Namibia does not rely heavily on donors, who in 2003 provided only 3.4 per cent of GDP (compared to 13.1 per cent in Tanzania). Partly for this reason, Namibia has been successful in ensuring that donors support indigenous priorities: *'When you're not aid-dependent, you can stay in charge.'* High-level meetings with donors were chaired by the minister, and donor proposals were worked on intensively within the ministry at the planning stage, so that pressure to import pet schemes which donors have implemented in other countries was resisted. Despite this, the Namibian side still had to assert itself from time to time. This was especially true, it appeared, in dealing with American donors, who *'can be quite hard to keep under control'*, having domestically generated objectives of their own which cut across the Ministry's – including, according to one senior official, a preference for expensive drugs manufactured by American companies rather than generic substitutes.[5]

From an outside perspective, Namibia sometimes seemed too ready to resent donors suggesting models from other countries. But it is in keeping with our emphasis on indigenous ownership of staff management in Swaziland and Sri Lanka (Chapters 6 and 8), and there was concrete evidence of its value. The Ministry of Health has used its position of strength to face down donors' preference for freestanding projects and to use their support to recruit and train more staff. One example was the 'parallel hiring scheme' run by the American CDC with support from USAID, where additional staff were appointed on the standard ministry terms. At the time of writing 13 doctors, ten nurses, ten pharmacists and ten data clerks had been recruited, and there was approval to go up to 27, 15, 15 and 15 respectively. Similarly, funding from CDC made it possible for the number of nurses trained to increase dramatically from the 50 that the Ministry of Education was prepared to fund to around the 200 that the Ministry believed it needed to train: *'CDC bridged the gap.'*

This style of support incurred a minimum transaction cost in money, time and expertise, because the government's administrative structures already existed. It should not be a surprise that Ministry staff seemed to appreciate it more than any other kind of donor assistance.

Conclusion: towards a new HR paradigm

Once we have noted the importance of resolving the strategic tension between long- and short-run objectives, and the political problem of commitment to a more radical approach to health needs, what HR action should be a priority, both in Namibia and in other countries? At a fundamental level, we suggest that this is a special case of the need for a performance paradigm which is geared to delivering public services rather than to reducing the size of the state, thus departing from the downsizing paradigm which has been dominant for most of the last quarter century: we develop that paradigm in the concluding chapter which follows this one.

In the health context, the priority is to estimate the staffing needed to scale up AIDS and TB provision and move towards the MDGs. There should first be an estimate of how far the current health staffing paradigm can be extended; in other words, how much scope there is to fill more vacancies through additional funding from central government and donors.

However, even with the extra funds that were scheduled to come from the Global Fund, debt relief and other initiatives, countries like Namibia will need a radically different staffing paradigm if they are to go beyond the fudged response that Namibia has made up to now. We saw that Botswana estimated that it would need, among other things, 179 per cent more pharmacists to administer ART. But this was a mechanical and completely unrealistic extrapolation from current arrangements: there are just not enough pharmacists to go around.

What shape might a new paradigm take? It would have to come from within the health system, where the necessary knowledge and the basic ownership of the problem reside. With that proviso, however, it should be accommodated within the basic strategic framework built up over 15 years, which should not be destabilized. Second, it should target middle and lower levels in the staffing hierarchy. African countries find it hard to retain the highly qualified staff whose training is so time-consuming and expensive, and the experience of using what Dovlo has called 'mid-level cadres' to substitute for those staff is positive. It seems appropriate to use job analysis and competence development to identify the precise skills that the new treatments will require, and to provide them to trainees at the lowest possible level, equivalent to Namibia's enrolled nurses and community counsellors. In every African country there is a large pool of unemployed people, notably recent school leavers, who have only basic qualifications. They can be trained quickly and cheaply, their training will not be sophisticated enough for other countries to want to poach them, and they are more likely to have roots in rural and poor areas that will make them want to stay there. There are probably also existing staff like Namibia's auxiliary nurses whose skills can be upgraded. There may also be public employees in low priority areas who can be retrained and redeployed.

Namibia's experience shows that such trainees need professional support and supervision. Staff at higher levels will need to take extra supervisory duties. 137 health staff had successfully completed Certificates in Management up to the time of writing in Namibia. However, the more urgent need is for short, intensive development programmes that will provide management skills that can be used immediately. It is very desirable that there is a performance management framework within which those skills can be used.

We conclude this final case study, therefore, with the possibility of a new paradigm for HR in governments like Namibia's which need to respond to the health crisis, and to move towards the MDGs to which most governments have committed themselves. It is absolutely in keeping with what we know about strategic management that a new strategic direction will mean a new public management and HR approach. It will include the elements that we have focused on in all our case studies: a strategic framework, since governments should proceed from a strategic sense of overall HR needs in the light of national policy objectives; line manager ownership, since lower level and relatively unqualified staff will have greater supervision needs; good employee selection to identify candidates who may lack normal qualification badges of achievement but who have relevant skills and the potential to acquire more; and a system of performance management for managers to supervise and support these new staff. But it is likely to be distinctive in giving pride of place to the deployment and pre-service training of middle- and lower-level health workers: training, which has been out of fashion for 15 years in development management, regains the importance it had in the early independence period. There is also room for creativity in organizational arrangements, just as Namibia has delegated management of its counselling scheme to an NGO, the Red Cross. In our final chapter we will look back at the experience of all the countries we have surveyed in this book in order to look forward to the new policy challenges that are facing developing countries and how the employees of government can help to meet them.

10
Conclusion: Improving HRM in Developing Country Governance

Our central chapters used case studies to explore particular themes which we now review, roughly in the order in which they have arisen in the course of the book, discussing them more broadly than we could in individual chapters.

Strategic human resource management

The SHRM model and its associated HR practices were a theme in all the case studies. Since SHRM is predicated on the existence of a *strategic framework* in the form of a mission statement or similar statement of organizational purpose translated into numerical strategic objectives or a full-fledged business plan, we were interested in whether such a framework existed and the extent to which there was *strategic integration* between it and the way staff were managed. We were also interested in *line manager ownership*, in the form of delegation of staffing authority to line ministries and agencies, and to line managers lower down.

The strategic framework

The strategic management framework is now widely disseminated. Apart from Morocco, the Francophone exception, all the countries we studied have at least the basic apparatus of mission statements. In the majority of cases, however, strategies existed only on paper in central ministries, or in the form of mission statements in line ministries. Underneath them, day-to-day management – Morocco's 'gestion courante' – continued much as before.

Where strategy was real, as it was in Malaysia and Namibia, it made a positive difference. Namibia's success in creating and training a cadre of enrolled nurses was a direct outcome of the national primary health care strategy. Malaysia's 'Vision 2020' led to the creation of central strategic agencies, and to the new prime minister's emphasis on performance indicators.

Two things distinguished Malaysia and Namibia. The first was a shared sense of political purpose. In 'power distant' Malaysia, purpose rained down from above, with the personal leadership of former Prime Minister Mahathir Mohamad being decisive. In Namibia it had a broader base, coming from many politicians' and senior officials' participation in the liberation struggle, and from the policy preparation that took place in that period.

However, Namibia faced a strategic dilemma. Its relatively strategic approach to managing its staff ought to give it an advantage in working towards the MDGs, which in this sense represent the application of strategic management on a global scale, with ambitious outcome targets for maternal mortality and so on. Yet we saw that this global strategy ironically cuts across the national strategy which Namibia has been pursuing with some success since independence, leading to tension between the government and some international donors. The dilemma has its roots in the meta- or political level, in the government's commitment to its established primary health strategy as opposed to a commitment to the health MDGs, or to a concerted effort against AIDS, about which Namibia has shared some of its neighbour South Africa's notorious ambivalence.

The second thing that distinguished Malaysia and Namibia was the capacity of the government machinery: the two governments could be confident that the machine would respond to a touch of the strategic tiller, because the framework of institutions was stable and functioning. Even in those two countries, though, strategy had its limits. Malaysia's framework was a little more apparent than real, as it served a legitimizing function as well as the ostensible substantive one. Namibia's framework in relation to health was more substantial. But even here, its elaborate HIV/AIDS strategy set targets only for activities, not results (in the jargon, output rather than outcome indicators). When the government did set (very modest) result targets, it was to meet the requirements of the Global Fund, rather than out of any spontaneous conviction.

Capacity could be equally notable in its absence. One reason why there was little evidence of strategy in Sri Lanka was that the government felt obliged to give its attention to strengthening basic staffing institutions such as the Public Service Commission. This suggests that there may be a reform sequencing issue: we will return to this point.

Strategic integration

There may also be a reform sequencing issue with strategic integration, the keystone of the SHRM model. The question of integration only arises if an overall strategy already exists. In the countries where strategy was rudimentary at best, namely all but Malaysia and Namibia, it is not surprising that we found little evidence of integration. But even in Malaysia and Namibia, integration was piecemeal. From time to time a policy area would become important – whether TQM in Malaysia or HIV/AIDS in Namibia – and the government would demand a HR response. This is very different from the systematic and comprehensive HR strategy, mirroring overall organizational strategy, that the SHRM literature assumes. Moreover, those piecemeal responses were not usually initiated by the HR function, and might even bypass them completely.

One reason for this that our case chapters did not highlight was the unimaginative rigidity of the HR function. We saw in Chapter 1 that 'strategy expert' is one of the four roles which HR specialists are supposed to play in Ulrich's (1998) widely quoted model, but there was little evidence of it in operation. From the insouciance of the HR official in Mauritius whose response to our question about major HR initiatives was *'Well, have there been any?'* through Morocco's 'finicky' Civil Service Ministry with its consuming interest in enforcing rules, to Sri Lanka, where the head of a line agency told us that *'We don't have any freedom, every aspect comes under the Establishment Code'*, the picture was of a central agency dedicated to policing conformity rather than facilitating performance. Only in Malaysia and Namibia did we have the sense that HR has a role to play in advancing government's strategic objectives.

In all the countries that we studied, HR was a general administrative function which conformed to the 'clerk of works' model of HR that we outlined in Chapter 1. At the time of an earlier study of Sri Lanka (McCourt, 2001a), the most senior official responsible for HR fortuitously had a Masters degree in Human Resource Management. By the time of our interviews in 2004, he had moved on, and his post was again occupied by a general administrator.

With none of the governments in this book taking the fully strategic approach that the textbooks commend, it seems clear that there is something wrong with the strategic model itself. The SHRM literature assumes a systematic and uniform mapping of strategic objectives on to staff management activities. But where strategy occurs, it is much more likely to be piecemeal, as in Malaysia and Namibia: particular HR responses to particular strategic priorities.

The HR literature shows little recognition of such a piecemeal approach, distinct as it is from the 'blueprint' approach which formerly monopolized discussion of strategic management, and which continues to dominate development thinking about strategy in the form of the well-known 'logical framework' technique. But it tallies with the strategic tradition to which we alluded in Chapter 1 and again in Chapter 9 (Lindblom, 1959; Mintzberg, 1989; Korten, 1980). Mindful of the data limitations that managers face, strategy in this tradition is an incremental process in which strategic thinking is more important than the strategic product, continually overtaken by events as that perforce is. A piecemeal approach in which there are particular HR responses to particular strategic priorities is arguably within that tradition.

This approach should not be seen as 'watered-down' strategy: instead, it means thinking strategically, and learning, throughout the strategy process, rather than doing all the thinking at the planning stage, with only minor adjustments thereafter if the strategy slips off track. It also means sensitivity to the political environment, in which party manifestos and government policies may stand for strategic objectives.

Line manager ownership and the institutional framework

Another reason why strategic integration was piecemeal at best in our study countries was the typically centralized but also fragmented structure of HR. Discussing line manager ownership entails discussing the institutional framework of staff management, the focus of Chapter 4, as it represents the formal division of responsibility between government agencies.

Division between central and local

The political argument for devolving responsibility is that local officials make better decisions because local people can shape them and hold officials to account. Yet a review of decentralization experience in several developing countries found that decisions were only properly 'pro-poor' in one region of one country (West Bengal in India), and even there it was because of the commitment of the central state government. Poverty orientation came from the top down rather than the bottom up (Crook and Sverrisson, 2001).

The public management argument for devolution is that line managers make better decisions because they know they will carry the can for their mistakes. As the 1980s report that paved the way for staffing devolution in the UK civil service put it,

> Too much authority is centralised ... this is wrong because it means that decisions are not being taken by those who have to live with them. (Cassels, 1983, p.36)

Yet there is also a view that devolving power to public managers who cannot or will not use it fairly will increase inefficiency and corruption (Schick, 1998).

In most countries all significant decisions were made by the Centre. In the historiographical terms we used in Chapter 8, there was some 'path dependence' here: decisions were centralized in Malaysia, for example, partly because they always had been, and governments had obtained the 'increasing return' of getting used to this way of operating. The effect of political decentralization, where it occurred, was more apparent than real: ostensible decentralization followed by covert recentralization in Sri Lanka, and a reinstatement of local authorities in Tanzania in which central government kept control of staffing decisions.[1]

Central control frustrated some managers, but reassured others. Awareness of bureaucratic pathologies was more often outweighed by the belief that central management was a bulwark against political influence. In a situation where *'Government officers' sound is very low, MPs' sound is very big'*, as a Sri Lankan official put it, only a strong central agency could provide a counterweight to the power of politicians. Sri Lanka was indeed the extreme case, where a constitutional amendment had consolidated the power of the PSC in the centre with strong support from line ministry staff and the trade unions. Crook and Manor (1998) found that while decentralization might initially increase corruption, in the long run it tended to decrease it as local scrutiny began to operate. But in the majority of our countries, civil servants and their unions believed otherwise, at least where staff management was concerned.

The two exceptions to the central control rule were Morocco and Namibia. In Namibia, despite some clawing back of central control in response to a budget squeeze, line ministries could advertise nationally for posts right up to the top, and central officials did not seem to object. Tellingly, the Ministry of Finance was relaxed, and was in fact making plans for further devolution, something that its Swazi counterpart on the other side of southern Africa could not begin to contemplate. In Francophone Morocco, however, it was the line minister who exercised the freedom to appoint, so that the potential for more responsive decision-making was negated by the breach in the separation between politics and administration (see below), with predictable results.

Division between line ministries and local managers

In countries where power is centralized in agencies like the PSC, there is no question of delegation to local managers within a line ministry, although this is the meaning that 'line manager ownership' usually has in the HR literature (see Guest, 1989). Yet even in Namibia, where line ministries do have a great deal of authority, they have passed little of it on to their local managers.

The central/local division of responsibility

We support the Cassels view that staffing decisions should be taken at the level that is affected by them, other things being equal – but other things rarely are. Table 10.1 suggests that staffing devolution will be viable to the extent that four factors have a positive value. The position in Mauritius, Sri Lanka and Namibia conforms to the table. We suggested in Chapter 3 that the arguments for and against devolution in Mauritius are quite finely balanced. Staffing was even more strongly centralized in Sri Lanka than it had been previously, but was relatively decentralized in Namibia. Malaysia, however, does not conform, for reasons we explain below when we discuss the influence of history.

Table 10.1 Factors affecting staffing devolution in Namibia, Mauritius and Sri Lanka

Factor	Mauritius	Sri Lanka	Malaysia	Namibia
How strong is the commitment to political decentralization or deconcentration?	Weak	Weak	Weak	Strong
Are staffing decisions free from political influence?	No	No	Yes	Yes
Is the periphery reasonably efficient relative to the Centre?	No	No	Yes	Yes
Is the periphery at least as fair as the Centre?	Yes	No	Yes	Yes
Is devolution viable?	**Possibly**	**No**	**Yes**	**Yes**

There is still scope for limited devolution even in countries where the position is generally unfavourable. However inefficient or corrupt the periphery might be, it is very hard to defend a position in which a line ministry has to get central permission to change the walking allowance paid to forest guards (as in Mauritius) or the design of official forms (as in Tanzania).

Staffing delegation, where viable, will only be fully effective if accompanied by budgetary delegation and a shift from ex-ante to ex-post controls of both staff and budgets, as one of our Malaysian interviewees suggested. And there is a final caveat: major pay decisions should continue to be made centrally. As we saw in Chapter 9, there was no appetite for devolving pay decisions even in Namibia's relatively devolved structure, given the strength of Namibia's trade unions and the bad experience of performance-related pay in the 1990s.

Divisions at the Centre: balkanization

Binary discussion of whether decisions ought to be central or local has been at the expense of considering where decisions should be made among the different agencies at the centre. In the Commonwealth countries of Mauritius, Tanzania, Swaziland, Sri Lanka and Malaysia, where decisions about all but very junior staff were centralized, responsibility was parcelled out among several agencies, see Table 10.2.

Perhaps because it was overlooked in the decentralization debate, this institutional settlement was very stable, having either remained intact (Mauritius and Malaysia), or re-emerged after flirtation with other models (Tanzania and Sri Lanka). But it created a balkanized or *'fragmented'* structure – to use a Mauritian Permanent Secretary's term –

Table 10.2   Responsibility for HR in central government agencies (Commonwealth model)

Agency	Functions
Office of the Prime Minister	overall government policy
Ministry of Finance	pay and pensions
Ministry for the Civil Service	deployment and conditions of service for public servants
Public Service Commission	appointment, promotion, transfer and discipline
National Administrative Staff College	training and development

which made strategic integration all but impossible, as each agency had its own priorities; especially so with the Commonwealth PSCs whose role was fixed by the national constitution. At a more basic level, fragmentation meant duplication of functions, as we saw in Tanzania.

Divisions at the Centre: politics and administration

In Tanzania and Swaziland the position was further complicated by the superimposed final authority of the president, prime minister or king, whether formal or informal. Chapters 4 and 6 indicated the problem that this created: the justified perception that staffing decisions would be secretive and arbitrary, and that civil servants' only effective right of appeal was outside the civil service, through the courts or the public ombudsman. The fact that Sri Lanka has gone to so much trouble to take this arbitrary power away from the politicians reinforces our argument in Chapters 4 and 6 that Tanzania and Swaziland ought to do the same, and that in this instance the public administration orthodoxy enjoining a strict separation between politics and administration is correct. However, in Chapter 7 we also saw that governments like Sri Lanka's and Tanzania's which deliberately politicized the civil service in the 1960s and 70s did so with the perfectly proper intention of transforming an aloof colonial civil service into one that would respond to development objectives. There will be little gain if restoring civil service independence just means reinstating the colonial aloofness, which politicians in any case may no more tolerate than they did in earlier years. The civil service must be politically independent, but also responsive to political objectives.

Downsizing and employment reform

It is appropriate to deal with this issue in the context of strategy, as one of Chapter 2's major conclusions was that employment reform needs to be approached in a strategic context. Certainly we found that there are emergency measures that some governments should take to cut costs and 'stop the bleeding', notably the elimination of 'ghost workers'; following Arogyaswamy *et al.* (1995), these are 'Stage One' of recovery. But we also found that in the private and public sectors of both industrialized and developing countries, downsizing programmes were only sustained when they were part of a recovery strategy (Stage Two of recovery). The empirical experience suggests that it is every bit as important to have strategic integration between overall government or agency strategy and downsizing as the literature tells us it is between strategy and the other HR activities like recruitment and selection.

Strategy is the meso-level in the governance model that we presented in Chapter 1 (Table 1.2). But the micro-level is also important. In a strong strategic framework, it is still important to consider management issues such as the desirability of focusing on cost savings rather than on reducing the number of jobs, since focusing on numbers may not deliver savings, and it will be regressive if lower-paid staff are disproportionately affected. Similarly, it is usually better to design a package for the victims of downsizing that puts cash in their hands rather than enrol them in elaborate but ineffectual retraining and employment schemes.

Table 10.3 is a summary of our findings on SHRM and associated HR practices.

Other HR activities: employee selection and performance management

We prioritized these activities so that we could explore them in detail, hoping that they would stand for the other activities that space obliged us to exclude (although we broke our own rule in Chapters 8 and 9, where we discussed affirmative action and training respectively).

Employee selection

We found three approaches here. The dominant one was the Commonwealth PSC approach, where following public advertising, a central agency acting on line agencies' behalf conducts academic-style examinations which lead to rigidly structured interviews at the end of which applicants are scored. Only in this last respect is the approach in line with professional 'good practice'. However, although this dispensation allowed Malaysia to operate a covert gender quota and flout the official race quota over many years, it is still relatively transparent, as shown by the support that public service trade unions tend to give it, even in Mauritius where the PSC has been a political football.

The second approach was Morocco's, where ministries could do as they pleased, allowing some to increase transparency, but others to fall prey to nepotism. This has led to an unlikely convergence between the trade union side and the World Bank, with both advocating a move to something like the Commonwealth PSC model, where recruitment would be centralized in a politically independent agency.

The third approach was Namibia's, where despite the government having impaled itself on the horns of an affirmative action dilemma, practice was transparent and decentralized, with ministries making

Table 10.3 Human resource management in study governments: summary findings

Country	Strategic HRM				HR activities	
	Strategy	Strategic integration	Line manager ownership	Employee selection	Performance management	Other
Mauritius	Mission statements only	None	Centralized	Politicized PSC open to nepotism; unskillful	PRP floated in 1987; new scheme piloted in 2004	
Tanzania	At ministry level only; donor-driven	None	Centralized	CSC under Presidential control	PA a 'dead letter'	
Morocco	Policies but not strategy	'clerk of works' HR	Ministries have power but don't delegate	Merit-based at middle level; some movement towards merit	Confidential reports; PA initiatives in some ministries	Downsizing launched in 2005
Swaziland	National Development Strategy with little momentum	None	Centralized	CSB under Prime Minister's control	Confidential reports: piloted scheme not adopted	
Sri Lanka	Mission statements only, except in donor-driven areas	None	Recentralization under PSC to combat patronage	Inflexible procedure to contain patronage	PA moribund; seniority promotion	

Table 10.3 Human resource management in study governments: summary findings – *continued*

Country	Strategic HRM				HR activities		
	Strategy	Strategic integration	Line manager ownership	Employee selection	Performance management		Other
Malaysia	Strong framework; piecemeal strategy	'Piecemeal integration'	Central control supporting affirmative action	Efficient, though affected by affirmative action	PRP scheme watered down; exam assessment		Affirmative action central to staff management
Namibia	Strong framework and strategic thinking; weak targets	'Piecemeal integration'	Line ministries in control, except over pay	Elaborate, driven by affirmative action	PRP scheme abandoned; new pilot scheme		Affirmative action is central; training and the 'skills mix'

their own appointments right up to Permanent Secretary, and the PSC acting as an aggressive watchdog in relation to appeals. Practice was also relatively skilful, with explicit procedures and guidance for recruiters to follow. However, it still did not go beyond traditional selection methods, with little use being made of tests or assessment centres.

Most of the energy devoted to employee selection has gone into increasing its transparency rather than its quality, or, to put it another way, into its institutional rather than professional dimension, even when the former has been at the expense of the latter. Sri Lanka's experience highlights this. In re-establishing the PSC as an independent constitutional body, the government opted to make integrity its exclusive objective. The system was less efficient than before; sophisticated selection methods were ruled out; but the civil service unions and most central officials considered this an acceptable price to pay.

Performance management

The starting point for all the countries discussed in this book, both Anglophone and Francophone, is what Commonwealth countries call the 'annual confidential report'. Since in reality it is no more than what a Mauritian report called an 'annual ritual', every country has attempted to replace it with some form of performance management. Moroccan and Sri Lankan officials were politically astute enough to introduce a simple scheme whose modest objective was to get managers to recognize their responsibility for staff performance, even if the schemes failed to stick because managers were unfamiliar with them and because political support was weak. Those officials were acting, unconsciously or otherwise, on the recognition, embodied in the HR and performance debate that we outlined in Chapter 1, that the ultimate role of staff management is to contribute to organizational performance. In a sense Mauritius, Malaysia and Namibia were taking that recognition to its logical conclusion when they introduced schemes which included a performance-related pay (PRP) element, modelled on the experience of influential governments like New Zealand's and the UK's. But because they were not aware of the negative aspects of that experience, they ended up repeating or even compounding those governments' mistakes, and also running into political difficulty in the shape of civil service union hostility.

So in Chapter 9 we said that Namibia's experiments with performance management took it down the bumpy trail blazed by Mauritius and Malaysia: the belated introduction of a scheme with a pay element that was intended to introduce the culture of performance, but which quickly succumbed to particularistic tendencies in the broader society, and also to the sheer inability of managers to deal fairly with staff; followed after a cooling-off period by the tentative re-introduction of a diluted scheme which emphasized employee development rather than pay but which had still to prove its worth. All three governments at the time of our research were still trying to rebuild the political capital which the earlier experiments had depleted. Their experiments had ironically made it harder to create a culture of performance.

A two-stage normative model of HRM

To say in the light of our cases that different countries will have different priorities might be true, but does not take us far. We think we can derive a model from our findings which accommodates country differences (Table 10.4). It is a normative model in that we cannot read off priorities for any individual country. Its two-stage structure derives from Arogyaswamy *et al.*'s corporate recovery model which we adopted in Chapter 2.[2]

The model accommodates both the countries that need to concentrate on the integrity of staffing and the institutional framework that will promote it (in our view, Swaziland, Tanzania, Morocco and Sri Lanka) and countries where lapses of integrity are exceptional rather than systemic, and where governments can concentrate on improving staff performance so to as to improve the quality of public services (Malaysia and Namibia). Mauritius has, as it were, a foot in both Stages, as institutions are weak, but credible initiatives to improve management quality in the form of the Action Plans have been taken under the government elected in 2000.

Legislation from simple secondary legislation right up to constitutional amendments is the main vehicle for change at Stage One. As well as its substantive value, such legislation can represent the irrevocable step that Chapter 6 suggested was the litmus test of political commitment to reform. Sri Lanka's Seventeenth Amendment (Chapter 7) was our clearest example of that.

A gloss on Figure 10.1 is that we saw in Chapter 2 that savings from the emergency actions to cut costs that constitute Stage One of corporate recovery have only been sustained when they have led to a second, strategic stage. Countries like Swaziland, Tanzania and Sri Lanka may need to concentrate initially on Stage One activities, but they should also have a vision of a Stage Two towards which Stage One

Table 10.4   A two-stage normative model of HRM

Stage	One	Two
Focus	Integrity	Performance
Method	Bureaucratic rule-following	Strategic human resource management
Institutions	Ensure framework of constitutional, primary and secondary legislation: • Staffing organizations (PSC etc.) • Respective roles of politicians and officials	Maintain (and devolve)
Strategy		
Strategic management	–	Set strategic/policy objectives
Strategic human resource management	–	Piecemeal harmonization of HR with objectives
Line manager ownership	Centralize to ensure rule following	Devolve to line ministries and line managers
Activities		
Downsizing/ employment reform	Emergency action to bring spending and budgets in line: remove ghosts etc.	Align staffing with objectives
Employee selection	Rigid procedures: interview scoring etc.	Professionalize: train managers, introduce tests etc.
Performance management	–	Introduce performance management linked to objectives but minus pay
(Other activities)	–	Training and other activities to support new objectives

will lead. Moreover, the Stage One activities of cost cutting and bureaucratic rule following are intrinsically unappealing. A vision of a performing civil service providing good services to citizens will help motivate governments to persevere with Stage One. That is one reason for our suggestion in Chapter 3 that modest actions to prepare the ground for Stage Two such as strengthening the HR function and training managers can accompany the Stage One actions; and it is one reason why the Moroccan reform team's role as a clearing house for

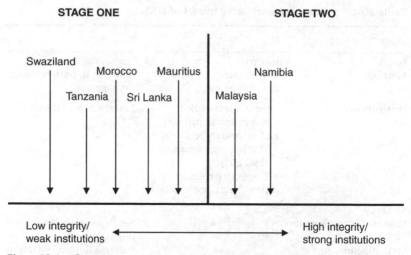

Figure 10.1   Countries at stage one and stage two of reform

line ministry initiatives such as introducing performance appraisal is useful, even if substantial results should not be expected.

Before moving on, we draw attention to the respective focus of the two stages of our model. Following Schick (1998), our model implies that it will be necessary to establish integrity before addressing performance; before addressing, in other words, the *quality* of staff management and of public services at large. But this creates a difficulty. Governments have committed themselves to the MDGs, and in Chapter 9 we argued, following Fukuyama, that achieving them will require a performing public service. That is not a problem for Namibia, the subject of Chapter 9, which we have located at Stage Two in our model; but it is definitely a problem for countries like Tanzania and Swaziland. However, we cannot dodge the logic of our model. Improvements to public services that advance the MDGs will only be sustained if a framework and a political and official culture of rule-following have first been established: *reculer pour mieux sauter* may be in order. To put the point concretely, Sri Lanka's reformers were right to beat a tactical retreat from the ineffectual 'Stage Two' activities of what in Chapter 7 we called the 'third wave' of Sri Lanka's reforms in favour of the 'Stage One' activity of putting the Public Service Commission and the other service commissions on a firm footing. Thus development advocates who wish to reach the sunlit uplands of the MDGs must first pass through the

Valley of Despond of HR and public service reform; or, to put it positively, HR and public service reform, far from being a parlour game of interest only to bureaucrats, becomes an integral preliminary stage in a strategy for achieving the MDGs.

The politics of HRM (Chapters 5, 6 and 7)

While Table 10.3 integrated the macro (institutional), meso (strategic) and micro (management) levels of our governance model, it omitted the political or meta-level. We turn our attention, therefore, to the final analytical task of this book, which is to integrate that level with the model we have just proposed in a comprehensive account of human resource management in developing country governments.

It would be possible – in fact it has been usual – to explain the trajectory of staff management in the public sector purely in management terms. We could confine ourselves, rather as we did earlier with performance management, to blaming failure on the choice of 'inappropriate' models, implying that an appropriate, properly contingent model would succeed. Similarly, we could apply standard organizational change notions such as 'resistance to change', as we suggested in Chapter 5. Certainly we should always prefer such parsimonious explanations where we can. But mechanical application of 'good practice' cannot occur when public management is politically contentious, as it is in all of our countries. Even where the political dispensation is stable, a political party may be determined to convince voters that it and it alone is able to deliver good public services, as the Barisan Nasional in Malaysia and the Labour party in the UK were both doing at the time of writing. There is no such thing as a politics-free public management, even if the political issues are starker when the political dispensation is fundamentally flawed.

Chapters 5 to 7 therefore tried to show why talking about staff management in purely management terms is inadequate. Whether the problem was the general preference for reacting rather than initiating, as in Morocco, or an absence of political will deriving from the 'dual' system of government, as in Swaziland, or the existence of a patronage system which politicians and officials feel obliged to stoke, as in Sri Lanka, all three cases had one thing in common: the failure of management reform had its roots in the political system.

We believe that this lesson is an important one that in some quarters is still not recognized: we must not go back to the contextless, apolitical and therefore fruitless civil service reform recipes of the 80s and 90s. But

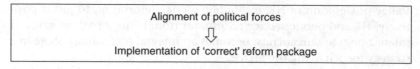

Figure 10.2   Politics and management: the DFID premise

strangely, by the time we wrote this final chapter it was a lesson that in other quarters we were in danger of over-learning. With a political scientist, Paul Wolfowitz, newly installed as President of the World Bank, and with the UK Department for International Development's (2005) ambitious multi-country report series on the political and social 'drivers of change', we no longer need to labour the importance of political analysis with readers who are aware of those agencies' work. The new danger is that analysis has tended to assume that the direction of causation is exclusively from politics to policy, institutions and management: get the politics right, and the appropriate reform measures will fall into place (Figure 10.2).

Thus the premise of DFID's 'drivers of change' project is that there is a 'correct' policy package, and it is just a question of getting the political actors to line up behind it:

> There is a broad agreement about the nature of the problems in Bangladesh and even on what needs to be done to promote broad-based poverty reduction in Bangladesh – civil service reform, reduce corruption, liberalise the economy ... bring about greater policy-focus and accountability ... privatise the SOEs, etc. But how to do this remains unclear for many actors. The central task that has emerged from the paper is how, over time, to strengthen underlying socio-economic processes and agents that will sustain pressure for pro-poor change across the wide agenda of policy and institutional reform and investments that are required for successful development. (Duncan *et al.*, 2002, p.8; see also Duncan *et al.*, 2003, p.1; and Ng'ethe *et al.*, 2004, p.3).

Now that is broadly in line with our analysis of Morocco, where we suggested that political action would be necessary before any management initiative could hope to succeed. But other cases in this book show how causation is often reciprocal. We make two points to support this view. First, we have seen that part of the reason for the difficulties with performance management in Mauritius, Malaysia and Namibia is that the version attempted included a PRP element which heightened particularistic tensions because most managers lacked the finesse to operate it properly, creating the suspicion that they favoured members of their own ethnic group. Yet there was no professional reason for them to make that mistake. The HRM literature shows that PRP is dispensable, and that worthwhile performance management is possible without it. A different version, minus PRP but including training or briefing for managers, might have succeeded in exactly the same political climate. This corroborates the World Bank's opinion, quoted in Chapter 2, that political will can be a function of the quality of advice that politicians receive from their officials and advisers.

Second, our view dovetails with the growing interest in 'policy networks' which proceeds from the recognition that policy emerges from a network of actors that includes politicians, but potentially also civil servants and non-state actors such as trade unions, NGOs and international donors (Perkin and Court, 2005; Rhodes, 1997). The origin of the Seventeenth Amendment to Sri Lanka's Constitution, discussed in Chapter 7, is an example of that.

So while studies of management need to be better informed politically than they have been in the past, policy-orientated studies of politics need to show an equal understanding of the machinery of policy, institutions and (human resource) management in order to bear fruit. Our preference for an approach to performance management which would be more politically acceptable because it would exclude pay, but which would still have the potential to improve civil service performance, is an example of that. So also is our recommendation in Chapter 6 that policymakers in Swaziland should frame a limited reform to the Civil Service Board that would detach it gently from the patronage system without disturbing the basic dual system of government. In the end, politics and management are interdependent, as Figure 10.3 shows.

| Alignment of political forces | ⇔ | Search for 'good enough' reform package |

Figure 10.3   Politics and management: reciprocal causation

Patronage (Chapter 7)

Patronage is a sub-set of political corruption, which following Johnston (1998) we defined as the abuse of public roles or resources for private benefit. While it has some desirable effects that include inducting citizens into the political process and rectifying bureaucratic injustices, they are outweighed by patronage's distortion of public resource allocations.

The preferred remedy to patronage has been institutional reform. In Sri Lanka, that reform, in the shape of the Seventeenth Amendment to the Constitution, was necessary, since rule-following bureaucracy is indeed one of patronage's 'countervailing forces', as scholars like Eisenstadt and Roniger have argued. Sri Lanka was right to reject alternative institutional remedies: administrative devolution would have made the problem worse, and political decentralization to the provinces had already done so. However, bureaucratic reform was still insufficient. The narrowness of the reform's political base and the legacy of suspicion between politicians and officials means that steps were needed to make officials more responsive to political control in order to strengthen politicians' commitment. The countervailing force of 'horizontal associations', or civil society as we have come to call it, could also have been deployed. In Sri Lanka no one had attempted to sell administrative reform: politicians were reluctant to abandon the pork barrel.

A further reason why institutional reform is insufficient is that, as we saw in Chapters 6 and 7, patronage in public staff management is part of a broader patronage system which also manifests itself in allocation of land, places at popular schools and other public resources. That system cuts across the institutional structure of government, so that the discrete reform of one part of the system such as staff management is like digging a trench in a bog: patronage seeps back in from other parts of the system. In the long run, our analysis of Sri Lanka, and also Mauritius and Swaziland, suggests that patronage will decrease as the countervailing forces increase in strength, as we saw with economic success in Mauritius and institutional strengthening in Sri Lanka. Chapter 7 showed that there are steps that governments can take to increase their strength.

Political commitment (Chapter 6)

The reciprocal relationship we have outlined between politics, institutions and management becomes particularly clear when we consider commitment, a concept that is at the interface between politics and management. Even after we have taken thorough account of the political economy of reform, commitment may still be necessary to carry a policy over the implementation threshold. That may be the reason why the same authors who find the concept unsatisfactory still end up using it themselves; and why, as with organizational culture (Barley *et al.*, 1988), commitment seems to be a concept where the academics who dislike it have to give way to the practitioners who find it indispensable.

In Chapter 6, therefore, we proposed a model of commitment and applied it to Swaziland's experience of staffing reform. Given the disappointing history of reform in countries like Mauritius, Morocco and Swaziland, observers and activists may find it useful to have a way of assessing whether a reform is going to succeed; and donors in particular may find it useful to have a way of assessing whether a particular reform proposal deserves their taxpayers' money. Moreover, using our model to pinpoint where a reform is weak gives a government the opportunity to strengthen it. It may be the reform's political base that needs strengthening, but it could also be the institutional framework or the detailed management content of the reform: action at any or all of the four levels in our governance model may be needed. We suggested just above that in Swaziland, the priorities are at the political and institutional levels. In Namibia, as we shall see, they are at the political and management levels.

Social and economic influences

A politically informed account of staff management increases its complexity, as we have just seen. As if this was not already demanding enough, our analysis in the individual case chapters suggested that we must also take account of social and economic influences. We support that with reference to Chapter 8, the most theoretically elaborate of our cases, where we listed five principal causes of the development of HR in the Malaysian civil service: the pervasive respect for authority, Malaysia's ethnic make-up, the stable and buoyant economy, the National Development Policy of 1990, and the personal role of former Prime Minister Mahathir Mohamad. Two of those causes are social, one economic and two political; all play a part, none is decisive on its own.

History (Chapter 8)

We contended in Chapter 8 that even after we have looked at staff management in a political, social and economic perspective, it may be valuable to add the time dimension of history. We reached that view through an exploration of the currently fashionable 'path dependence' and 'punctuated equilibrium' theories of economic and public policy history. We found that path dependence had a certain explanatory force when applied to Malaysia, where the structure of Malaysia's civil service was settled in the early 1950s and withstood the shocks of independence in 1957, the civil upheaval of May 1969, the ensuing New Economic Policy of 1971 and the subsequent National Development Policy of 1990 onwards. Many managers think it appropriate in this power-distant society, even though it militates against line manager ownership.

Malaysia's civil service structure of course resembles that of the other Commonwealth countries in some respects, notably in the role of its Public Service Commission. But it is a strength of the path dependence analysis that it can also explain Morocco's roughly opposite structure. Morocco's 'administrative feudalism', in which line ministries have a good deal of power, is as stable – as firm a 'path' – as Malaysia's opposite system. Borrowed in a hurry from France just after independence, the Moroccan system allows great disparities in pay and conditions between ministries, influenced by the power of the *corps* around which they are organized, and it has resisted the advice of the World Bank and of staff associations to centralize staffing on the Commonwealth model.

However, path dependence is also limited as an account of political and administrative history. When applied to countries on a negative path, whether we are talking about clientelism in southern Italy or economic stagnation in Spain or Bolivia, path dependence has the fatalistic character of the famous last line of Scott Fitzgerald's *The Great Gatsby*: 'So we beat on, boats against the current, borne back ceaselessly into the past' (1990, p.172). This is the fatalism that Houtzager and Moore objected to when they insisted that even 'relatively small groups of politicians and bureaucrats' might be enough to get a country off a negative path (2003, see especially p.3, p.13 and p.278).[3] But Malaysia's experience shows that paths can be good things to be on. Malaysia was lucky that the basic structure of the civil service withstood the shocks of independence and the 1969 riots.

A more profound limitation is that the 'path' and 'punctuated equilibrium' metaphors[4] provide over-simple accounts of history. We have followed the historians Bloch, Braudel and Carr in expecting to find multiple historical causes. In Chapter 8 we identified six such causes of the development of Malaysia's civil service: respect for authority, the tripartite ethnic mix, an Anglo-Saxon orientation, the health and stability of the economy, the effect of the National Development Policy of 1990 and the personal influence of former Prime Minister Mahathir Mohamad. The structure of the civil service has remained stable, and somewhat path dependent, through the half-century since independence, but its content has changed incrementally and out of recognition as a result of those six causes, with no single cause being decisive.

Path dependence can explain stability, which we have neglected, but not change. A more wide-ranging survey of historical development such as ours identifies further obstacles to change, to be sure, but also dynamic possibilities that policymakers can turn to their advantage. The solidity of the civil service structure explains why staff management remains centralized in Malaysia, even though staffing devolution would appear viable in terms of Table 10.1. But in a society which respects authority and in a public service with an Anglo-Saxon orientation, a prime minister can use the authority which Mahathir Mohamad bequeathed to his successor to make changes to that structure, capitalizing on the prestige that the Anglo-Saxon devolved civil service model holds in Malaysian eyes by consciously emulating it.

However, such a survey must be done for every country individually. Malaysia happens to be a country where Houtzager and Moore's 'small group of politicians and bureaucrats' can get its way and is likely to want to. By contrast, in Morocco's segmented society the king hesitates to impose his possibly limited authority, despite which other political actors still tend to wait for him to make the first move in the prevailing atmosphere of 'attentisme'. The executive authority that Malaysia can take for granted is problematic in Morocco.

In general, we hope that we have justified our belief that 'We must add the depth of time to studies that so singularly lack it' (Plumb, 1966, p.142) in order to correct what the political scientist Sydney Tarrow (1996, p.396) has called 'the presentism of much social science work'. Of course country-level historical analysis may lead us to conclude that a given country's 'path' is ingrained, and that change is unlikely. As we have seen, that is not always a bad thing. But we have managed to find potential for positive change even in countries like Morocco and Swaziland about which we might be entitled to feel pessimistic. In unpromising circumstances we may still manage to make 'hope and history rhyme', in the words of the Irish poet Seamus Heaney (1998, p.330).

Towards 'total explanation' and 'thick description' in governance

We believe that recognizing the importance of political, social and economic influences on public staff management propels us towards what, echoing the French historian Fernand Braudel's concept of 'total history' which we invoked in Chapter 8, we will call a 'total explanation' of politics, institutions, policy, strategy and management, because that is what will be necessary to produce reforms that will stick and that will make a difference. It may be that the successful reformer will be like Braudel's 'true man of action',

> who can measure most nearly the constraints upon him, who chooses to remain within them and even to take advantage of the weight of the inevitable, exerting his own pressure in the same direction. All efforts against the prevailing tide of history – which is not always obvious – are doomed to failure. (1973, pp.1243–4[5])

This view constrains the role of the individual, but it does not negate it. There is still room for a gifted and determined leader to make a difference, as we saw in Chapter 8 that Mahathir Mohamad managed to do.

But there is no calibration that the reformer can use to measure the constraints upon him (or her). Drawing on a normative model such as the SHRM model, or indeed our own two-stage model of public HRM, to produce a reform programme is not the same as applying a formula. We do not want to underestimate the practical and political skills that a reformer needs, but in this context his or her task – and certainly the task of the scholar who wishes to help the reformer – is essentially the task of an ethnographer as Clifford Geertz has portrayed it:

> Ethnography is thick description. The ethnographer is faced with ... a multiplicity of complex conceptual structures, many of them superimposed upon or knotted into one another, which are at once strange, irregular and explicit ... Doing ethnography is like trying to read ... a manuscript – foreign, faded, full of ellipses, incoherencies, suspicious emendations and tendentious commentaries. (Geertz, 1973, p.10)

Like the ethnographer, the reformer or scholar finds himself or herself having to weigh up evidence which is every bit as flawed as the ethnographer's. The best way at this final stage of our book of illustrating how the reformer should 'read' governance is probably to point to the way we have conducted our analysis in earlier chapters. However, the specific example of the structure of government in Swaziland may be helpful. As we noted in Chapter 6, at first glance that structure is a standard Westminster one, complete with prime and cabinet ministers who are supported by the usual ministries. Yet a 'thick description' reveals that this façade disguises the reality of a dual system of government in which the 'traditional' side calls the shots. Understanding the role which the standard Westminster model plays in Swaziland is the starting point for framing a meaningful reform. Professional initiatives like performance management which have worked well elsewhere are likely to fail in Swaziland, and may even compound the political problem by depleting the scarce reserve of political capital. It is in this sense that 'vice may be virtue uprooted', to repeat the words of David Jones that we quoted in Chapter 1.

Governance priorities and interactions between levels

Stage One and Stage Two priorities

We now complete our analytical task by synthesizing our findings in terms of the four levels of our governance model, taking the opportunity to summarize the main policy implications of our analysis of the individual cases at the same time. On this occasion we present countries in the order in which they appear in Figure 10.1, as this serves to emphasize how priorities are increasingly at meso and micro levels as countries move from Stage One to Stage Two (Table 10.5).

Interactions between levels

Presenting our findings in Table 10.5 highlights the interaction, or reciprocal causation, between levels (see Figure 10.3). The priorities we have suggested for each country at the macro level illustrate this important point. It would be possible to apply a single template to every country's institutional framework, and then read off priorities mechanically. This has a diagnostic value, as with the OECD checklists that we used in Chapter 4 to assess Tanzania's primary and secondary legislation. But it will lead to impractical recommendations that countries do not 'own', of the kind that resulted in the World Bank assessing 40 per cent of its own civil service reform projects up to the late 1990s as unsatisfactory at completion, as we saw in Chapter 2.

Table 10.5 Governance priorities and interactions between levels

Level	Swaziland	Tanzania	Morocco	Sri Lanka	Mauritius	Malaysia	Namibia
(Stage)	One	One	One	One → Two	One/Two	Two	Two
Meta (politics)	Autonomy within autocracy	End presidential discretion	Break the political stalemate	Autonomous responsiveness	Further reduce ethnic competition	–	Commitment to scaling up action on AIDS
Macro (institutions)	Restore Civil Service Board independence	Delegation from politicians to officials; end duplication among central agencies	Royal Commission?	Consolidate autonomy and strengthen responsiveness	Autonomy and pilot devolution	Start to devolve	Extend devolution via programme budgeting
Meso (policy and strategy)	–	–	–	(After consolidation): Revive ministry reviews	Extend Action Plans	Continue 'piecemeal' SHRM	Resolve tension between existing strategy and scaling-up of health plans
Micro (HR management)	–	(Training of 'mid-level cadres'?)	Downsizing; Centre continuing to broke line ministry initiatives	(After consolidation): Professionalize HR	Extend performance management pilots	Continue professional improvements	Training of 'mid-level cadres'

Instead of recommending a single universal institutional framework, we have offered tailored priorities based on our 'reading' of the cases. Our approach to devolution is an example of that. At one extreme, we have suggested that fundamental contradictions in Swaziland's dual system of government mean that devolution will not be a priority until there is political agreement to make civil service independence a reality. At the other extreme, we have suggested that Namibia's political stability and successful experience with devolution justify extending devolution, using the pilot programme budgeting scheme as a vehicle. In the middle, as it were, we have suggested that consolidating civil service autonomy in Sri Lanka requires, paradoxically, making the civil service more responsive to political objectives in order for politicians to have confidence in administrators and not start to undermine the Seventeenth Amendment reform as they have undermined previous reforms.

HR and other governance reforms

In Chapter 1 we expressed the hope that taking a broad view of the political, social, economic and historical influences on staff management would allow us to extend the scope of our conclusions to other areas of governance. It seems to us now that in Tables 10.4 and 10.5 we could substitute other governance topics. Narrowly, we could substitute the management of other resources: all the points we have made about the viability of taking a strategic or politically informed view of human resource management also apply to financial and information management (see for example Heeks, 2005). More broadly, we could substitute other areas of governance reform: proposals to reform customs and revenue collection or the judiciary or intergovernmental relations in terms of the balance between central and local powers all appear equally likely to require a sequencing of reform where fundamental political and institutional actions combined with rudimentary management actions lead to on to a political settlement in which more elaborate management actions can be taken to improve the quality of the judiciary or of revenue collection as the case may be. Thus we hope that readers whose interest in governance is broader than the one that this book has mostly taken have indeed found something to repay their study, as we hoped in Chapter 1 that they would.

Conclusion: institutional settlements and performance cultures

Mistress Gloria was always saying to me softly ... Agu make sure you study book enh? If you are studying hard you can be going to the university to be Doctor or Engineer … I am liking school very much and always thinking about going until the war is coming. (Iweala, 2005, p.35)

We opened the book with a 'Third World' novelist of the last generation, and we close it with a writer of the next one. The narrator of the young Nigerian novelist Uzodinma Iweala's *Beasts of no nation* has been a scholarly boy, but when his school closes he is press-ganged as a child soldier into a war he barely understands. He suffers and commits atrocities. At the end of the novel he has achieved an ambiguous redemption, enrolled in a rehabilitation programme but traumatized and struggling to reconcile what he has done and had done to him with the Christian values of his upbringing.

As in William Golding's *Lord of the flies*, a descent into savagery fills the vacuum that a school's collapse has left behind. Far from the state being 'predatory', the teachers that it employs – and we should recall that education is everywhere the biggest function of government apart from defence – have given order and purpose to children's lives. That connection tolls like a bell throughout the novel – Iweala, like Lampedusa (see Chapter 6), uses repetition to drive home his point: 'Then they are stopping school because there is no more government' (p.35); 'One day, they are closing school because there is no more government (p.71); 'There is no more school' (p.77).[6] Mistress Gloria, the Head Teacher who has picked out Agu's potential from among the sea of faces in her one-room rural primary school, and Agu's own father, whom Iweala has also made a teacher, present a positive image of public employees that is missing from the downsizing literature of the 80s and 90s. An atomized society is in no position to create private organizations or throw up private individuals to take the place of Agu's school and its head teacher.

The staffing institutions like the Public Service Commissions of Commonwealth countries are an important block in that project of building, or rebuilding, states which Fukuyama and others have seen as one of our most pressing public tasks. Whether or not the MDGs which came to the fore in the second half of our research project and which we focused on in Chapter 9, will be realized, it seems clear that without public institutions and public services they certainly will not be. The acid test of a rarefied analysis like ours is whether it has the potential to make a difference to the way the Mistress Glorias of this world do their jobs. We hope that this book has shown how an institutional settlement that promotes rule following can set the scene for a culture of performance which will allow public employees to steer Agu's real-life counterparts towards a life in which they can develop rather than destroy the societies in which they are growing up.

Notes

Chapter 1 Introduction: The Human Factor in Governance

1 'Although nature is subject to diminishing returns, man is subject to increasing returns. Knowledge is the most powerful engine of production; it enables us to subdue nature and satisfy our wants.' (Marshall, 1890; quoted in Meier and Stiglitz 2001)

2 That distinction is elaborated in McCourt (2001b).

3 This section gives a necessarily compressed account of a large and well-established area of theory and practice. Readers unfamiliar with it may wish to consult a standard HRM textbook such as McCourt and Eldridge (2003).

4 The other elements of Guest's (1989) version of the HRM model are commitment, in the sense of staff commitment to the organization's aims, and flexibility, in the sense of having a workforce that can increase or decrease in line with increasing or decreasing demand for the organization's products or services (*numerical flexibility*) and where staff can take on new responsibilities as the organization's needs change (*functional flexibility*). We have not included them in our research framework for reasons of space, but functional flexibility is an issue in Chapter 9, where we report on HR in the Namibian health service.

5 In case there are readers unfamiliar with these, we are using 'employee selection' to refer to the processes by which organizations appoint staff to fill vacancies, whether at entry level or higher promotion levels, and whether the appointees come from outside or inside the organization (Cooper *et al.*, 2003). We are using 'performance management' (sometimes known as 'performance appraisal') to refer to the processes by which organizations manage the performance of their employees, usually centering on an annual meeting between a manager and a subordinate at which the previous year's performance is reviewed and objectives and individual development goals for the coming year may be set (Armstrong and Baron, 1998). We are not concerned with performance management at the level of government agencies.

6 The other HR activities which appear in most textbook treatments are human resource planning, job analysis (or competence development, as it is increasingly called), pay (or 'reward management'), training and employee relations (which refers to the management of the relationship between the employer and its staff, usually *via* a trade union or unions). Once again we have not included them in our research framework for reasons of space, though training is discussed in Chapter 9 on Namibia.

Chapter 2 HRM as Downsizing: From Cost to Strategy

1 This, however, is untrue of the literature on structural adjustment, of which employment reform is a sub-set in many countries (see, for example, Nelson, 1990). But that debate is outside the scope of this chapter.

2 Although choice of 'instruments' was a factor in both the downsizing litera-ture and our field interviews, they are not discussed further in this chapter, which concentrates on the design of reform. Nunberg (1994) provides an inventory of instruments; see also McCourt (1998a).

3 These measures were destined to run into the sand, as we shall see in Chapter 7.

4 Pay compression can be more apparent than real. The compression ratio of 1:6.8 in Uganda changed to 1:100 after non-monetary allowances and benefits were included (Government of Uganda, 1994).

5 This was also true in Poland (Redman and Keithley, 1998).

Chapter 3   Mauritius: Economic Growth and Strategic Human Resource Management

1 The victory of the 'Social Alliance', led by former Prime Minister Navinchandra Ramgoolam, in the general election of July 2005 came too late to be incorporated into our text. It was also too early to say what differ-ence, if any, it would make to staff management in the government.

Chapter 4   Tanzania: Laws and Institutions

1 Readers may wish to compare this section with the discussion of politiciza-tion in Sri Lanka in Chapter 7.

2 Trade Unions Ordinance (Amendment) Act, 1962; Trade Disputes (Settlement) Act, 1962; Civil Service (Negotiating Machinery) Act, 1962.

3 Both presidents have been men, so we use masculine pronouns and adjectives to refer to them.

4 We discuss this syndrome of reforms spawning further reforms in more detail in the Swaziland chapter in this book.

5 Subsequent to our field research, the Civil Service Commission was retitled the Public Service Commission, and the Civil Service Department was restyled the President's Office Public Service Management.

6 From this point we will use 'line ministries' as a shorthand for 'line ministries and Regions', since Tanzania's regional administrations (as distinct from its local councils) have the same structural relationship with central government as line ministries. See also earlier footnote on the retitling of CSC and CSD.

Chapter 5   Morocco: The Politics of HRM

1 Similar claims were still being made in Britain as recently as the start of the reign of the current Queen, who remains the formal Head of the Church of England (Jones, 1973).

2 In Morocco's case, this view is enshrined in the French colonial distinction between the *bilad al-siba* (zone of rebellion) and the *bilad al-makhzan* (zone of government) (Pennell, 2000).

3 There is a little of the French reverence for the *grande école* graduate, which allowed the *Enarque* Dominique de Villepin to be appointed prime minister in 2005 without the encumbrance of an election.

4 However, as we completed this chapter observers were starting to talk about an 'Arab spring', excited by developments such as the decision of Egypt's President Mubarak to allow opponents to challenge him in the presidential elections of September 2005 (Beeston, 2005). It was too early when we wrote to say if those developments, partly induced by a *soi-disant* pro-democracy American administration, would have a lasting impact, and they are in any case peripheral to this chapter.

5 Quotations from interviews and from other French and Arabic sources are translated by the authors.

6 This was its new title at the time of writing. It was still known as the Civil Service Ministry (in French, Ministère de la Fonction Publique) at the time of our interviews.

7 This is the English for 'tatillon', the word used in a UNDP evaluation of the reform programme: see Proulx (1999, p.41).

8 This may be a Francophone feature, since the same thing happens in Benin: see Kiragu and Mukandala (2004).

9 Staff reported that an unanticipated consequence for those ministries that have improved their practice is to raise the expectations of staff appointed, only to dash them when the appointee comes face to face with the less glamorous reality of Moroccan public administration.

10 We will see in a later chapter that Sri Lanka corrected a similar mistake by moving reform into the President's Office, the strategic centre of government. It is unclear where Morocco's strategic centre might be located, if not in the Palace.

Chapter 6   Swaziland: Political Commitment

1 The author has added his own pebble to the pile. In a project memorandum prepared for a bilateral donor in 1995, he wrote that 'The greatest potential constraint to the proposed project is uncertainty about (the government's) commitment to reform.'

2 Though none of them is statistically rigorous. Only Johnson and Wasty and Campos and Esfahani have carried out tests of statistical significance. But Johnson and Wasty (1993, p.23) do not detail their results, while Campos and Esfahani's preferred variables, with the partial exception of political turnover, are not corroborated by the other studies.

3 Goal-setting theory also corroborates the importance of the voluntary and explicit elements of commitment, while the publicity element is corroborated by Asch's (1956) classic conformity studies.

4 Among the antecedents, 'leadership' corresponds to 'visionary leadership' in Williamson (1994) and also relates to 'executive authority' as discussed by Nelson and 'expression of political will' in Johnson and Wasty (1993). 'Strong political base' corresponds to the item of the same name in Williamson (1994), and also relates to Nelson's 'executive authority', and to 'political turnover' in Campos and Esfahani (2000). The derivation of the remaining antecedents should be self-evident. 'Administrative capacity' includes the capacity of the laws and institutions which are the framework for administrative action.

5 The influence of history on HRM in government is something that we will consider theoretically and at greater length in Chapter 8.

6 In Chapter 7 we will see that the official's counterpart in Sri Lanka had made an uncannily similar observation.

7 Average score on a questionnaire item administered to 30 senior officials asking 'What political will exists to carry out staffing reform?' was 3.0 on a four-point scale, where point 1 represented high commitment.

8 This is in contrast with other studies, such as Mosley *et al.* (1991) which argues that the problem of commitment only arises at the implementation stage, at which they found slippage of over 40 per cent on structural adjustment loan conditions. Our judgement is that, at least where civil service reform is concerned, Swaziland has acted in good faith with its donor partners, who consequently had no criticism to make on this score in our interviews.

9 'Traditional' and 'modern' will not appear in quotation marks after this point so as to avoid cluttering the page. But readers should remember that the traditions in question are partly invented (Levin, 1991), while 'what is modern is not necessarily more desirable' (Lister and George, 1985, p.42). Moreover, identifying the dividing line between traditional and modern elites with the boundary between the two halves of the dual system is a simplification: one may assume that many individuals on both sides of government are ambivalent about merit and patronage.

10 Few steps are ever wholly irrevocable. As Salancik (1977, p.5) observes, 'Even a vasectomy can be undone.' But the cost of policy reversal can be prohibitive, either politically or financially.

Chapter 7   Sri Lanka: Political Patronage

1 The common-sense explanation of administrative incapacity is not convincing here. Despite administrative blunders which we detail in this chapter, the government has managed to make major administrative changes from time to time, notably the Thirteenth and Seventeenth Amendments to the Constitution (see below). Sri Lanka appears on the 60th percentile of countries worldwide for 'government effectiveness' in the World Bank's governance index, against an average placing on the 48th percentile for countries in South Asia; while the average placing for lower middle-income countries like Sri Lanka is only on the 42nd percentile (Kaufmann *et al.*, 2003).

2 Studies of patronage and clientelism had their heyday between 1975 and 1985, with relatively little having appeared thereafter. However, recent studies such as Villarreal's (2002) do continue to employ the concepts introduced in the earlier studies, suggesting that this is one of those rare instances in the social sciences where research has tailed off because something has actually been established, obviating the need for further basic enquiry.

3 From here on we will use 'brokers', 'broking' and 'brokerage' as shorthand for 'brokers of political patronage' etc.

4 'So universal was the plaguing of Ministers on behalf of friends and relatives that in 1760 a tender mother who wished to see her son in Parliament thought it useful to point out to (the Duke of) Newcastle that her son would have no such requests to make' (Namier, 1929, p.23). And old British habits die hard: in 2004, four government departments insisted on continu-

ing to allow their Ministers to vet shortlists for official appointments even after the Commissioner for Public Appointments had told them to stop (Office for Public Appointments, 2004).

5 It seems relevant at this point to invoke the ascriptive/achievement distinction that we introduced in Chapter 3.

6 Putnam consequently excludes voting in elections from his measure of 'civicness', clientelistic politics – and, incidentally, also the Catholic religion – apparently representing the wrong kind of civil society.

7 The fate of performance appraisal is discussed later in the chapter.

8 Perhaps this is one reason why Sri Lanka's attempts at decentralization have mostly been half-hearted. Decentralization as such is outside the scope of this chapter. Readers may consult Oberst (1986). Shaw (1999) is particularly instructive on the process by which such initiatives fall short of their original intentions.

9 Support for this view came just as we were completing this chapter from the report of the UK government's Commission for Africa which states that 'Donors must change their behaviour and support the national priorities of African governments rather than allowing their own procedures and special enthusiasms to undermine the building of a country's own capacity' (2005 p.12).

10 A corollary is that initiatives to increase the responsiveness or poverty orientation of government are not likely to succeed without the kind of attention that Sri Lanka has been giving to the institutional framework of government.

Chapter 8   Malaysia: History and Path Dependence

1 Space precludes a detailed account of the origins and ramifications of the path dependence notion. Hirsch and Gillespie (2001) will supplement our brief description.

2 In a pessimistic conclusion based on no visible evidence, the Nobel prize winner North asserts that 'In Spain, personalistic relationships are still the key to much of the political and economic exchange. They are the consequence of an evolving institutional framework that produces neither political stability nor consistent realization of the potential of modern technology'. Most readers will be aware of Spain's economic success in the 15 years since North's book was published.

3 It is surprising how little curiosity path dependence scholars display about mainstream historiography, despite their insistence on the importance of history. Their citations, such as they are, are exclusively to economic historians, and they show no awareness of theoretical questions. See Gardiner (1974) and Marwick (2001) for an introduction to these questions.

4 The allusion is to Kuhn's (1962) account of scientific development, where long periods of 'normal science' are punctuated by revolutionary 'paradigm shifts' which rewrite the basic rules. We are grateful to Sterman and Wittenberg (1999) for spotting the analogy. Mahoney and Snyder, along with North and one or two others, have resorted to another analogy, with the notion of 'punctuated equilibria' in evolutionary biology popularized by Stephen Jay Gould (Eldredge, 1985). Since analogy is a legitimate form of scholarly argument, it is

worth observing that Gould's notion, which postulates occasional quantum jumps in evolution, has been challenged, notably by Richard Dawkins (1986), who upholds the orthodox Darwinian account of gradual evolution.

5 By contrast, Schilling (1998, p.283) suggests in a business context that firms' adoption of a technology can be a 'function of strategic choices made by the firm.'

6 Malaysia is ranked 39th out of 144 countries in Transparency International's 2004 Corruption Perceptions Index. Other rankings for the region: Indonesia, 133; Myanmar, 142; Philippines, 102; Singapore, 5; Thailand, 64; Vietnam, 102.

7 In fact Henderson (1999) has suggested that Malaysia is what Evans (1995) calls an 'intermediate state', only partly complying with the bureaucratic ideal (the contrast is with Japan, South Korea and Taiwan). But we think our point still stands.

8 Though this was an area where change was more apparent than real. The government claimed to have slowed the rate of increase to 0.2 per cent between 1989 and 1995. But once privatization is excluded, the remaining 'core civil service' actually increased by 7.7 per cent. This is similar to Britain, where again the government claimed to have reduced numbers dramatically, whereas when privatization was excluded, the number of civil servants was roughly the same on the day Mrs Thatcher left office as on the day she arrived.

9 'Vire' is public sector jargon for moving money from one budget to another.

10 This allows those allergic to Carlyle's 'great man' view of history to argue that we are entitled to ask what it was about Malaysia that allowed Mahathir's writ to run as far as it did; or that Malaysians' need for a strong leader was going to conjure up, if not Mahathir himself, then someone very like him.

11 It is intriguing, but outside the scope of this chapter, to say whether the same goes for the history of technology where the path dependence view originated.

12 Our view implies that it is sometimes better to stay on the path one is on already. This is in contrast to Mahoney, North and Putnam's assumption that 'lock-in' is always a bad thing; that Latin America, Spain and southern Italy would have done better if they had been able to get out of their historical rut. We return to this issue in our final chapter.

Chapter 9 Namibia: The Human Resource Crisis in Health in Africa

1 These are MDGs 4, 5 and 6. See United Nations (2005a) for a report on progress towards meeting the MDGs. See Wyss (2004a) for a review of HR implications of the health MDGs.

2 In a disturbing study of the effect on nurses of looking after HIV/AIDS patients (carried out by one of the Ministry of Health's HR staff), one nurse said: *'Let me tell you the truth, we do not do any sterile dressing procedure in this ward any longer. And we don't wash patients any more. Their relatives do that. We don't make their beds or even dust the rooms as it is supposed to be, and this pains me a lot. What will God think of me? I took a vow to this profession.'* (Pendukeni, 2004, pp.44–5).

3 We hope it is not pedantic to point out that the Plan incorrectly uses the word 'outcome' to refer to activities such as increasing condom use rather than the results that the activities are designed to obtain.
4 Significantly, UK spending on overseas training resurfaced in the form of the 'Chevening Scheme', administered by the Foreign Office, partly as a way of buying the good will of the future 'movers and shakers' trained under the scheme's auspices. The Foreign Office was no doubt mindful that the US President at the time, Bill Clinton, had spent a Rhodes Scholarship year at Oxford University.
5 We could not verify the official's statement. However, just as we were finishing this chapter the US Ambassador to the United Nations was pressing to have the following phrase deleted from the draft of a United Nations summit agreement: 'encourage pharmaceutical companies to make anti-retroviral drugs affordable and accessible in Africa' (Borger, 2005).

Chapter 10   Conclusion: Improving HRM in Developing Country Governance

1 Tanzania was carrying out a local government reform programme whose effects were still unclear at the time of our research.
2 See also the World Bank's (2003) similarly structured model, based on the work of Manning and Parison (2003).
3 Robert Putnam endearingly allows an Italian regional president to express the same reaction in his well known *Making democracy work*: 'This is a counsel of despair! You're telling me that nothing I can do will improve our prospects for success. The fate of the reform was sealed centuries ago' (Putnam, 1993, p.183).
4 For an account of theories as metaphor, see McCourt (1997).
5 There is a remarkable similarity with the view of history that Tolstoy expounds in *War and peace*, in which Prince Andrey says about Russia's Napoleonic war leader, General Kutuzov, that he 'knows that there is something stronger and more important than his will – that is the invisible march of events, and he can see them, can grasp their significance, and, seeing their significance, can abstain from meddling, from following his own will, and aiming at something else' (2002, p.851). Also see David (1985, p.333).
6 This is no mere literary conceit. We remind readers that in Chapter 7 we traced a connection between patronage, including in public employment, and civil war in Sri Lanka.

References

Abed, G. *et al.* (1998) *Fiscal reforms in low income countries: Experience under IMF-supported programs*, Washington DC: International Monetary Fund, Occasional Paper #160.

Abrahamsen, R. (2000) *Disciplining democracy: Development discourse and good governance in Africa*, London: Zed.

ADB (Asian Development Bank) (2004) *Review of governance and public management for Sri Lanka*, Manila: Asian Development Bank.

Administrative Reforms Committee (1987–88) *Reports of the Administrative Reforms Committee*, Colombo: Government of Sri Lanka.

Ahmad, A., N. Mansor and A. Ahmad (2003) *The Malaysian bureaucracy: Four decades of development*, Kuala Lumpur: Prentice-Hall.

Ahmed, N. (1988) 'Experiments in local government reform in Bangladesh', *Asian Survey*, 28: 813–29.

Ajzen, I. (1988) *Attitudes, personality and behavior*, Milton Keynes: Open University Press.

Alarkoubi, K. (1999) *Organizational change in Morocco: The case of human resource management in the Ministry of Equipment*, Manchester: Institute for Development Policy and Management, MSc. dissertation.

Alderman, H., S. Canagarajah and S. Younger (1994) 'Consequences of permanent layoff from the civil service: Results from a survey of retrenched workers in Ghana', in D. Lindauer and B. Nunberg (eds) *Rehabilitating government: Pay and employment reform in Africa*, Washington DC: World Bank, 211–37.

Al-Hayat (2002) 'New government accelerates privatization', *Al-Hayat*, Rabat, November 14 2002.

Allen, K. (2005) 'HIV drug target "will not be met"', *BBC News*, http://news.bbc.co.uk/1/hi/health/4629933.stm, accessed June 28 2005.

Allum, P. (1973) *Politics and society in postwar Naples*, Cambridge: Cambridge University Press.

Amnesty International (2002) *Annual report 2002: Morocco and Western Sahara*, http://web.amnesty.org/web/ar2002.nsf/mde/morocco!Open, accessed March 8 2003.

Amnesty International (1999) *Annual report 1999: Morocco and Western Sahara*, http://www.amnesty.org/ailib/aireport/ar99/mde29.htm, accessed March 8 2003.

Anand, S. and T. Baernighausen (2003) *Human resources and health outcomes*, Joint Learning Initiative, Working Paper 7–2.

Andaya, B. and L. Andaya (2001) *A history of Malaysia*, Basingstoke: Palgrave.

Anthony, W., P. Perrewé and K. Kacmar (1993) *Strategic human resource management*, Fort Worth, TX: Dryden.

Appelbaum, E. and R. Batt (1994) *The new American workplace: Transforming work systems in the United States*, Ithaca, NY: Cornell.

Argyle, M. (1989) *The psychology of work*, Harmondsworth: Penguin.

Armstrong, M. and A. Baron (1998) *Performance management: The new realities*, London: Institute of Personnel and Development.

Arogyaswamy, K., V. Barker and M. Yasai-Ardekani (1995) 'Firm turnarounds: An integrative two-stage model', *Journal of Management Studies*, 32: 493–525.

Arthur, W. (1989) 'Competing technologies, increasing returns, and lock-in by historical events', *Economic Journal*, 99, 394: 116–31.

Asch, S. (1956) 'Studies of independence and conformity: A minority of one against a majority', *Psychological Monographs*, 70 (9, whole No. 416).

Ashurst, M. (1998) 'An African success story', *Banker*, 148, 870: 47–50.

Azam, J. and C. Morrisson (1994) *The political feasibility of adjustment in Côte d'Ivoire and Morocco*, Paris: OECD.

Bale, M. and T. Dale (1998) 'Public sector reform in New Zealand and its relevance to developing countries', *World Bank Research Observer*, 13, 1: 103–22.

Baloro, J. (1994) 'The development of Swaziland's constitution: Monarchical responses to modern challenges', *Journal of African Law*, 38, 1: 19–34.

Bana, B. (2004) *Human resource management in the Tanzanian civil service*, University of Manchester: PhD thesis.

Banfield, E. (1958) *The moral basis of a backward society*, Glencoe: Free Press.

Barley, S., G. Meyer and D. Gash (1988) 'Cultures of culture: Academics, practitioners, and the pragmatics of normative control', *Administrative Science Quarterly*, 33: 24–60.

Barnes, P. (1997) 'Lessons of reform in the Ontario civil service', *Public Administration and Development*, 17: 27–32.

Barry, N. (2000) *An introduction to modern political theory*, New York: Palgrave.

Barsoux, J. and P. Lawrence (1990) *Management in France*, London: Cassell.

Bates, R. (1993) 'A reply', *World Development*, 21: 1077–81.

Baumol, W., A. Blinder and E. Wolff (2003) *Downsizing in America: Reality, causes and consequences*, New York: Russell Sage Foundation.

Becker, B. and B. Gerhart (1996) 'The impact of human resource management on organizational performance', *Academy of Management Journal*, 39: 779–801.

Becker, H. (1960) 'Notes on the concept of commitment', *American Journal of Sociology*, 66: 32–40.

Beckett, S. (1952) *En attendant Godot*, Paris: Editions de Minuit.

Beer, M. *et al.* (1985) *Human resource management: A general manager's perspective*, New York: Free Press.

Beeston, R. (2005) 'Sleeping giant of the Arab world awakens to democracy', *The Times*, June 15: 36.

Benn, H. (2005) 'Foreword', in DFID *Partnerships for poverty reduction: Rethinking conditionality*, http://www.dfid.gov.uk/pubs/files/conditionality.pdf, iii.

Bennett, A. (1991) 'Downsizing doesn't necessarily bring an upswing in corporate profitability', *Wall Street Journal*, June 6: B1, B4.

Berlin, I. (1978) *Karl Marx: His life and environment*, Oxford: Oxford University Press.

Bhopal, M. and C. Rowley (2002) 'The State in employment: The case of Malaysian electronics', *International Journal of Human Resource Management*, 13: 1165–85.

Blau, P. (1964) *Exchange and power in social life*, New York: Wiley.

Bloch, M. (1954) *The historian's craft*, Manchester: Manchester University Press.

Booth, A. (1983) *Swaziland: Tradition and change in a Southern African kingdom*, Boulder, CO: Westview.

Borger, J. (2005) 'Road map for US relations with rest of the world', *The Guardian*, August 27: 19.

Boston, J., J. Martin, J. Pallot and P. Walsh (1996) *Public management: The New Zealand model*, Oxford: Oxford University Press.

Bouachrine, T. (2001) 'Peu de réalisations et inflation de discours', *Gazette du Maroc*, March 14 2001: 10.

Bowman, L. (1991) *Mauritius: Democracy and development in the Indian Ocean*, Boulder, CO: Westview.

Braudel, F. (1990) *The identity of France, Volume II: People and production*, London: Fontana.

Braudel, F. (1973) *The Mediterranean and the Mediterranean world in the age of Philip II*, London: Collins.

Bretton Woods Project, Action Aid, AFRODAD, Christian Aid, Development Gap, One World Trust and World Development Movement (2005) *Kept in the dark: The World Bank, the IMF and parliaments*, http://ifiwatchnet.org/doc/keptinthedark.pdf, accessed July 11 2005.

Brewster, C. and A. Hegewisch (1994) *Policy and practice in European human resource management: The Price Waterhouse Cranfield survey*, London: Routledge.

Brockner, J., S. Grover, T. Reed, R. DeWitt and M. O'Malley (1987) 'Survivors' reactions to layoffs: We get by with a little help from our friends', *Administrative Science Quarterly*, 32: 526–41.

Brødsgaard, K. (2002) 'Institutional reforms and the *Bianzhi* system in China', *China Quarterly*, 170: 361–86.

Brow, J. (1996) *Demons and development: The struggle for community in a Sri Lankan village*, Tucson: University of Arizona Press.

Bryceson, D. (1988) 'Household, hoe and nation: The development policy of the Nyerere era', in M. Hodd *Tanzania after Nyerere*, London: Pinter, 36–48.

Brytting, T. (1994) 'The ethics of giving notice', *Business Ethics: A European Review*, 3, 2: 93–100.

Buchan, J. and M. Dal Poz (2002) 'Skills mix in the health care workforce: Reviewing the evidence', *Bulletin of the World Health Organization*, 80: 575–80.

Burgoyne, J. (1994) 'Stakeholder analysis', in C. Cassell and G. Syman (eds) *Qualitative methods in organizational research*, London: Sage, 187–207.

Burns, J. (2003) '"Downsizing" the Chinese state: Government retrenchment in the 1990s', *China Quarterly*, 175: 775–802.

Burton, J., C. Joubert, J. Harrison, and C. Athayde (1993) *Evaluation of ODA project in support of Ghana's civil service reform programme: Volumes I and II*, London: ODA Evaluation Department.

Cabinet Office (1996) *Civil service statistics*, London: HMSO.

Cai, Y. (2002) 'The resistance of Chinese laid-off workers in the reform period', *China Quarterly*, 170: 327–44.

Caiden, G. (1970) *Administrative reform*, London: Allen Lane.

Camdessus, M. (1999) 'Second generation reform: Reflections and new challenges', *http:www.imf.org/external/np/speeches/1999/110899.htm*, accessed June 6 2000.

Cameron, K. (1994) 'Strategies for successful organizational downsizing', *Human Resource Management*, 33: 189–211.

Campbell, J. (1964) *Honour, family and patronage: A study of institutions and moral values in a Greek mountain community*, Oxford: Oxford University Press.

Campos, J. and H. Esfahani (2000) 'Credible commitment and success with public enterprise reform', *World Development*, 28: 221–43.

Carr, E. (1987) *What is history?*, London: Penguin.

Carroll, B. and T. Carroll (1997) 'State and ethnicity in Botswana and Mauritius: A democratic route to development?, *Journal of Development Studies*, 33: 464–86.

Carroll, B. and S. Joypaul (1993) 'The Mauritian senior public service since independence: Some lessons for developing and developed nations', *International Review of Administrative Sciences*, 59: 423–40.

Cascio, W., C. Young and J. Morris (1997) 'Financial consequences of employment-change decisions in major U.S. corporations', *Academy of Management Journal*, 40: 1175–89.

Case, W. (2002) 'Malaysia: Semi-democracy with strain points', in W. Case (ed.) *Politics in South east Asia*, Richmond: Curzon, 99–146.

Case, W. (1995) 'Malaysia: Aspects and audiences of legitimacy', in M. Alagappa (ed.) *Political legitimacy in South East Asia*, Stanford: Stanford University Press, 69–107.

Cassels, J. (1983) *Review of personnel work in the civil service: Report to the prime minister*, London: HMSO.

Chalos, P. and C. Chen (2002) 'Employee downsizing strategies: Market reaction and post announcement financial performance', *Journal of Business, Finance and Accounting*, 29: 847–70.

Chaudhry, S. (1994) 'Selected discussion points', in S. Chaudhry, G. Reid, and W. Malik (eds) *Civil service reform in Latin America and the Caribbean*, Washington DC: World Bank, 199–202.

Chew, D. (1990) 'Internal adjustments to falling civil service salaries: Insights from Uganda', *World Development*, 18: 1003–14.

Child, J. (1972) 'Organizational structure, environment and performance: The role of strategic choice', *Sociology*, 6: 1–22.

Choi, J. (2003) 'Ethnic and regional politics after the Asian economic crisis: A comparison of Malaysia and South Korea', *Democratization*, 10: 121–34.

Chowdhury, A. and I. Islam (1996) 'The institutional and political framework of growth in an ethnically diverse society: The case of Malaysia', *Canadian Journal of Development Studies*, 17: 487–512.

Claisse, A. (1987) 'Makhzen traditions and administrative channels', in W. Zartman (ed.) *The political economy of Morocco*, New York: Praeger, 34–58.

Clapham, C. (ed.) (1982) *Private patronage and public power*, London: St. Martin's.

Clark, P. and M. Rowlinson (2004) 'The treatment of history in organisation studies: Towards an "historic turn"?', *Business History*, 46: 331–52.

Clark, T. (1994) 'Clientelism, U.S.A.: The dynamics of change', in L. Roniger and A. Güneş-Ayata (eds) *Democracy, clientelism and civil society*, Boulder, CO: Lynne Rienner, 121–44.

Clay, E. and B. Schaffer (1984) *Room for manoeuvre: An exploration of public policy in agriculture and rural development*, London: Heinemann.

Clement, J. (1990) 'Maroc: Les atouts et les défis de la monarchie', in B. Kodmani-Darwish (ed.) *Maghreb: Les années de transition*, Paris: Masson, 59–93.

Cleveland, J., K. Murphy and R. Williams (1989) 'Multiple uses of performance appraisal: Prevalence and correlates', *Journal of Applied Psychology*, 74: 130–5.

Collier, R. and D. Collier (1991) *Shaping political arenas: Critical junctures, the labor movement and regime dynamics in Latin America*, Princeton: Princeton University Press.

Collins, A. (1998) 'The ethnic security dilemma: Evidence from Malaysia', *Contemporary Southeast Asia*, 20: 261–78.

Commission for Africa (2005) *Our common interest: Report of the Commission for Africa*, http://www.commissionforafrica.org/english/report/thereport/cfafull-report.pdf, accessed March 20 2005.

Conway, J., R. Jako and D. Goodman (1995) 'A meta-analysis of interrater and internal consistency reliability of selection interviews', *Journal of Applied Psychology*, 80: 565–79.

Cook, M. (1998) *Personnel selection: Adding value through people*, Chichester: John Wiley.

Cooke, F. (2000) 'Manpower restructuring in the stateowned railway industry of China: The role of the state in human resource strategy', *International Journal of Human Resource Management*, 11: 904–24.

Coomaraswamy, A. (2003) 'The politics of institutional design: An overview of the case of Sri Lanka', in S. Bastian and R. Luckham (eds) *Can democracy be designed? The politics of institutional choice in conflict-torn* societies, London: Zed, 145–69.

Cooper, D., I. Robertson and G. Tinline (2003) *Recruitment and selection: A framework for success*, London: Thomson.

Corkery, J. and A. Land (1996) *Civil service reform in the context of structural adjustment*, Maastricht: European Centre for Development Policy Management.

Courier (1999) 'Interview with Obed Dlamini', *The Courier*, 174: 49–50.

Courier (1998) 'An eclectic society', *The Courier*, 170: 14–17.

Court, J., P. Kristen and B. Weder (1999) *Bureaucratic structure and performance: First Africa survey results*, Tokyo: United Nations University.

Crook, R. and J. Manor (1998) *Democracy and decentralization in South Asia and West Africa*, Cambridge: Cambridge University Press.

Crook, R. and A. Sverrisson (2001) *Decentralization and poverty alleviation in developing countries: A comparative analysis or, Is West Bengal unique?*, Falmer: Institute of Development Studies, Working Paper 130.

Crouch, H. (1996) *Government and society in Malaysia*, Ithaca: Cornell University Press.

Daniel, J. and J. Vilane (1986) 'Swaziland: Political crisis, regional dilemma', *Review of African Political Economy*, 35: 54–67.

David, P. (1985) 'Clio and the economics of QWERTY', *American Economic Review Proceedings*, 75: 332–7.

Dawkins, R. (1986) *The blind watchmaker*, London: Longman.

De Giorgio, E. (2000) 'Mauritius: A role model for Africa', *African Business*, 254, 31–2.

De Korte, D., P. Mazonde and E. Darkoh (2004) *Introducing anti-retroviral therapy in the public sector in Botswana*, Geneva: World Health Organization.

De Meuse, K., P. Vanderheiden and T. Bergmann (1994) 'Announced layoffs: Their effect on corporate financial performance', *Human Resource Management*, 33: 509–30.

De Silva, K. (1993a) 'Politics and the political system', in K. De Silva (ed.) *Sri Lanka: Problems of governance*, New Delhi: Konark, 3–41.

De Silva, K. (1993b) 'The bureaucracy', in K. De Silva (ed.) *Sri Lanka: Problems of governance*, New Delhi: Konark, 83–98.

Department for International Development (2005) *Drivers of change*, http://www.grc-exchange.org/g_themes/politicalsystems_drivers.html, accessed May 25 2005.

Devotta, N. (2003) 'Sri Lanka's political decay: Analysing the October 2000 and December 2001 parliamentary elections', *Commonwealth and Comparative Politics*, 41, 2: 115–42.

Dia, M. (1996) *Africa's management in the 1990s and beyond: Reconciling indigenous and transplanted institutions*, Washington DC: World Bank.

Dlamini, S. (1999) 'Vision for the future', *New African*, January 28–29.

Dlamini, M. (1992) 'Administrative reform and civil service in Swaziland: Gap between promise and performance', *Indian Journal of Public Administration*, 38, 2: 169–86.

Doriye, J. (1992) 'Public office and private gain: An interpretation of the Tanzanian experience', in M. Wuyts, M. Mackintosh and T. Hewitt (eds) *Development policy and public action*, Oxford: Oxford University Press, 91–113.

Dovlo, D. (2004) 'Using mid-level cadres as substitutes for internationally mobile health professionals in Africa: A desk review', *Human Resources for Health*, 2, 7.

Downs, A. (1995) *Corporate executions: The ugly truth about layoffs – how corporate greed is shattering lives, companies, and communities*, New York: AMACOM.

Dubey, A. (1997) *Government and politics in Mauritius*, Delhi: Kalinga.

Duncan, A., H. Macmillan and N. Simutanyi (2003) *Drivers of pro-poor change: An overview*, http://www.grc-exchange.org/g_themes/politicalsystems_drivers.html, accessed May 25 2005.

Duncan, A., I. Sharif, P. Landell-Mills, D. Hulme and J. Roy (2002) *Bangladesh: Supporting the drivers of pro-poor change*, http://www.grc-exchange.org/g_themes/politicalsystems_drivers.html, accessed May 25 2005.

Dunsire, A. and C. Hood (1989) *Cutback management in public bureaucracies*, Cambridge: Cambridge University Press.

Earthtrends (2005) *Economic indicators – Mauritius*, http://earthtrends.wri.org/pdf_library/country_profiles/Eco_cou_480.pdf, accessed August 31 2005.

Economist (2004) 'The slow march to reform', *Economist*, August 7 2004: 49.

Economist (2003) 'Celebrating 30 oppressive years: Swaziland's monarchy', *Economist*, May 17 2003: 62.

Economist (2003) 'Offshore and upbeat: Mauritius changes government', *Economist*, September 22 2003: 66.

Economist (2002) 'The Palace and the politicians: Morocco's election', *Economist*, September 28 2002: 68.

Economist (1999) 'Reggae rage in Mauritius', *Economist*, February 27 1999: 43.

Economist (1998) 'Zhu takes on the red-tape army', *Economist*, March 14 1998: 83.

Economist (1996a) 'A half-African success story', *Economist*, December 14 1996: 45.

Economist (1996b) 'The year downsizing grew up', *Economist*, December 21 1996: 115–17.

Economist (1995) 'Good havens', *Economist*, September 30 1995: 122.

Economist Intelligence Unit (1999) *Country profile: Mauritius, Seychelles*, London: Economist Intelligence Unit.

Eickelman, D. (1998) *The Middle East and Central Asia: An anthropological approach*, Upper Saddle River, NJ: Prentice-Hall.

Eisenhardt, M. (1989) 'Building theories from case study research', *Academy of Management Review*, 14: 532–50.

Eisenstadt, S. and L. Roniger (1984) *Patrons, clients and friends*, Cambridge: Cambridge University Press.

Eldredge, N. (1985) *Time frames: The rethinking of Darwinian evolution and the theory of punctuated equilibrium*, New York: Simon and Schuster.

El-Messaoudi, A. (1996) 'Le profil du ministre Marocain au début des années 90', *Maghreb Review*, 21: 77–94.

Embong, A. (2002) *State-led modernization and the new middle class in Malaysia*, London: Palgrave.

Emsley, I. (1996) *The Malaysian experience of affirmative action: Lessons for South Africa*, Cape Town: Human and Rousseau.

Eriksen, T. (1998) *Common denominators: Ethnicity, nation-building and compromise in Mauritius*, Oxford: Berg.

Eriksson, K., A. Majkgard and D. Sharma (2000) 'Path dependence and knowledge development in the internationalization process', *Management International Review*, 40, 307–28.

Esman, M. (1972) *Administration and development in Malaysia: Institution building and reform in a plural society*, Ithaca: Cornell University Press.

Evans, P. (1998) 'Transferable lessons? Re-examining the institutional prerequisites of East Asian economic policies', *Journal of Development Studies*, 34, 6: 66–86.

Evans, P. (1995) *Embedded autonomy: States and industrial transformation*, Princeton, NJ: Princeton University Press.

Evans, P. and J. Rauch (1999) 'Bureaucracy and growth: A cross-national-analysis of the effects of "Weberian" state structures on economic growth', *American Sociological Review*, 64: 748–65.

Evans, R. (1997) *In defence of history*, London: Granta.

Evans-Pritchard, E. (1940) *The Nuer: A description of the models of livelihood and political institutions of a Nilotic people*, Oxford: Oxford University Press.

Ferguson, J. (1990) *The anti-politics machine: 'Development', depoliticization and bureaucratic power in Lesotho*, Cambridge: Cambridge University Press.

Ferguson, N. (1997) *Virtual history*, London: Pan.

Fernando, E. (1982) 'The public service and the political environment in Sri Lanka', *International Review of Administrative Sciences*, 3, 4: 363–7.

Fitzgerald, S. (1990) *The great Gatsby*, London: Penguin.

Fombrun, C., N. Tichy and M. Devanna (1984) *Strategic human resource management*, New York: Wiley.

Fosh, P. (1978) 'Attitudes of East African white-collar workers to income inequalities', *International Labour Review*, 117, 1: 99–108.

Fourie, D. (1998) 'Government contracting and official capacity: Reflections with reference to South Africa', *Asian Journal of Public Administration*, 20, 2: 233–48.

Fukuyama, F. (2004) *State building: Governance and world order in the 21st century*, Ithaca, NY: Cornell University Press.

Ganguly, S. (1997) 'Ethnic policies and political quiescence in Malaysia and Singapore', in M. Brown and S. Ganguly (eds) *Government Policies and Ethnic Relations in Asia and the Pacific*, Cambridge, MA: MIT Press, 233–72.

Gardiner, P. (ed.) (1974) *The philosophy of history*, Oxford: Oxford University Press

Geertz, C. (1973) 'Thick description: Toward an interpretive theory of culture', in C. Geertz *The interpretation of culture*, New York: Basic Books, 3–30.

Gellner, E. (1981) *Muslim societies*, Cambridge: Cambridge University Press.

Gellner, E. and J. Waterbury (eds) (1977) *Patrons and clients in Mediterranean societies*, London: Duckworth.

Gerschenkron, A. (1968) 'On the concept of continuity in history', in *Continuity in history and other essays*, Cambridge, MA: Harvard University Press, 11–39.

Gildea, R. (2002) *Marianne in chains: In search of the German occupation of France 1940–45*, London: Macmillan.

Global Fund to Fight AIDS, Tuberculosis and Malaria (2004) *Portfolio of grants in Namibia*, www.theglobalfund.org/portfolio.aspx?lang=en&countryI=NMB#HIV/AIDS, accessed September 5 2005.

Gomez, E. and K. Jomo (1997) *Malaysia's political economy: Politics, patronage and profits*, Cambridge: Cambridge University Press.

Government of Ghana (1992) *Redeployment management committee: Status programme for 1992 and work programme for 1993*, Accra: Government of Ghana.

Government of Ghana (1987) *Programme of actions to mitigate the social costs of adjustment*, Accra: Government of Ghana.

Government of Malaysia (1991) *Report of the special committee of the Cabinet on salaries for the public sector*, Kuala Lumpur: Government of Malaysia.

Government of Mauritius (2000) *Reform of the civil service: Report of the standing committee on civil service reform*. Port-Louis: Government of Mauritius.

Government of Namibia (1998) *Vision 2030*, http://www.npc.gov.na/vision/pdfs/Summary.pdf, accessed July 24 2005.

Government of South Africa (1998) *Developing a culture of good governance: Report of the Presidential Review Commission on the reform and transformation of the public service in South Africa*, http://www.polity.org.za/html/govdocs/reports/presreview/, accessed April 7 2003.

Government of South Africa (1997) *White Paper on transforming service delivery*, *Government Gazette*, No. 18340, October 1997.

Government of South Africa (1995) *White Paper on the transformation of the public service*, *Government Gazette*, No. 16838, November 1995.

Government of Sri Lanka (1998) *Administrative reforms circular no. 2: Improvement of systems and procedures in ministries and departments*, Colombo: Presidential Secretariat.

Government of Sri Lanka (1987) *Report of the Administrative Reforms Committee*, vols. 1–10, Colombo: Government of Sri Lanka.

Government of Swaziland (2005) *Public sector management programme*, http://www.gov.sz/home.asp?pid=1953#achievements, accessed March 9 2005.

Government of Swaziland (1999a) *National development strategy: Vision 2022, Key macro and sectoral strategies*, Mbabane: Government of Swaziland.

Government of Swaziland (1999b) *Public Sector Management Programme annual report*, Mbabane: Government of Swaziland.

Government of Tanzania (1965) *Report of the Commission on the establishment of a democratic one-party state*, Dar es Salaam: Government Printer.

Government of Uganda (1996) *Uganda civil service reform programme: Status report 11*, Kampala: Ministry of Public Service.

Government of Uganda (1994) *Management of change: Context, vision, objectives, strategy and plan*, Kampala: Ministry of Public Service.

Government of Uganda (1990) *Report of the Public Service Review and Reorganisation Commission*, Kampala: Government of Uganda.

Graham, C. (1994) *Safety nets, politics and the poor: Transitions to market economies*, Washington DC: Brookings Institute.

Greene, G. (1984) *Getting to know the General: The story of an involvement*, London: Bodley Head.

Greene, G. (1978) *The human factor*, London: Bodley Head.

Greenhalgh, L. and R. McKersie (1980) 'Cost-effectiveness of alternative strategies of cut-back management', *Public Administration Review*, 40: 575–84.

Guardian (Tanzania) (2003) *Guardian*, February 19.

Guest, D. (1997) 'Human resource management and performance: A review and research agenda', *International Journal of Human Resource Management*, 8: 263–76.

Guest, D. (1989) 'Personnel and HRM: Can you tell the difference?', *Personnel Management*, 21, 1: 48–51.

Gulhati, R. (1990) 'Who makes economic policy in Africa and how?', *World Development*, 18: 1147–61.

Gulhati, R. and R. Nallari (1990) *Successful stabilization and recovery in Mauritius*, Washington DC: World Bank.

Güneş-Ayata, A. (1994) 'Clientelism: Premodern, modern and postmodern', in L. Roniger, and A. Güneş-Ayata (eds) *Democracy, clientelism and civil society*, Boulder, CO: Lynne Rienner, 19–28.

Hague, R. and M. Harrop (2001) *Comparative government and politics: An introduction*, New York: Palgrave.

Hall, S. (1999) 'India's manufactured exports: Comparative structure and prospects', *World Development*, 27: 1769–86.

Hammoudi, A. (1997) *Master and disciple: The cultural foundations of Moroccan authoritarianism*, Chicago: University of Chicago Press.

Heaney, S. (1998) 'Voices from Lemnos', in *Opened ground: Poems 1966–1996*, London: Faber and Faber, 327–32.

Heaver, R. and A. Israel (1986) *Country commitment to development projects*, Washington DC: World Bank Discussion Paper No. 4.

Heeks, R. (2005) *Implementing and managing eGovernment: An international text*, London: Sage.

Heenan, D. (1994) 'Postcards from the edge', *Journal of Business Strategy*, 15, 5: 14–16.

Henderson, J. (1999) 'Uneven crises: Institutional foundations of East Asian economic turmoil', *Economy and Society*, 28: 327–68.

Henderson, J., D. Hulme, H. Jalilian and R. Phillips (2003) 'Bureaucratic effects: "Weberian" state structures and poverty reduction', University of Manchester: Chronic Poverty Research Centre Working Paper No. 31.

Henkoff, R. (1990) 'Cost cutting: How to do it right', *Fortune*, April 9: 26–33.

Higgins, M. (1982) 'Limits of clientelism: Towards an assessment of Irish politics', in C. Clapham (ed.) *Private patronage and public power*, London: St. Martin's, 114–41.

High-level forum on the health MDGs (2005) *Addressing Africa's health workforce crisis: An avenue for action*, http://www.hlfhealthmdgs.org/Documents/AfricasWorkforce-Final.pdf, accessed July 15 2005.

Hilderbrand, M. (2002) 'Capacity building', in C. Kirkpatrick, R. Clarke and C. Polidano (eds) *Handbook of development policy and management*, Cheltenham: Edward Elgar, 323–32.

Hilley, J. (2001) *Malaysia: Mahathirism, hegemony and the new opposition*, London: Zed.

Hirsch, P. and J. Gillespie (2001) 'Unpacking path dependences: Differential valuations accorded history across disciplines', in R. Garud and P. Karnøe (eds) *Path dependence and creation*, Mahwah, NJ: Lawrence Erlbaum, 69–90.

Hobsbawm, E. and G. Rudé (1969) *Captain Swing*, London: Lawrence and Wishart.

Hofstede, G. (1980) *Culture's consequences: Differences in work-related values*, London: Sage.

Hourani, A. (1991) *A history of the Arab peoples*, London: Faber and Faber.

House, R., P. Hanges, M. Javidan, P. Dorfman and V. Gupta (2004). *Culture, leadership, and organizations: The GLOBE study of 62 societies*, Thousand Oaks, CA: Sage.

Houtzager, P. and M. Moore (eds) (2003) *Changing paths: International development and the new politics of inclusion*, Ann Arbor, MI: University of Michigan Press.

Hulme, D. (1995) 'Projects, policies and professionals: Alternative approaches for project identification and project planning', *Agricultural Systems*, 47: 211–33.

Hulme, D. (1990) *The effectiveness of British aid for training*, London: Action Aid.

Huselid, M. (1995) 'The impact of human resource management practices on turnover, productivity and corporate financial performance', *Academy of Management Journal*, 38: 635–70.

Hutton, W. (1995) *The state we're in*, London: Jonathan Cape.

Hyden, G., J. Court and K. Mease (2004) *Making sense of governance: Empirical evidence from 16 developing countries*, Boulder, CO: Lynne Rienner.

IMF (International Monetary Fund) (2004a) *2003 Article IV consultation: Staff report*, www.imf.org, accessed May 27 2004.

IMF (2004b) *IMF Concludes 2003 Article IV consultation with Malaysia*, www.imf.org, accessed May 10 2004.

IMF (2004c) *IMF concludes 2003 Article IV consultation with Swaziland*, http://www.imf.org/external/np/sec/pn/2004/pn0461.htm, accessed March 9 2005.

Irwin, T. (1996) 'An analysis of New Zealand's new system of public sector management', in OECD, *Performance management in government: Contemporary Illustrations*, Paris: OECD, Public Management Occasional Paper No. 9, pp. 7–32.

Isenman, P. (1980) 'Basic needs: The case of Sri Lanka', *World Development*, 20: 119–31.

Iweala, U. (2005) *Beasts of no nation*, London: John Murray.

Jaspars, J., F. Fincham and M. Hewstone (eds) (1983) *Attribution theory and research: Conceptual, developmental and social dimensions*, London: Academic Press.

Jayanntha, D. (1992) *Electoral allegiance in Sri Lanka*, Cambridge: Cambridge University Press.

Jayarajah, C. and W. Branson (1995) *Structural and sectoral adjustment: World Bank experience 1980–1992*, Washington DC: World Bank Operations Evaluation study.

JLI (Joint Learning Initiative) (2004) *Human resources for health: Overcoming the crisis*, Cambridge, MA: Harvard University.

Joffe, G. (1988) 'Morocco: Monarchy, legitimacy and succession', *Third World Quarterly*, 10, 1: 201–28.

Johnson, G., K. Scholes and R. Whittington (2004) *Exploring corporate strategy: Text and cases*, London: FT Prentice Hall.

Johnson J. and S. Wasty (1993) *Borrower ownership of adjustment programmes and the political economy of reform*, Washington DC: World Bank Discussion Paper No. 199.

Johnston, M. (1998) 'Fighting systemic corruption: Social foundations for institutional reform', *European Journal of Development Research*, 10, 1: 85–104.

Jomo, K. and P. Todd (1994) *Trade unions and the state in peninsular Malaysia*, Kuala Lumpur: Oxford University Press.

Jones, D. (1974) 'The tribune's visitation', in D. Jones *The Sleeping Lord and other fragments*, London: Faber and Faber, 42–58.

Jones, D. (1973) *Epoch and artist: Selected writings*, London: Faber.

Joubert, C. and A. Zoubi (1995) *Report of a mission to the kingdom of Swaziland on public sector management review*, New York: United Nations, Department for Development support and Management Services.

Jupp, J. (1978) *Sri Lanka: Third World democracy*, London: Frank Cass.

Kamoche, K. (1996) 'Strategic human resource management within a Resource-Capability view of the firm', *Journal of Management Studies*, 33: 213–33.

Kaufmann, D. (1999) *Governance redux: The empirical challenge*, http://www.worldbank.org/wbi/governance/pubs/govredux.html, accessed June 17 2004.

Kaufmann, D., A. Kraay and M. Mastruzzi (2005) *Governance matters IV: Governance indicators for 1996–2004*, http://info.worldbank.org/governance/kkz2004/sc_chart.asp, accessed May 10 2005.

Kaufmann, D., A. Kraay, and M. Mastruzzi (2003) *Governance Matters III: Governance Indicators for 1996–2002*, http://info.worldbank.org/governance/kkz2002/sc_chart.asp, accessed April 26 2004.

Khaleghian, P. and M. Gupta (2005) 'Public management and the essential public health functions', *World Development*, 33: 1083–99.

Khoo, B. (2003) *Beyond Mahathir: Malaysian politics and its discontents*, London: Zed.

Kiesler, C. (1971) *The psychology of commitment: Experiments linking behavior to belief*, New York: Academic Press.

Kiesler, C. and J. Sakamura (1966) 'A test of a model for commitment', *Journal of Personality and Social Psychology*, 3: 349–53.

Killick, T. (1998) *Aid and the political economy of policy change*, London: Routledge.

Kiragu, K. (1998) 'The civil service pay reform: Issues and options', in S. Rugumamu (ed.) *Civil service reform in Tanzania: Proceedings of the National Symposium*, Dar es Salaam: University Consultancy Bureau, 129–67.

Kiragu, K. and R. Mukandala (2004) *Pay reform and policies report*, Paris: OECD Development Assistance Committee.

Kitchen, R. (1989) 'Administrative reform in Jamaica: A component of structural adjustment', *Public Administration and Development*, 9: 339–55.

Klein, P. (1997) 'Downsizing government: Size and institutionalist principles', *Journal of Economic Issues*, 31: 595–604.

Klitgaard, R. (1997) '"Unanticipated consequences" in anti-poverty programs', *World Development*, 25: 1963–72.

Korten D. (1980) 'Community organisation and rural development: A learning process approach', *Public Administration Review* (September/October).

Kotter, J. (1979) 'Choosing strategies for change', *Harvard Business Review*, March/April 1979.

Kozlowski, S., G. Chao, E. Smith and J. Hedlund (1993) 'Organizational downsizing: Strategies, interventions and research implications', in C. Cooper and I. Robertson (eds) *International Review of Industrial and Organizational Psychology, Volume 8*, Chichester: John Wiley, 263–332.

Krugman, P. (1994) *Peddling prosperity: Economic sense and nonsense in the age of diminished expectations*, New York: W. W. Norton.

Kuhn, T. (1962) *The structure of scientific revolutions*, Chicago: University of Chicago Press.

Kuper, H. (1980) *An African aristocracy: Rank among the Swazi*, New York: Africana.

Kuruvilla, S. and C. Erickson (2002) 'Change and transformation in Asian industrial relations', *Industrial Relations*, 41: 171–227.

Lampedusa, T. (1963) *Il gattopardo ('The leopard')*, Milan: Feltrinelli.

Landé, C. (1977) 'The dyadic basis of clientelism', in S. Schmidt, L. Guasti, C. Landé and J. Scott (eds) *Friends, followers and factions: A reader in political clientelism*, Berkeley: University of California Press, xiii–xxxvii.

Latham, G. and E. Locke (1991) 'Goal-setting: A motivational technique', in R. Steers and L. Porter (eds) *Motivation and work behavior*, New York: McGraw-Hill, 357–70.

Lee, T. (1999) *Using qualitative methods in organizational research*, Thousand Oaks, CA: Sage.

Legum, C. (1988) 'The Nyerere years: A preliminary balance sheet', in M. Hodd (ed.) *Tanzania after Nyerere*, London: Pinter, 3–11.

Leveau, R. (1985) *Le fellah Marocain, défenseur du trône*, Paris: Presses de la fondation nationale des sciences politiques.

Levin, R. (1991) 'Swaziland's Tinkhundla and the myth of Swazi tradition', *Journal of Contemporary African Studies*, 10, 2: 1–23.

Levy, B. (1993) 'An institutional analysis of the design and sequence of trade and investment policy reform', *World Bank Economic Review*, 7: 247–62.

Li, J., J. Moy and B. Sun (2004) 'The effects of local environments on employment system: Reform and organizational downsizing in China', Hong Kong: Hong Kong Baptist University BRC Papers on Human Resource Studies.

Lienert, I. and J. Modi (1997) *A decade of civil service reform in sub-Saharan Africa*, Washington DC: International Monetary Fund, Working Paper.

Lindauer, D. and B. Nunberg (eds) (1994) *Rehabilitating government: Pay and employment reform in Africa*, Washington DC: World Bank.

Lindblom, C. (1959) The science of muddling through, *Public Administration Review*, 19: 78–88.

Linton, R. (1936) *The study of man*, New York: Appleton-Century.

Lister, L. and B. George (1985) 'The role of tradition in the recent political and economic development of Swaziland', *Manchester Papers on Development*, 1, 3: 30–44.

Long, P. (1986) *Performance appraisal revisited*, London: Institute of Personnel Management.

Love, K., R. Bishop, D. Heinisch and M. Montei (1994) 'Selection across two cultures: Adapting the selection of American assemblers to meet Japanese job performance demands', *Personnel Psychology*, 47: 837–46.

Lumbanga, M. (1995) 'Report on the joint donors and government meeting on the Civil Service Reform Programme', President's Office, CSD. Dar es Salaam.

Macduffie, J. (1995) 'Human resource bundles and manufacturing performance: Organizational logic and flexible production systems in the world auto industry', *Industrial and Labor Relations Review*, 48: 197–221.

Mahoney, J. (2003) 'Long-run development and the legacy of colonialism in Spanish America', *American Journal of Sociology*, 109: 50–106.

Mahoney, J. (2001) 'Path-dependent explanations of regime change: Central America in comparative perspective', *Studies In Comparative International Development*, 36: 111–41.

Mahoney, J. and R. Snyder (1999) 'Rethinking agency and structure in the study of regime change, *Studies in Comparative International Development*, 34, 2: 3–32.

Mail and Guardian (2005) 'Small show for stayaway', *Mail and Guardian*, January 28 2005.

Mallaby, S. (2005) *The world's banker: A story of failed states, financial crises and the wealth and poverty of nations*, New Haven, CT: Yale University Press.

Manning, N. and N. Parison (2004) *International public administration reform: Implications for the Russian Federation*, Washington DC: World Bank.

Manning, N. and N. Parison (2003) *International public administration reform: Implications for the Russian Federation*, Washington: World Bank, http://worldbank.org/publicsector/civilservice, accessed September 9 2004.

Mansor, N. and M. Ali (1998) 'An exploratory study of organizational flexibility in Malaysia: A research note', *International Journal of Human Resource Management*, 9: 506–15.

Marais, O. (1973) 'The ruling class in Morocco', in I. Zartman (ed.) *Man, state and society in the contemporary Maghreb*, London: Pall Mall, 181–200.

Marwick, A. (2001) *The new nature of history: Knowledge, evidence, language*, Basingstoke: Macmillan.

Mathiason, N. (2005) 'Elvis of economics takes a bow', *The Observer*, Business, March 20: 11.

Matlosa, K. (1998) 'Democracy and conflict in post-apartheid southern Africa: Dilemmas of social change in small states', *International Affairs*, 74: 319–37.

Mauritius News (2005) 'Communalism is dead in Mauritius', *Mauritius News*, March 2005, http://www.mauritius-news.co.uk/, accessed March 6 2005.

Mawhood, P. (1983) *Local government in the Third World: The experience of tropical Africa*, Chichester: John Wiley.

Maxwell, S. (2005) *The Washington Consensus is dead! Long live the meta-narrative!*, London: Overseas Development Institute, Working Paper 243.

McCourt, W. (2003) 'Political commitment to reform: Civil service reform in Swaziland', *World Development*, 31: 1015–31.

McCourt, W. (2001a) 'Finding a way forward on public employment reform: A Sri Lankan case study', *Asia Pacific Journal of Human Resources*, 39, 1: 1–22.

McCourt, W. (2001b) 'Moving the public management debate forward: A contingency approach', in W. McCourt and M. Minogue (eds) *The internationalization of public management: Reinventing the Third World state*, Cheltenham: Edward Elgar, 220–53.

McCourt, W. (2001c) 'The new public selection? Anti-corruption, psychometric selection and the New Public Management in Nepal', *Public Management Review*, 3: 325–44.

McCourt, W. (2001d) 'The NPM agenda for service delivery: A suitable model for developing countries?', in W. McCourt and M. Minogue (eds) *The internationalization of public management: Reinventing the Third World state*, Cheltenham: Edward Elgar, 107–28.

McCourt, W. (1998a) 'Civil service reform equals retrenchment? The experience of staff retrenchment in Ghana, Uganda and the United Kingdom', in M. Minogue, C. Polidano and D. Hulme (eds) *Beyond the New Public Management: Changing ideas and practices in governance*, Cheltenham: Edward Elgar, 172–87.

McCourt, W. (1998b) *Employment and pay reform: A guide to assistance*, London: Department for International Development.

McCourt, W. (1997) 'Using metaphors to understand and to change organizations: A critique of Gareth Morgan's approach', *Organization Studies*, 18, 511–22.

McCourt, W. and D. Eldridge (2003) *Global human resource management: Managing people in developing and transitional countries*, Cheltenham: Edward Elgar.

McCourt, W. and A. Ramgutty-Wong (2003) 'Limits to strategic human resource management: the case of the Mauritian civil service', *International Journal of Human Resource Management*, 14: 600–18.

McCourt, W. and N. Sola (1999) 'Using training to promote civil service reform: A Tanzanian local government case study', *Public Administration and Development*, 17: 435–76.

McGreal, C. (2000) 'Swazis begin national strike', *Guardian*, 13 November: 18.

McKinley, W., C. Sanchez and A. Schick (1995) 'Organizational downsizing: constraining, cloning, learning', *Academy of Management Executive*, 9, 3: 32–44.

Means, G. (1996) 'Soft authoritarianism in Malaysia and Singapore', *Journal of Democracy*, 7, 4: 103–17.

Means, G. (1991) *Malaysian politics: The second generation*, Oxford: Oxford University Press.

Meisenhelder, T. (1997) 'The developmental state in Mauritius', *Journal of Modern African Studies*, 35: 279–97.

Meier, G. and J. Stiglitz (eds) (2001) Frontiers of development economics: The future in perspective, Oxford: Oxford University Press.

Mellahi, K. and G. Wood (2004) 'HRM in Malaysia', in P. Budhwar (ed.) *Managing human resources in Asia-Pacific*, London: Routledge, 201–20.

Meyer, J. and N. Allen (1997) *Commitment in the workplace: Theory, research and application*, Thousand Oaks, CA: Sage.

Meyer-Stamer, J. (1998) 'Path dependence in regional development: Persistence and change in three industrial clusters in Santa Catarina', *World Development*, 26: 1495–511.

Milliman, J., S. Nason, E. Gallagher, P. Huo, M. Von Glinow and K. Lowe (1998) 'The impact of national culture on human resource management practices: The case of performance appraisal', in S. Prasad (ed.) *Advances in international comparative management*, Greenwich, CT: JAI Press, 157–83.

Milne, R. and D. Mauzy (1999) *Malaysian politics under Mahathir*, London: Routledge.

Ministère de la Fonction Publique (1998) *Résumé du rapport: Groupe d'Etude sur la gestion des ressources humaines*, Rabat: Ministère de la Fonction Publique.

Ministry of Civil Service Affairs and Administrative Reforms (2004) *Action Plan 2004–2005*, http://civilservice.gov.mu, accessed March 6 2005.

Ministry of Civil Service Affairs and Administrative Reforms (2001) *Action Plan 2001–2003*, http://civilservice.gov.mu/actionpl.htm, accessed March 6 2005.

Ministry of Economic Development and Regional Co-operation (1997) *Vision 2020: The national long-term perspective study*, Port-Louis: Ministry of Economic Development and Regional Co-operation.

Ministry of Health and Social Services (2004) *Personnel procedures manual*, Windhoek: Ministry of Health and Social Services.

Minns, J. (2001) 'Of miracles and models: The rise and decline of the developmental state in South Korea', *Third World Quarterly*, 22: 1025–43.

Minogue, M. (1992) 'Mauritius: Economic miracle or developmental illusion?', *Journal of International Development*, 4: 643–7.

Minogue, M. (1976) 'Public Administration in Mauritius', *Journal of Administration Overseas*, 15, 3: 160–6.

Mintzberg, H. (1989) 'Crafting strategy', in H. Mintzberg *Mintzberg on management*, New York: Free Press, 25–42.

Mintzberg, H. (1983) *Structure in fives: Designing effective organizations*, New York: Prentice Hall.

Mirguet, O. (2005) 'Les cachots secrets d'Hassan II', *Libération*, June 9: 38–9.

Montgomery, J. and M. Esman (1966) *Development administration in Malaysia*, Kuala Lumpur: Government of Malaysia.

Moore, M. (2000) 'Political underdevelopment: What causes "bad governance"?', *Public Management Review*, 3: 385–418.

Moore, M. (1994) '"Guided democracy" in Sri Lanka: The electoral dimension', *Journal of Commonwealth and Comparative Politics*, 32: 1–30.

Moore, M. (1985) *The state and peasant politics in Sri Lanka*, Cambridge: Cambridge University Press.

Morgan, D. (1997) *Focus groups as qualitative research*, Thousand Oaks, CA: Sage.

Morgan, G. (1986) *Images of organization*, Newbury Park, CA: Sage.

Mosley, P., J. Harrigan and J. Toye (1991) *Aid and power: The World Bank and policy-based lending*, Vol. 2, *Case studies*, London: Routledge.

Moussa, F. (1988) 'Existe-t-il un modèle Maghrébin d'administration?', in A. Claisse and J. Leca (eds) *Le Grand Maghreb: Données socio-politiques et facteurs d'intégration des états du Maghreb*, Paris: Economica, 148–72.

Mowday, R., L. Porter and R. Steers (1982) *Employee-organization linkages: The psychology of commitment, absenteeism and turnover*, New York: Academic Press.

Mukandala, R. (1992) 'To be or not to be: The paradoxes of African bureaucracy in the 1990s', *International Review of Administrative Science*, 58: 526–55.

Munson, H. (1993) *Religion and power in Morocco*, New Haven: Yale.

Musa, M. (1999) *The Malay dilemma revisited: Race dynamics in modern Malaysia*, Gilroy, CA: Merantau.

Museveni, Y. (1997) *Sowing the mustard seed: The struggle for freedom and democracy in Uganda*, London: Macmillan.

Mwaikusa, J. (1998) 'Revisiting the legal framework for civil service reform in Tanzania', in S. Rugumamu (ed.) *Civil service reform in Tanzania: Proceedings of the National Symposium*, Dar es Salaam: University of Dar es Salaam, 168–77.

Najem, T. (2001) 'Privatization and the state in Morocco: Nominal objectives and problematic realities', *Mediterranean Politics*, 6, 2: 51–67.

Namibian (2005) 'Swazi king says he's no absolute monarch', *The Namibian*, June 3: 10.

Namier, L. (1929) *The structure of politics at the accession of George III*, London: Macmillan.

Navaratnam, R. (2003) *Malaysia's economic challenges: A critical analysis of the Malaysian economy, Governance and Society*, London: Asean Academic Press.

Ncholo, P. (1997) *Presentation to the Presidential Review Commission on the transformation of the public service*, Pretoria: Department of Public Service and Administration.

Nelson, J. (ed.) (1990) *Economic crisis and policy choice*, Princeton, NJ: Princeton University Press, 321–61.

NEPAD (New Partnership for African Development) (2004) *Country self-assessment for the African peer review mechanism*, http://www.nepad.org/2005/files/documents/156.pdf, accessed July 13 2005.

Nevin, T. (1999) 'Swaziland: Blessings of a compact economy', *African Business*, January 1999: 15–20.

Ng'ethe, N., G. Williams and M. Katumanga (2004) *Strengthening the incentives for pro-poor policy change: An analysis of drivers of change in Kenya*, http://www.grc-exchange.org/g_themes/politicalsystems_drivers.html, accessed May 25 2005.

Nithiyanandam, V. (2000) 'Ethnic politics and Third World development: Some lessons from Sri Lanka's experience', *Third World Quarterly*, 21: 283–311.

Noda, T. and D. Collis (2001) 'The evolution of intraindustry firm heterogeneity: Insights from a process study', *Academy Of Management Journal*, 44: 897–925.

North, D. (1990) *Institutions, institutional change and economic performance*, Cambridge: Cambridge University Press.

Nsouli, S., S. Eken, K. Enders, V. Thai, J. Decressin and F. Cartiligia (1995) *Resilience and growth through sustained adjustment: The Moroccan experience*, Washington: IMF, Occasional Paper No. 117.

Ntukamazina, D. (1998) 'Civil service reforms in Tanzania: A strategic perspective', in S. Rugumamu (ed.) *Civil service reform in Tanzania: Proceedings of the National Symposium*, Dar es Salaam: University of Dar es Salaam, 44–60.

Nunberg, B. (1997) *Re-thinking civil service reform: An agenda for smart government*, Washington DC: World Bank.

Nunberg, B. (1994) 'Experience with civil service pay and employment reform: An overview', in D. Lindauer and B. Nunberg, *op. cit.*, 119–59.

Nyerere, J. (1977) *The Arusha Declaration: Ten years after*, Dar es Salaam: Government Press.

Nyerere, J. (1975) 'A decade of progress 1961–1971, TANU: Ten years after', in *Tanzania Notes and Records*, No. 76, Dar es Salaam: Tanzania Society.

Nyerere, J. (1962) *Democracy and the party system*, Dar es Salaam: Government Press.

Oberst, R. (1986) 'Admnistrative conflict and decentralization: The case of Sri Lanka', *Public Administration and Development*, 6: 163–74.

OECD (Organization for Economic Co-operation and Development) (2004) *Issues and developments in public management – country reports*, http://www.oecd.org/document/17/0,2340,en_2649_37421_2732241_1_1_1_37421,00.html, accessed September 21 2004.

OECD (2002) *International migration of physicians and nurses: Causes, consequences, and health policy implications*, Paris: OECD.

OECD (1996) *The civil service legislation contents checklist*, SIGMA Papers, No. 5, http://www.oecd.org/puma/sigmaweb/pubs, accessed May 7 2003.

OECD (1995) *Governance in transition: Public management reforms in OECD countries*, Paris: OECD.

OECD (1994) *Public management developments*, Paris: OECD.

Office for Public Appointments (2004) *Annual report*, http://www.ocpa.gov.uk/pages/downloads/pdf/OCPA_Annual_Report_2004.pdf, accessed July 15 2004.

Office of Public Service (1995) *The strategic management of agencies: Full report and case studies*, London: HMSO.

Pandit, N. (1996) *A meta-analysis of the corporate turnaround literature*, Manchester: Manchester Business School, Working Paper No. 326.

Parasuraman, B. (2003) *Malaysian industrial relations: A critical analysis*, Petaling Jaya: Pearson.

Patterson, M., M. West, R. Lawthorn and S. Nickell (1997) *The impact of people management practices on business performance*, London: Institute of Personnel and Development, Issues in People Management No. 22.

Peak, M. (1996) 'An era of wrenching corporate change', *Management Review*, 85, 7: 45–9.

Pendukeni, M. (2004) *The impact of HIV/AIDS on health care provision: Perceptions of nurses currently working in one regional hospital in Namibia*, Cape Town: University of the Western Cape MSc. thesis.

Pennell, C. (2000) *Morocco since 1830*, London: Hurst.

Perkin, E. and J. Court (2005) *Networks and policy processes in international development: A literature review*, London: Overseas Development Institute, Working Paper 252, http://www.odi.org.uk/RAPID/Publications/Documents/WP252.pdf, accessed November 12 2005.

Perkins, D. (1987) 'What can CEOs do for displaced workers?', *Harvard Business Review*, November 1987: 90–3.

Peters, T. and R. Waterman (1982) *In search of excellence: Lessons from America's best-run companies*, London: Harper and Row.

Pfeffer, J. (1998) *The human equation: Building profits by putting people first*, Boston, MA: Harvard Business School.

Pfeffer, J. (1992) *Managing with power: Politics and influence in organizations*, Boston, MA: Harvard Business School Press.

Plumb, J. (1966) *The death of the past*, London: Macmillan.

Polidano, C. (1995) 'Should administrative reform commissions be decommissioned?', *Public Administration*, 73: 455–71.

Polidano, C. and D. Hulme (1999) 'Public management reform in developing countries: Issues and outcomes', *Public Management*, 1: 121–32.

Pratt, C. (1976) *The critical phase in Tanzania, 1945–68: Nyerere and the emergence of the socialist strategy*, Cambridge: Cambridge University Press.

PRB (Pay Research Bureau) (2003) *Review of pay and grading structures and conditions of service in the public sector*, http://ncb.intnet.mu/dha/prb/report.htm, accessed March 6 2005.

PRB (1998) *Review of pay and grading structures and conditions of service in the public sector*, Port Louis: Government of Mauritius.

Pressman, J. and A. Wildavsky (1979) *Implementation: How great expectations in Washington are dashed in Oakland*, Berkeley: University of California Press.

Pritchett, and M. Woolcock (2004) 'Solutions when the solution is the problem: Arraying the disarray in development', *World Development*, 32: 191–212.

Pronk, J. (1996) 'Preface', in P. De Haan and Y. van Hees (eds) *Civil service reform in sub-Saharan Africa*, The Hague, Netherlands: Ministry of Foreign Affairs: 7.

Proulx, D. (1999) *Programme national de modernisation et d'amélioration des capacités de gestion de l'administration*, Rabat: UNDP.

Public Service Commission (2004) *Annual report*, Windhoek: Public Service Commission.

Pugh, D. and D. Hickson (1976) *Organizational structure in its context: The Aston Programme I*, London: Gower.

Purcell, J. (1995) 'Corporate strategy and its link with human resource management strategy', in J. Storey (ed.) *Human resource management: A critical text*, London: Thomson, 63–86.

Puthucheary, M. (1987) 'The administrative elite', in Z. Ahmad (ed.) *Government and politics of Malaysia*, Singapore: Oxford University Press, 94–110.

Putnam, R. (1993) *Making democracy work: Civic traditions in modern Italy*, Princeton, NJ: Princeton University Press.

Radipati, B. (1993) 'Swaziland today: Law and politics under King Mswati III', *Année Africaine*, 1992–93: 243–67.

Rama, M. (2002) 'The gender implications of public sector downsizing: The reform program of Vietnam', *World Bank Research Observer*, 17, 2: 167–89.

Randell, G. (1994) 'Employee appraisal', in K. Sisson (ed.) *Personnel management: A comprehensive guide to theory and practice in Britain*, Oxford: Blackwell, 221–52.

Rauch, J. and P. Evans (2000) 'Bureaucratic structure and bureaucratic performance in less developed countries', *Journal of Public Economics*, 75: 49–71.

Redding, G. (2002) 'The capitalist business system of China and its rationale', *Asia Pacific Journal Of Management*, Singapore: 19, 2/3, 221–49.

Redman, T. and D. Keithley (1998) 'Downsizing goes east? Employment restructuring in post-socialist Poland', *International Journal of Human Resource Management*, 9: 274–95.

Regulska, J. (1997) 'Decentralization or deconcentration: Struggle for political power in Poland', *International Journal of Public Administration*, 20: 643–80.

Rhodes, R. (1997) *Understanding governance: Policy networks, governance reflexivity and accountability*, Buckingham: Open University Press.

Rigby, D. (2002) 'Look before you lay off', *Harvard Business Review*, April: 20–21.

Roach, S. (1996) 'The hollow ring of the productivity revival', *Harvard Business Review*, 74, 6: 81–9.

Robinson, D. (1990) 'Public-sector pay: The case of Sudan', in J. Pickett and H. Singer (eds) *Towards economic recovery in sub-Saharan Africa*, London: Routledge, 92–105.

Rodrik, D. (1989) 'Promises, promises: Credible policy reform via signalling', *Economic Journal*; 99: 756–72.

Rodrik, D. (1996) 'Understanding economic reform policy', *Journal of Economic Literature*, 34: 9–41.

Roniger, L. and A. Güneş-Ayata (eds) (1994) *Democracy, clientelism and civil society*, Boulder, CO: Lynne Rienner.

Root, H., G. Hodgson and G. Vaughan-Jones (2001) 'Public administration reform in Sri Lanka', *International Journal of Public Administration*, 24: 1357–78.

Rose, L. (1992) *The politics of harmony: Land dispute strategies in Swaziland*, Cambridge: Cambridge University Press.

Rose, R. (1985) *Public employment in Western nations*, Cambridge: Cambridge University Press.

Rose-Ackerman, S. (2004) 'Governance and anti-corruption', in B. Lomborg (ed.) *Global crises, global solutions*, Cambridge: Cambridge University Press, 301–44.

Rosen, L. (1979) 'Social identity and points of attachment: Approaches to social organization', in C. Geertz, H. Geertz and L. Rosen *Meaning and order in Moroccan society*, Cambridge: Cambridge University Press, 19–122.

Rouban, L. (1999) 'Senior civil servants in France', in E. Page and V. Wright (eds) *Bureaucratic elites in Western European states: A comparative analysis of top officials*, Oxford: Oxford University Press, 65–89.

Ruggles, P. and M. O'Higgins (1987) 'Retrenchment and the new Right: A comparative analysis of the impacts of the Thatcher and Reagan administrations', in M. Rein, G. Esping-Andersen and L. Rainwater (eds) *Stagnation and renewal in social policy: The rise and fall of policy regimes*, London: Sharpe, 160–90.

Russell, M. (1986) 'High status, low pay: Anomalies in the position of women in Swaziland', *Journal of Southern African Studies*, 12: 293–307.

Sachs, J. (2005) *The end of poverty: Economic possibilities for our time*, New York: Penguin.

Sahdev, K., S. Vinnicombe and S. Tyson (1999) 'Downsizing and the changing role of HR', *International Journal of Human Resource Management*, 10: 906–23.

Said, E. (2003) *Orientalism*, London: Penguin.

Salancik, G. (1977) 'Commitment and the control of organizational behavior and belief', in B. Staw and G. Salancik (eds) *New directions in organizational behavior*, Malabar, FL: Krieger, 1–54.

Sallinger-McBride, J. and L. Picard (1986) 'Patrons versus planners: The political contradictions of integrated rural development in Swaziland', *Journal of Contemporary African Studies*, 5, 1/2: 119–44.

Sampson, A. (2004) *Who runs this place? The anatomy of Britain in the twenty-first century*, London: John Murray.

Sarji, A. (1995) *The civil service of Malaysia: Towards efficiency and effectiveness*, Kuala Lumpur: Government of Malaysia.

Sater, J. (2002) 'The dynamics of state and civil society in Morocco', *Journal of North African Studies*, 7, 3: 101–18.

Sbih, M. (1977) *Les institutions administratives du Maghreb*, Paris: Hachette.

Schiavo-Campo, S. (1996) 'Reforming the civil service', *Finance and Development*, September 1996: 10–13.

Schiavo-Campo, S., G. de Tommaso and A. Mukherjee (1997) *An international statistical survey of government employment and wages*, Washington DC: World Bank, Policy Research Working Paper No. 1806.

Schick, A. (1998) 'Why most developing countries should not try New Zealand's reforms', *World Bank Research Observer*, 13, 1, 123–31.

Schilling, M. (2002) 'Technology success and failure in winner-take-all markets: The impact of learning orientation, timing, and network externalities', *Academy Of Management Journal*, 45: 387–98.

Schilling, M. (1998) 'Technological lockout: An integrative model of the economic and strategic factors driving technology success and failure', *Academy Of Management Review*, 23: 267–84.

Schmidt S., L. Guasti, C. Landé and J. Scott (eds) (1977) *Friends, followers and factions: A reader in political clientelism*, Berkeley: University of California Press.

Schmidt, F. and J. Hunter (1977) 'Development of a general solution to the problem of validity generalization', *Journal of Applied Psychology*, 62: 529–40.

Scott, J. (1985) *Weapons of the weak: Everyday forms of peasant resistance*, New Haven: Yale University Press.

Scott, J. (1972) 'The erosion of patron-client bonds and social change in rural Southeast Asia', *Journal of Asian Studies*, 23: 5–37.

Scott, J. (1968) *Political ideology in Malaysia*, New Haven: Yale University Press.

Shafie, H. (1996) 'Malaysia's experience in implementing the new performance appraisal system', *Public Administration and Development*, 16: 341–52.

Sharma, K. (1998) 'Development administration in Malaysia: Contribution of Tan Sri Dato' Seri Ahmad Sarji', *Public Administration and Development*, 18: 431–7.

Shastri, A. (1997) 'Government policy and the ethnic crisis in Sri Lanka', in M. Brown and S. Ganguly (eds) *Government policies and ethnic relations in Asia and the Pacific*, Cambridge, MA: MIT Press, 129–63.

Shaw, J. (1999) ' A World Bank intervention in the Sri Lankan welfare sector: The National Development Trust Fund', *World Development*, 25: 827–38.

Siffin, W. (1966) *Thai bureaucracy: Institutional change and development*, Honolulu: East-West Center.

Slatter, S. (1984) *Corporate Recovery*, Harmondsworth: Penguin.

Smith, B. (1985) *Decentralization: The territorial dimension of the state*, London: Allen and Unwin.

Smith, M. and I. Robertson (1993) *The theory and practice of systematic staff selection*, London: Macmillan.

Snoussi, B. (2001) *Les grands textes de la Fonction Publique*, Casablanca: Les Editions Maghrébines.

Solinger, D. (2002) 'Labour market reform and the plight of the laid-off proletariat', *China Quarterly*, 170: 304–26.

Sonko, K. (1994) 'A tale of two enterprises: Swaziland's lessons for privatization', *World Development*, 22: 1083–96.

Spencer, J. (1990) *A Sinhala village in time of trouble*, New Delhi: Oxford University Press.

Stepforward (2003) *AIDS Programme in Tanzania*, http://www.stepforward-forchildren.org/countries/tanzania.htm, accessed July 9 2003.

Sterman, J. and J. Wittenberg (1999) 'Path dependence, competition, and succession in the dynamics of scientific revolution', *Organization Science*, 10: 322–41.

Stevens, A. (1997) 'Persistent effects of job displacement: The importance of multiple job losses', *Journal of Labor Economics*, 15: 165–88.

Stevens, M. (1994a) 'Preparing for civil service pay and employment reform: A primer', in D. Lindauer and B. Nunberg, *op. cit.*, 103–15.

Stevens, M. (1994b) 'Public expenditure and civil service reform in Tanzania', in D. Lindauer and B. Nunberg, *op. cit.*, 62–81.

Storey, J. (1995) 'Human resource management: Still marching on, or marching out?', in J. Storey (ed.) *Human resource management: A critical text*, London: Thomson, 3–32.

Straussman, J. and M. Zhang (2001) 'Chinese administrative reforms in international perspective', *International Journal of Public Sector Management*, 14, 5: 411–22.

Subramaniam, A. (2001) 'Mauritius: A case study', *Finance and Development*, 38, 4: 22–5.

Sutton, R. (1987) 'The process of organizational death: Disbanding and reconnecting', *Administrative Science Quarterly*, 32: 542–69.

Taib, A. and M. Ismail (1982) 'The social structure', in E. Fisk and H. Osman-Rani (eds) *The political economy of Malaysia*, Kuala Lumpur: Oxford University Press, 104–24.

Taib, M. and J. Mat (1992) 'Administrative reforms in Malaysia: Toward enhancing public service performance', *Governance*, 5: 423–37.

Tarrow, S. (1996) 'Making social science work across space and time: A critical reflection on Robert Putnam's *Making democracy work*', *American Political Science Review*, 90: 389–97.

Tarrow, S. (1967) *Peasant communism in southern Italy*, New Haven: Yale University Press.

Taylor, H. (1992) 'Public sector personnel management in three African countries: Current problems and possibilities', *Public Administration and Development*, 12: 193–207.

Tessler, M. (1987) 'Image and reality in Moroccan political economy', in W. Zartman (ed.) *The political economy of Morocco*, New York: Praeger, 212–42.

Thomas, J. and M. Grindle (1990) 'After the decision: Implementing policy reforms in developing countries', *World Development*, 18: 1163–81.

Thompson, M. (2001) 'Whatever happened to "Asian values"?', *Journal of Democracy*, 12, 4: 154–65.

Ting, Y. (1996) 'Workforce reductions and termination benefits in governments: The case of advance notice', *Public Personnel Management*, 25, 2: 183–98.

Titmuss, R. and B. Abel-Smith (1968) *Social policies and population growth in Mauritius*, London: Frank Cass.

Todd, P. and D. Peetz (2001) 'Malaysia's industrial relations at century's turn: Vision 2020 or a spectre of the past?', *International Journal of Human Resource Management*, 12: 1365–82.

Tolstoy, L. (2002) *War and peace*, New York: Random House.

Tomaney, J. (1990) 'The reality of workplace flexibility', *Capital and Class*, 40: 29–60.

Tordoff, W. (1967) *Government and politics in Tanzania*, Dar es Salaam: East African Publishing House.

Tsikata, Y. (2001) *Owning economic reforms: A comparative study of Ghana and Tanzania*, New York: World Institute for Development Economics Research, Discussion Paper No. 2001/53.

Turner, M. (1989) '"Trainingism" revisited in Papua New Guinea', *Public Administration and Development*, 9: 17–28.

Tyson, S. and A. Fell (1986) *Evaluating the personnel function*, London: Hutchinson.

Ulrich, D. (1998) 'A new mandate for human resources', *Harvard Business Review*, January/February 1998, 124–35.

UNAIDS (Joint United Nations Programme on HIV/AIDS) (2004) *Report on the global AIDS epidemic*, www.unaids.org/Bangkok/2004/GAR2004_html/GAR2004_00_en.htm, accessed September 1 2005.

UNDP (United Nations Development Programme) (2004) *Human development report 2004*, New York: Oxford University Press.

UNICEF (United Nations Children's Fund) (2002) *Situation analysis of children in Tanzania*, Dar es Salaam: UNICEF.

United Nations (2005a) *The Millennium Development Goals report*, http://www.unmillenniumproject.org/documents/overviewEngHighRes1-23.pdf, accessed June 13 2005.

United Nations (2005b) *Unlocking the human potential for public sector performance: World Public Sector Report 2005*, New York: United Nations.

United Republic of Tanzania (2003) *Tanzania economic survey*, http://www.tanzania.go.tz/economicsurvey/part1/domesticeconomy.htm, accessed January 2 2004.

United Republic of Tanzania (2002) *Civil Service Circular No.1*, Dar es Salaam: Civil Service Department, President's Office, Ref. No. MUF. C/AC/46/205/01.

United Republic of Tanzania (2001) *Civil Service Circular No.1*, Dar es Salaam: Civil Service Department, President's Office, Ref. No. C/AC/46/205/01/169.

United Republic of Tanzania (1999) *Medium-term strategic plan 1999–2004*, Dar es Salaam: Civil Service Department, President's Office.

United Republic of Tanzania (Planning Commission) (2000) *Poverty reduction strategy paper*, http://www.tanzania.go.tz/povertyf.html, accessed May 8 2003.

Van der Gaag, J., M. Stelcner and W. Vijverberg (1989) 'Wage differentials and moonlighting by civil servants: Evidence from Cote d'Ivoire and Peru', *World Bank Economic Review*, 3, 1: 67–95.

Villarreal, A. (2002) 'Political competition and violence in Mexico: Hierarchical social control in local patronage structures', *American Sociological Review*, 67: 477–98.

Vorozheikina, T. (1994) 'Clientelism and the process of political democratization in Russia', in L. Roniger, and A. Güneş-Ayata (eds) *Democracy, clientelism and civil society*, Boulder, CO: Lynne Rienner, 105–20.

Wade, R. (1989) 'Recruitment, appointment and promotion to public office in India', in P. Ward (ed.) *Corruption, development and inequality*, London: Routledge, 73–109.

Wade, R. (1985) 'The market for public office, or why India is not better at development', *World Development*, 13: 467–97.

Walters, M. (ed.) (1995) *The performance management handbook*, London: Institute of Personnel and Development.

Wamalwa, W. (1976) *Report of the Commission of Enquiry (Structure, conditions of service and remuneration of the public service of the kingdom of Swaziland)*, Mbabane: Government of Swaziland.

Warner, M. (1993) 'Human resource management with "Chinese characteristics", *International Journal of Human Resource Management*, 4: 45–66.

Wass, V. (1996) 'Who controls selection under "voluntary" redundancy? The case of the redundant mineworkers payments scheme', *British Journal of Industrial Relations*, 34: 249–65.

Waterbury, J. (1993) *Exposed to innumerable delusions: Public enterprise and state power in Egypt, India, Mexico and Turkey*, Cambridge: Cambridge University Press.

Waterbury, J. (1970) *The commander of the faithful: The Moroccan political elite – a study in segmented politics*, London: Weidenfeld and Nicholson.

Weingrod, A. (1977) 'Patrons, patronage and political parties', in S. Schmidt, L. Guasti, C. Landé and J. Scott (eds) *Friends, followers and factions: A reader in political clientelism*, Berkeley: University of California Press, 323–37.

Weiss, M. (1999) 'What will become of *reformasi?* Ethnicity and changing political norms in Malaysia', *Contemporary Southeast Asia*, 21: 424–50.

Wescott, C. (1999) 'Guiding principles on civil service reform in Africa: An empirical review', *International Journal of Public Sector Management*, 12, 2: 145–70.

Whetten, D. and K. Cameron (1994) 'Organizational-level productivity initiatives: The case of downsizing', in D. Harris (ed.) *Organizational linkages: Understanding the productivity paradox*, Washington DC: National Academy Press, 262–90.

Whitehead, L. (1990) 'Political explanations of macroeconomic management: A survey', *World Development*, 18: 1133–46.

WHO (World Health Organization) (2005) *Health a key to prosperity: Success stories in developing countries*, www.who.int/inf-new/aids2.htm, accessed September 1 2005.

Wijesinghe, D. (1997) *Administrative reforms: International perspectives and the case of Sri Lanka*, Colombo: Government of Sri Lanka.

Wijeweera, B. (1989) 'Policy developments and administrative changes in Sri Lanka: 1948–1987', *Public Administration and Development*, 9: 287–300.

Williamson, J. (1994) *The political economy of policy reform*, Washington DC: Institute for International Economics.

Willis, M. (2002) 'Political parties in the Maghrib: The illusion of significance', *Journal of North African Studies*, 7, 2: 1–22.

Wolfensohn, J. (1999) 'A proposal for a comprehensive development framework', Memorandum to the Board, Management and Staff of the World Bank Group, January 21 1999.

World Bank (2004a) *Country assistance strategy: Ghana*, http://web.worldbank.org/WBSITE/EXTERNAL/COUNTRIES/AFRICAEXT/GHANAEXTN/0,,menuPK:351965~pagePK:141132~piPK:141105~theSitePK:351952,00.html, accessed March 20 2005.

World Bank (2004b) *Minimizing negative distributional effects of public sector downsizing*, Washington DC: World Bank, PREM note No. 84.

World Bank (2004c) *Sri Lanka: Country brief*, http://www.worldbank.lk/WBSITE/EXTERNAL/COUNTRIES/SOUTHASIAEXT/SRILANKAEXTN/0,,contentMDK:20133668~pagePK:141137~piPK:217854~theSitePK:233047,00.html, accessed July 19 2005.

World Bank (2003) *World Development Report 2004: Making services work for poor people*, New York: Oxford University Press.

World Bank (2002) *Tanzania public expenditure review FY O2: Report of fiscal evelopments and public expenditure management issues*, http://www-wds.worldbank.org/servlet/WDSIBankServlet?pcont=details&eid=000094946_02091704122721, accessed January 15 2004.

World Bank (2000a) *Country assistance strategy: Uganda*, http://web.worldbank.org/WBSITE/EXTERNAL/COUNTRIES/AFRICAEXT/UGANDAEXTN/0,,menuPK:374950~pagePK:141132~piPK:141105~theSitePK:374864,00.html, accessed March 20 2005.

World Bank (2000b) *Morocco in brief*, http://lnweb18.worldbank.org/mna/mena.nsf, accessed March 26 2003.

World Bank (1999) *Poverty reduction strategy papers – operational issues*, http://www.imf.org/external/np/pdr/prsp/poverty1.htm.

World Bank (1998a) *Assessing aid: What works, what doesn't, and why*, Washington DC: World Bank.

World Bank (1998b) *Public expenditure management handbook*, Washington DC: World Bank, Poverty and Social Policy Department.

World Bank (1997) *World development report 1997: The changing role of the state*, New York: Oxford University Press.

World Bank (1996a) *Growing faster, finding jobs: Choices for Morocco*, Washington DC: World Bank Middle East and North Africa Economic Studies, http://www-wds.worldbank.org/servlet/WDS_IBank_Servlet?pcont=details&eid=00000926 5_3961214182006, accessed July 1 2003.

World Bank (1996b) *Sri Lanka: Public expenditure review*, Washington DC: World Bank.

World Bank (1989) *Mauritius: Managing success*, Washington DC: World Bank.

World Bank Institute (2005) *Governance and anti-corruption*, http://www.worldbank.org/wbi/governance/, accessed July 11 2005.

Wright, P. and G. McMahan (1992) 'Theoretical perspectives for strategic human resource management', *Journal of Management*, 18: 295–320.

Wu, M. (1990) *The Malaysian legal system*, Petaling Jaya: Pearson.

Wyss, K. (2004) 'An approach to classifying human resources constraints to attaining health-related Millennium Development Goals', *Human Resources for Health*, 2, 11.

Yin, R. (1994) *Case study research: design and methods*, London: Sage.

Younge, G. (2005) 'Pressure grows on Chicago's Teflon mayor', *The Guardian*, August 13.

Younger, S. (1996) 'Labour market consequences of retrenchment for civil servants in Ghana', in D. Sahn (ed.) *Economic Reform and the Poor in Africa*, Oxford: Clarendon Press, 185–202.

Zakaria, H. (1989) 'Malaysia: Quasi democracy in a divided society', in L. Diamond, J. Linz and S. Lipset (eds) *Democracy in developing countries: Asia*, Boulder, CO: Lynne Rienner, 347–81.

Zartman, W. (1987) 'King Hassan's new Morocco', in W. Zartman (ed.) *The political economy of Morocco*, New York: Praeger, 1–33.

Name Index

Subject Index